Essential Elements

Essential Elements
Contracts, Torts, and Criminal Law

Meredith Muller

CAROLINA ACADEMIC PRESS
Durham, North Carolina

ISBN   978-1-5310-1376-9
eISBN 978-1-5310-1377-6
LCCN 2018967177

Carolina Academic Press, LLC
700 Kent Street
Durham, North Carolina 27701
Telephone (919) 489-7486
Fax (919) 493-5668
www.cap-press.com

Printed in the United States of America

This book is dedicated to my students who worked tirelessly to study for both the FYLSE and the Bar Exam. They trusted me as well as the process, even though they often wanted to give up. They spent many precious hours with books instead of family and friends in an effort to pass. I am honored to have been a small part of their success and am proud to have been their Professor. My hope is that this book helps other equally determined students beyond the confines of my classroom. You can do this!

Contents

MULTIPLE CHOICE TESTING

RULE STATEMENTS

List of Figures

Foreword

A Special Message for Students Preparing for the FYLSE

by Dean Steven Bracci*

The information shared in this book will help as you prepare for your final exams in your substantive courses. Understanding the concepts contained in this book will also help put you in a strong position achieve your ultimate goal of succeeding on the bar exam.

For those students that may be subject to California's First Year Law Students' Exam, or "FYLSE," I'd like to share some additional information and advice. As you may already know, the FYLSE is a one-day test covering the three first year subjects of Torts, Contracts, and Criminal Law. Law students who are required to take the FYLSE must pass the exam at the end of their first year of law study to continue with their legal education.

The FYLSE represents the longest single day of law testing administered in California, and one of the longest testing days used by any state law testing authority in the country. Students must answer 4 essays in a morning session lasting four hours, and then, following a lunch break, students must answer 100 multiple choice questions in a three-hour session.

The starting point in preparing for the FYLSE and other Bar Examinations is a thorough understanding of the applicable law. This means not only knowing rules and concepts, but also understanding how the rules and concepts interrelate. Ideally, the flowcharts you will encounter in this book along with a well-developed outline of each subject will help you in this regard.

---

* Dean Bracci is a well-known lecturer and has been teaching law since 1979. He is an expert in examination techniques and has conducted writing and test-taking seminars nationwide.

However, to pass such an exam, students must not only know the applicable law but must also possess the skills necessary to succeed on each portion of the exam. Over the years, I've worked with many students who had a good working knowledge of the applicable law but were for the most part unsure as to how to apply that knowledge to a fact pattern. Mastering the application portion of the equation takes a great deal of practice to develop the necessary skills.

On the essays, this means demonstrating the ability to "think like a lawyer," which means to show the ability to differentiate between discussible and non-discussible issues, explain the law applicable to the particular issue, and discuss how the facts of the question need to be considered to support a logical conclusion. On the multiple-choice portion, this means possessing the ability to apply the law to a fact pattern and select the best answer from four alternative choices. This book will help you develop those skills if you take the time to practice as suggested.

It is not easy to pass the FYLSE. It will take many hours of study to succeed. Unfortunately, when students finish their finals, the natural tendency is to "let down" and take a break from the intense study of preparing for the finals. However, it is essential that the finals be viewed as merely a "stepping stone" to passing the FYLSE. You must work to improve even more so that you will be ready.

Professor Meredith Muller is extremely gifted in helping students master these skills. For many years, Professor Muller has worked with students preparing for both the California Bar Exam and the FYLSE. She has succeeded in greatly improving performance. She is one of the most knowledgeable people in the country with regard to bar study, and an excellent source of information on how a student should maximize preparation for exams.

Whether you are studying for your final exams, the FYLSE, or bar exam, we all congratulate you on your success to date and wish you the best of luck.

Acknowledgments

It takes a village to write a book. I am so very grateful for my village and would like to thank them all for their support.

First, to my scientist husband: I apologize that you had to learn everything you never wanted to know about Contracts, Torts, and Criminal Law while helping me format and edit this book. You always stand beside me when I need a partner, behind me when I need support, and in front of me when I need a hero. You are my everything.

Second, I'd like to thank my mentors. Jack Goetz, you started it all by giving an idealistic young lawyer a chance. Thank you for seeing the teacher in me. Greg Brandes, you taught me how to teach and helped me grow. Thank you for teaching me patience and grace. Steve Bracci, you are the source of my ambition. I always said, when I grow up, I want to be Steve Bracci. Thank you for giving me my moxie.

Third, I'd like to thank my peers. Alana DeGarmo, Stacey Sharp, Doug Holden, and Jeffrey Van Detta, thank you for your friendship, guidance, and support. When the ship sinks, true friends don't jump.

Finally, I truly thank God for my family, friends, and many blessings sometimes disguised as obstacles. Sometimes God puts a Goliath in your life to help you find the David within.

Contracts

1

Introduction

The courses in the First Year of Law School are giant puzzles that you must put together piece by piece without first looking at the picture on the front of each box. The images start to take shape towards the middle of the course but do not become completely clear until you take a step back and review each course in its entirety.

This book is not a complete study of Contracts, Torts, or Criminal Law. You've paid your law school tuition for that. It is also not a comprehensive outline. Rather, it is a book that will help you understand how each piece of the puzzle fits together. It will also help you to translate your knowledge when tested. Students often know the law, just not in an organized enough way to write a solid essay. Mastering essays also takes practice. Therefore, this book includes several practice essays on each subject.

Students who perform poorly on multiple choice tests also often know the law, but need to better understand how the law is tested before mastering the method. Therefore, this book also contains a chapter on multiple choice testing strategy.

Having said that, I've come across many students that perform poorly on both essay and multiple-choice exams because they simply do not know the law well enough. If you find yourself in this category, I strongly encourage you to review the substance of your courses before attempting any of the practice exercises in this book. Commercial outlines and flashcards may also help.

If you have done everything you can to learn and memorize the law on your own and still don't fully understand the concepts, you may need a tutor. I personally established PassTheFYLSE.com to help in this regard. You can use it to schedule some time with a tutor or to submit the practice essays found in this book for individual review. The site is located at *PassTheFYLSE.com*.

2

Contracts Overview & Formation

Let's get down to business and focus on the first puzzle: Contracts. To make sure you fully understand how each piece fits together, we will follow handy flowcharts. I suggest memorizing them if you do not already have a good organizational understanding of the subject.

Contracts is divided into three main areas: **Formation**, **Performance**, and **Remedies**. Later, we will cover the topics of Third Party Beneficiaries, Assignments and Delegation.

For now, just know that anytime you see a contracts problem, you should make sure it is properly **Formed**. If it is not, it is not valid and no performance is due.

If it is properly formed, then look to see if performance is waived or excused. If it is not waived or excused, then **Performance** is due. If one of the parties fails to perform or performs poorly, then he is in breach of contract.

If there is a breach of contract, then you would determine what **Remedies** are available to the non-breaching party in order to compensate him for the breach.

Sounds simple, right? It can get pretty complicated, but having this general structure in your mind will help when you sit down to confront a fact pattern.

This first look shows the picture on the outside of the puzzle box. When analyzing a contracts problem that raises the issue of formation, use this flowchart as a sort of mental checklist to help you spot issues in the fact pattern. This does not mean that you will discuss every contract formation issue in every essay. Rather, it just means that you are less likely to miss an issue that is raised by the facts if you are prepared for it.

Figure 2.1 Contracts

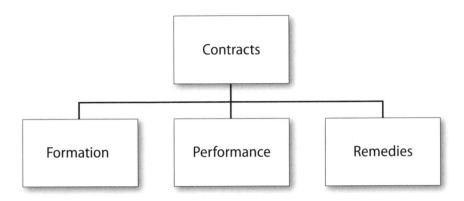

From here, we'll take the first topic, **Formation**, and break it down further.

In order to properly form a contract, there must be mutual assent, which is established through offer and acceptance. There must also be consideration, which is established through a bargained for exchange, promissory estoppel, restitution or quasi-contractual theory. Finally, there must be no defenses to formation present.

Figure 2.2 Contract Formation

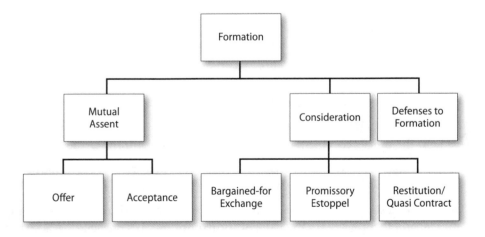

From here, we "unpack" the element of mutual assent. The issues we look for are 1) whether a valid offer was made and communicated to an identified offeree that manifests an objective intent to be bound and contains all material terms; 2) whether that offer is still open, in which case revocation, rejection, or UCC 2-205 may be an issue; and 3) whether a valid acceptance was made that either mirrored the offer or contained additional terms, and whether non-conforming goods were shipped.

Figure 2.3 Mutual Assent

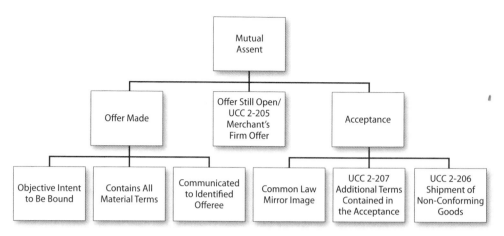

We can further unpack the "offer still open" issue, which often arises if the mailbox rule is triggered. You will want to discuss this if you see facts indicating that the offeror attempted to revoke the offer before it could be accepted or that the offeree rejected the offer before accepting it. As long as you know the that an acceptance is effective upon dispatch, and a revocation or rejection is effective upon receipt, you can analyze the facts to see which came first in order to determine whether the offer was still open when it was accepted.

Figure 2.4 Is the Offer Still Open? The Mailbox Rule

Is the Offer Still Open?
The Mailbox Rule

Rules:
1. An **ACCEPTANCE** is effective upon **DISPATCH**.
2. A **REVOCATION** or **REJECTION** is effective upon **RECEIPT**.

Always look to see what came first: Acceptance or Rejection/Revocation. As long as the Acceptance was **dispatched** before the Rejection/Revocation was **received**, the Acceptance will take precedence. **EXCEPTION:** If the Rejection was received prior to the Acceptance and **relied upon**, it will take precedence over the otherwise effective Acceptance.

UCC 2-207 may also be an issue if you find that the acceptance contains additional terms. You can use the following flowcharts to work through this complicated statute in an effort to determine whether a contract is formed as well as whether the additional terms become part of the contract.

Figure 2.5 Acceptance Contains Additional Terms: UCC 2-207

What happens if additional terms are included in the acceptance of a contract for the sale of goods?

Apply UCC 2-207 and ask yourself two questions:

1. Is the potential acceptance a definite and seasonable expression of acceptance?
2. Is the potential acceptance expressly conditioned on agreement to the additional or different terms?

If you answer:

Then look to **2-207(2)** to see what happens to the Additional Terms. If you answer in **ANY OTHER COMBINATION**, then no contract arises from the communications between the parties, and you need to look at **2-207(3)** to determine the outcome.

Figure 2.6 Acceptance Contains Additional Terms: UCC 2-207(2)

If you answered "Yes" to Question 1 and "No" to Question 2 in Figure 2.5, then a contract is formed by the communication of the parties. UCC 2-207(2) now lets you know what happens to the additional terms in this situation.

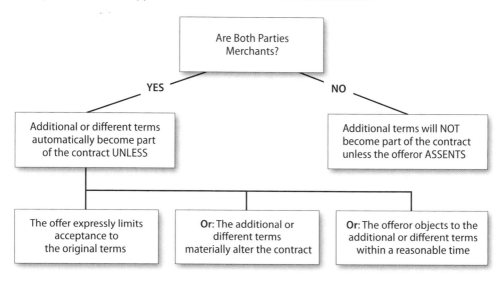

Figure 2.7 Acceptance Contains Additional Terms: UCC 2-207(3)

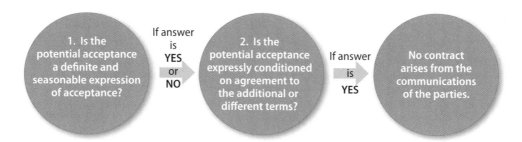

If the conduct of the parties is sufficient to indicate the existence of an agreement, then a contract will exist, and the terms of the contract will consist of any terms upon which the communications agree, while conflicting terms are knocked out. Any gaps in the terms of the contract will be filled using UCC gap-filler rules.

Contract Modification is a different issue, although many students confuse it with UCC 2-207. The key is to determine whether there are additional terms contained in the acceptance, in which case UCC 2-207 applies, or if a party attempts to modify the terms of a contract after acceptance, in which case the rules of contract modification apply. When determining whether a contract modification is valid, you need to consider both mutual assent and consideration. You may also need to consider the Statute of Frauds if the attempted modification was not in writing.

Figure 2.8 Contract Modifications: UCC 2-209

What is required for a valid modification?	Under the Common Law?	Under the UCC?
Is Mutual Assent required?	Yes	Yes
Is Consideration required?	Yes (Look out for the Unanticipated Difficulties Exception.)	No, as long as the modification is requested in good faith.
If the contract states that it can only be modified in writing, is an oral modification allowed?	Yes, unless the contract as modified falls within the Statute of Frauds. In this case, it must be in writing or otherwise satisfy the statute.	No. Additionally, if the contract as modified falls within the Statute of Frauds, it must be in writing or otherwise satisfy the statute.

After establishing mutual assent and consideration (or a consideration substitute,) you will have a valid, enforceable contract unless a defense to formation exists. Therefore, you need to work through your mental checklist to see if the facts raise any defenses. Here are the main defenses.

Figure 2.9 Defenses to Formation

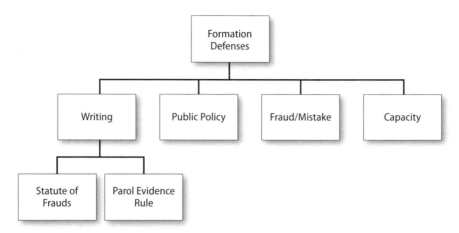

The issue of "Writing" includes two main topics, the Statute of Frauds and the Parol Evidence Rule. Many students confuse these concepts, but they are actually pretty easy to learn. Just remember that the Statute of Frauds protects you **before** the contract is written by not enforcing certain oral contracts that are not reduced to writing. The Parol Evidence Rule protects you **after** the contract has been reduced to writing by not allowing certain oral evidence that is not contained in the writing. Of course, there are exceptions to these rules. The following charts guide you through the process of analyzing a Statute of Frauds issue or a Parol Evidence issue.

Whenever you encounter an **oral** contract, ask yourself first whether it is covered by the Statute of Frauds, whether it has been reduced to writing, and if it was not, whether an exception applies.

Figure 2.10 Statute of Frauds

Certain types of contracts must be in writing in order to be enforceable.

Type of Contract?	Is It in Writing?	Is There an Exception?
Contracts subject to the statute include: 1. Contracts made in consideration of **Marriage**; 2. Contracts that, by their terms, cannot be completed within a **Year**; 3. Contracts for the sale of any interest in **Land**; 4. Contracts made by **Executors** to pay the debt of an estate; 5. Contracts for the sale of **Goods** over $500; and 6. **Suretyships** (contracts guaranteeing the debt of another).	Yes: Enforceable No: Unenforceable, unless an Exception applies. What constitutes a Sufficient Writing? Common Law: Signed by defendant; contains all essential terms. UCC: Signed (except between merchants, it can be signed by the sender); quantity term.	If an exception applies, the contract does not have to be in writing in order to be enforceable. **Exceptions:** **Goods**: merchant's confirming memo exception **Land**: part performance (money plus improvements or money plus possession) **Year**: Detrimental reliance exception **Suretyship**: main purpose rule

Whenever you encounter a **written** contract, and a party seeks to introduce evidence of a prior or contemporaneous agreement, you will need to work through the Parol Evidence Rule to determine whether that evidence can be introduced. Note that this is very different from a party trying to change the terms of a contract after it has been formed. In that case, you would need to discuss modification. It is also very different from a situation wherein the offeree tries to add terms to the acceptance. In that case, you would need to either discuss the mirror image rule or UCC 2-207.

If the Parol Evidence Rule is an issue, you first ask whether there is a writing. If there is, you need to determine whether the writing is a total integration. If it is, look to see if an exception applies.

Figure 2.11 Parol Evidence Rule

Once a contract is reduced to writing, it will control.

Is There a Writing?	Is It a Total Integration?	Is There an Exception?
Yes: The Parol Evidence Rule will prohibit introduction of prior or contemporaneous oral agreements that differ or contradict the terms of a writing that is considered to be a "total integration."	**Corbin** "Surrounding Circumstances." The court will admit evidence on the issue of integration to determine whether the writing is a total integration. **Williston** "Four Corners" Rule. Taking the document as a whole, does it, on its face, appear to be a total integration?	1. Collateral agreements 2. Consistent additional terms (partial integrations, both common law and UCC) 3. Explain the meaning of terms (even in a total integration under the UCC)

3

Performance & Remedies

Once a valid, enforceable contract has been formed, it must be properly performed, unless performance can be excused or discharged. Otherwise, the non-performing or poorly performing party will be in breach of contract.

To examine the issue of performance, we must examine the facts for issues concerning conditions, discharge, and breach.

Figure 3.1 Performance

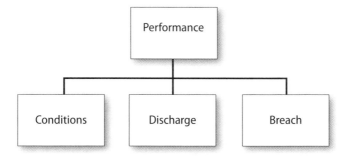

Let's start with Conditions. First, ask yourself whether there are any conditions. If so, identify them as express, implied, or constructive. Then, ask whether they have been satisfied. If there are conditions that have not been satisfied, check to see if they have been waived or excused. If they have not been waived or excused, then the non performing party may be labeled as a breachor.

Figure 3.2 Conditions

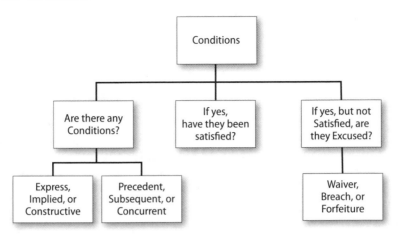

Contracts can also be discharged to avoid labeling the non-performing party as a breachor. Contracts can be discharged under the doctrines of impossibility, severe impracticability, and frustration of purpose. Impossibility is generally triggered by illegality, death or destruction. Just be sure to pay attention to see if a party assumed the risk of loss.

Figure 3.3 Discharge

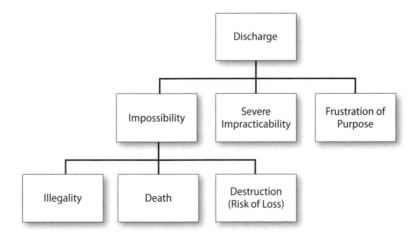

Once we have determined that a valid contract has been formed, that any conditions have been satisfied or excused, and that performance has not been discharged, we need to examine the issue of breach.

Here, most of the time, you will be dealing with a present breach, meaning that a party failed to perform or performed poorly. However, look out for issues involving anticipatory repudiation, wherein the breachor evidences his intent not to perform in advance of the performance date. In those cases, you may need to address adequate assurances or retraction under the UCC.

If the breach is a present breach, you need to determine whether it is minor or material. If it is minor, the non-breaching party must still perform and sue for damages caused by the breach. If it is material, the non-breaching party may suspend his performance and sue for damages.

You may also see an issue arise with regard to whether the breaching party is entitled to relief. This will depend on whether the breach is material, minor, or total. If the breach is total, the breachor may be able to argue that the contract was divisible or that he is entitled to restitution.

Figure 3.4 Breach

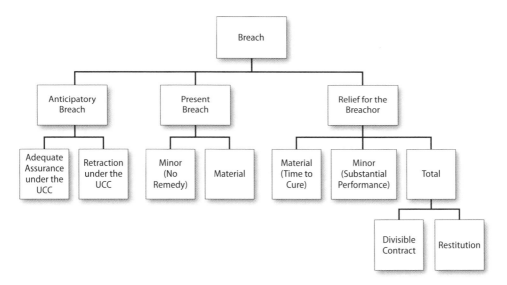

Possible remedies for breach include damages, restitution, injunction, rescission, and reformation. Usually, remedies is a small part of a contracts question, but should you encounter a fact pattern that begs close analysis of this issue, use the charts below to work through each type.

Figure 3.5 Remedies

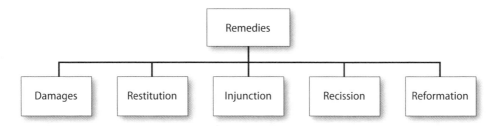

The general measure of damages is the product of natural, consequential, and incidental damages minus the cost and loss avoided.

Damages can come in the form of liquidated damages, expectation damages, or reliance damages. With expectation damages, you put the party in a position he would have been in had the contract been properly performed and consider both natural damages and consequential damages. The Damages chart shows the natural standard damages in four different types of contracts: Real Property, Goods, Employment, and Construction Contracts.

Figure 3.6 Damages

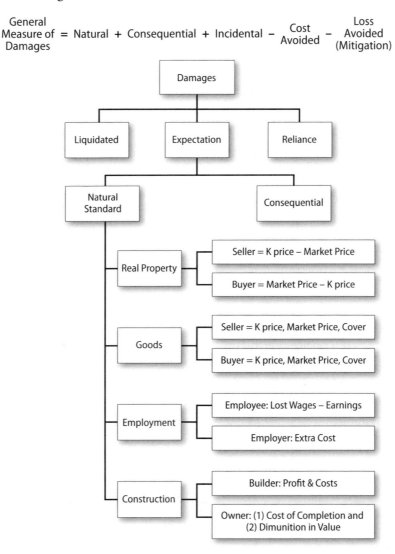

$$\text{General Measure of Damages} = \text{Natural} + \text{Consequential} + \text{Incidental} - \text{Cost Avoided} - \text{Loss Avoided (Mitigation)}$$

With Restitution, you'll need to determine what grounds entitle you to restitution, as well of what measure of recovery is warranted. The grounds include Mistake, Breach, and Unenforceable Contract.

Figure 3.7 Restitution

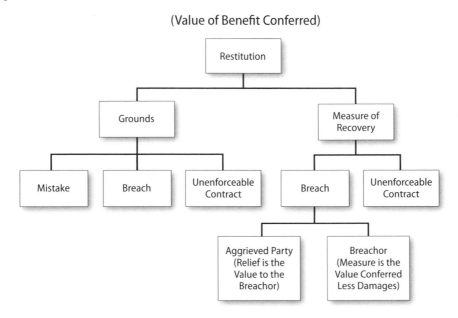

Finally, we may have to deal with equitable remedies including Injunction, Rescission, and Reformation. Rescission and Reformation are pretty self-explanatory, but if you are dealing with an injunction, you need to make sure you know the requirements for the grant of specific performance. There must be a definite and certain contract, an inadequate remedy at law, feasibility of enforcement, mutuality of remedy, and lack of defenses.

Figure 3.8 Injunction, Rescission, and Reformation

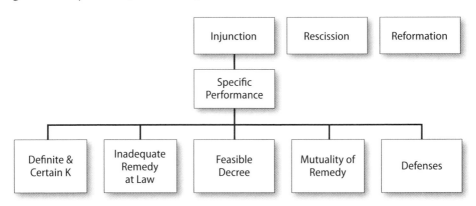

4

Third Party Beneficiaries, Assignments & Delegation

We're almost done completing the Contracts puzzle. This chapter provides an overview of Third Party Rights, Assignment and Delegation. When dealing with these topics, we do so in terms of Formation, Performance and Remedies.

Let's discuss Third Party Beneficiaries First. A third party beneficiary, or "3PB," exists when the parties enter into an agreement for the benefit of a third person.

When the contract is formed, the third person is either an intended or incidental 3PB. An intended 3PB may be either a Creditor or a Donee Beneficiary. It is important to note here that an incidental 3PB has no rights.

Performance comes into play when one of the original parties tries to modify or rescind the contract in a way that affects the 3PB. If the 3PB's rights have vested, the 3PB may be able to sue. If they have not yet vested before the modification or rescission, his rights are terminated.

If the contract is breached, the question then becomes whether the 3PB is entitled to remedies. If the original Promisee sues the Promisor, a creditor 3PB is entitled to recover, but a Donee 3PB is not entitled to money damages. If the 3PB sues the Promisor, the Promisor's defenses are good against the 3PB. If the 3PB sues the Promisee, a creditor 3PB can recover on the underlying promise while a Donee 3PB will not be able to recover.

Figure 4.1 Third Party Beneficiaries

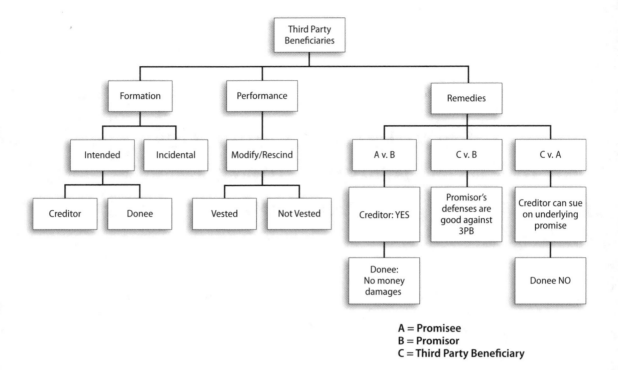

Again, we'll deal with the assignments of rights and the delegation of duties in terms of Formation, Performance, and Remedies.

Formation issues regarding assignments may include effective prohibitions against assignments, an increase of the Obligor's duty or risk, and existing or expected future rights. Performance issues include the effect of the assignment and revocation and priorities. Remedies are addressed by first determining the parties involved in a lawsuit. An Assignee can have a direct cause of action against the Obligor, and the Obligor can assert the same defenses he could assert against the Assignor. The Assignee could also sue the Assignor under a theory of implied warranties.

Formation issues regarding delegations include whether a duty is delegable and consideration. The issue for performance therefore becomes the effect of the delegation. Remedies can then be examined in terms of who is suing who and whether there has been a novation. When the Obligee sues the Obligor, he can recover if there has been a delegation, but not a novation. The Obligee can sue the Delagatee in a direct cause of action, and the Delagatee has the same defenses as the Delegator. If the Delegator sues the Delagatee, it is a general breach issue.

Figure 4.2 Assignment of Rights

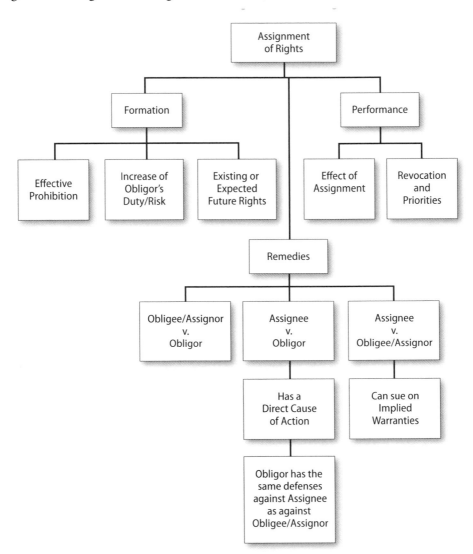

Figure 4.3 Delegation of Duties

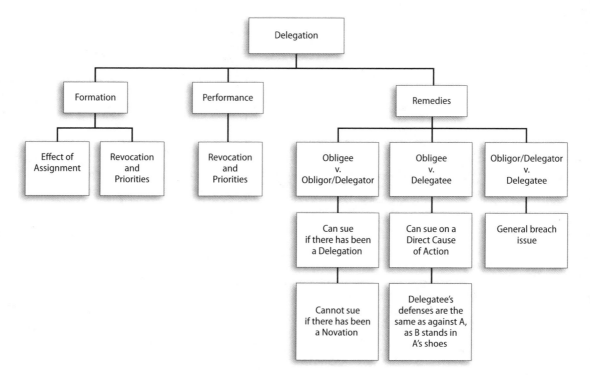

Whew! That's it for Contracts! Now it's time to practice! You will find practice essays and sample answers as well as practice multiple choice questions and answer explanations in a later chapter. Be sure to complete all of the practice questions on your own before referring to the sample answers to assess your work. Again, if you find yourself too far off track, review the substantive law and try again. After all, mastery takes lots of practice!

Torts

5

Torts Overview & Intentional Torts

Now that we have completed our review of Contracts, let's turn to another first-year puzzle: The Law of Torts.

Torts is divided into four main areas. The first is Intentional Torts, wherein the Defendant acts intentionally to harm Plaintiff in some way. The second, and perhaps most important part of the course, is Negligence. Negligence is found when Plaintiff is injured as a result of Defendant's unreasonable conduct. We then study the law of Strict Liability, which can result from Defendant's act or from a defective product. The subject wraps up with the study of Defamation. Once we work through each of these areas, we'll focus on available Remedies.

Let's begin with the first topic, Intentional Torts, and break it down further. Intentional Torts result in injury to a person or to a person's property. Intent can be proven by showing either desire or knowledge to a substantial certainty. Intent can also be transferred from person to person and tort to tort. Also, there are Defenses to Intentional Torts.

Figure 5.1 Torts

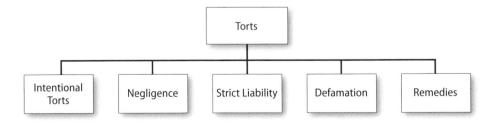

Figure 5.2 Intentional Torts

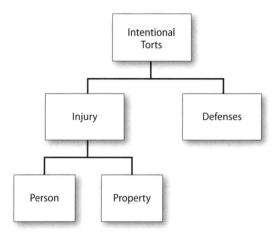

INTENT: (1) Desire, (2) Substantial Certainty, and (3) Transferred

Now let's unpack the various ways a Plaintiff can claim an intentional tort when there is personal injury. There are three of them. The first is that a plaintiff can suffer bodily injury, which can be caused by battery, assault, or false imprisonment. The second is injury to emotions, which results from Intentional Infliction of Emotional Distress. The third is injury to a plaintiff's Reputation and Privacy, which is caused by Defamation (which we will discuss separately in some detail), Invasion of Privacy, and the torts of Malicious Prosecution, Wrongful Institution of Civil Proceedings, and Abuse of Process.

Figure 5.3 Intentional Torts: Injury to Person

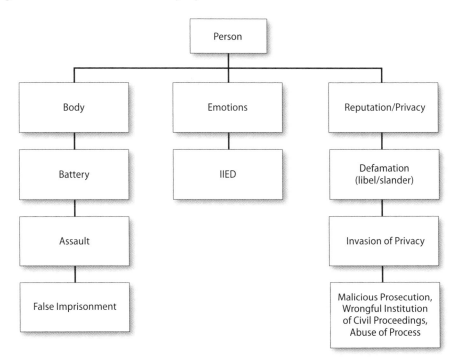

Working through the chart, focusing on bodily injury, we'll start with our first Intentional Tort. Battery is an intentional touching that results in harm or offense. Therefore, a prima facie case for battery requires showing:

1) intent, which can be shown by desire or knowledge to a substantial certainty;

2) touching; and

3) harm or offense.

When working through an intentional torts problem, it is essential that you unpack each one of these elements separately and completely. For example, discuss intent first by explaining which facts show that Defendant acted with intent. Then, discuss what facts evidence a touching. Finally, explain which facts show that harm or offense occurred as a result. If you can't satisfy ALL of the elements, there is no battery.

Figure 5.4 Battery

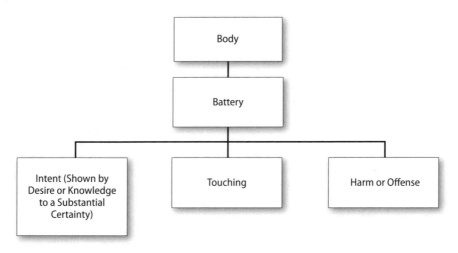

The next Intentional Tort is Assault. Assault occurs when Defendant intentionally places another in reasonable apprehension of an immediate battery. Again, as you can see, there are three elements you must prove here to make a case for assault:

1) intent;

2) reasonable apprehension; and

3) immediate battery.

Be on the lookout for facts that may indicate that Plaintiff's apprehension wasn't reasonable or that a battery was not imminent. In such cases, there is no assault.

Figure 5.5 Assault

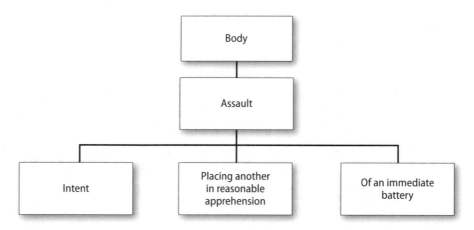

False imprisonment is our next Intentional Tort. It results when Defendant intentionally confines another to a bounded area. Be on the lookout for facts that indicate that Plaintiff is free to leave.

Figure 5.6 False Imprisonment

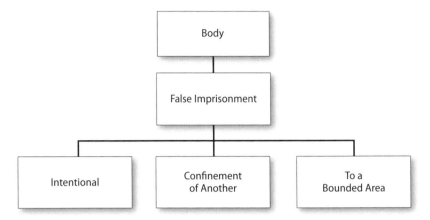

We now move on to Emotional Injury. The applicable Intentional Tort here is Intentional Infliction of Emotional Distress ("IIED.") IIED occurs when:

1) Defendant acts intentionally or recklessly;

2) Defendant's conduct was extreme and outrageous;

3) Defendant's act is the cause of such distress; and

4) Plaintiff suffers severe emotional distress as a result of defendant's conduct.

Keep in mind that third persons can also recover for IIED as long as:

1) the third person is present at the time of the incident, and that presence must be known to the defendant; and

2) the third person must either be a member of the injured person's immediate family; or

3) suffer bodily harm as a result of the emotional distress caused by witnessing the incident.

Figure 5.7 Intentional Torts: Injury to Emotions and Intentional Infliction of Emotional Distress

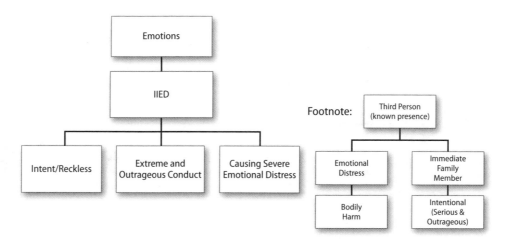

We now turn to Invasion of Privacy. There are four ways in which a Plaintiff can prove invasion of privacy. They are:

1) Intrusion into the Plaintiff's seclusion;

2) Public revelation of private facts;

3) Commercial appropriation; and

4) Portraying the plaintiff in a false light.

Figure 5.8 Invasion of Privacy

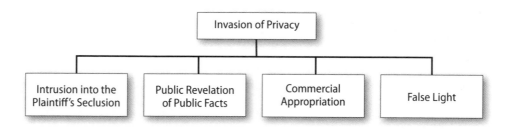

Let's take a closer look at the elements of each privacy tort. Intrusion into Seclusion requires proof that Defendant intentionally intruded upon the plaintiff's private affairs, the intrusion would be highly offensive to a reasonable person, Plaintiff had a reasonable expectation of privacy, and the intrusion caused Plaintiff mental anguish or suffering.

Figure 5.9 Intrusion into Plaintiff's Seclusion

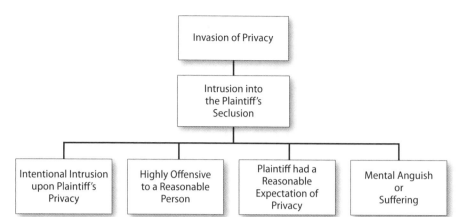

The next two privacy torts are Public Revelation of Private Facts and Commercial Appropriation. Public Revelation of Private Facts requires proof that Defendant intentionally publicized (to the public at large) a matter concerning Plaintiff's private life. It also has to be highly offensive to a reasonable person and cannot be a matter of legitimate public concern. Commercial Appropriation requires Defendant to intentionally misappropriate the name or likeness of another for his own use or benefit.

Figure 5.10 Public Revelation of Private Facts and Commercial Appropriation

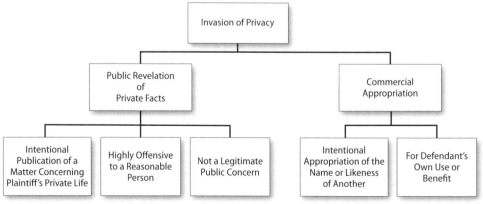

Finally, Portraying Plaintiff in a False Light is very similar to Defamation, which we'll discuss in detail later. False light is proven by showing the Defendant gave publicity to a private matter concerning Plaintiff, placing Plaintiff in a publicly false light. That light must be highly offensive to a reasonable person, and Defendant must have acted with knowledge or reckless disregard of the falsity of the claim.

Figure 5.11 False Light

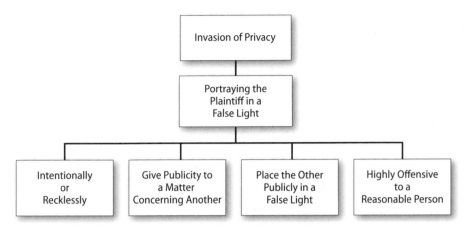

Keep a lookout for Constitutional issues that may arise with these privacy torts as well. We'll take a closer look at those when we discuss defenses.

This concludes our discussion of intentional injury to a person. We'll move on now to torts that arise from the intentional injury of property. There are three property interests that apply:

1) Real Property;

2) Personal Property; and

3) Business.

Figure 5.12 Intentional Torts against Property

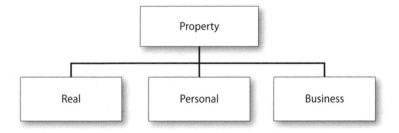

There are two ways in which a Defendant can interfere with Real Property. They are Trespass to Land and Nuisance, which can be either public or private. When dealing with trespass to land, remember the effect of mistake. Intent is shown when Defendant invades Plaintiff's land with knowledge that a trespass would result. It generally doesn't matter if Defendant is mistaken with regard to fact or law unless the jurisdiction follows the innocent trespasser rule.

Figure 5.13 Injury to Real Property

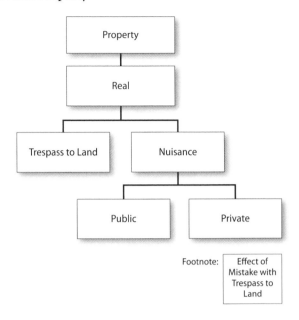

This brings us to the interference with personal property, which results in either Trespass to Chattel or Conversion. The effect of mistake is also applicable to Conversion.

Figure 5.14 Injury to Personal Property

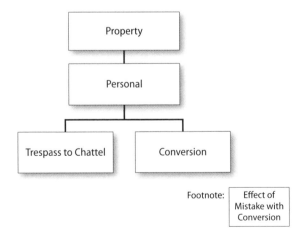

Finally, Deceit and Inducing Breach of Contract and Interfering with a Prospective Business Advantage round out the intentional torts involving property.

Figure 5.15 Intentional Torts against Business Interest

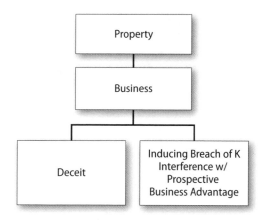

Now let's move on to Defenses to Intentional Tort. There are four main defenses:

1) Consent;

2) Authority;

3) Defense of _____; and

4) Necessity.

Figure 5.16 Defenses to Intentional Torts

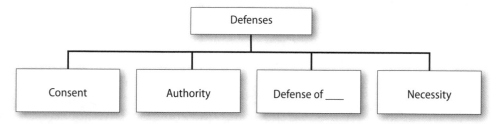

First, a Defendant may be able to claim that Plaintiff consented to the conduct. Watch out for situations where the scope of consent might be limited, where the consent was obtained by fraud or where consent may be illegal. The Defense of Authority includes Discipline, Arrest and the Shopkeeper's Privilege.

Figure 5.17 Consent and Authority

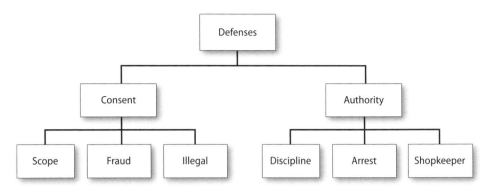

Now let's complete the blank space in the "Defense of" category. A Defendant may be able to defend himself against an intentional tort claim by arguing self-defense, defense of others, or defense of property. Finally, Defendant may also be able to claim either public or private necessity as a defense to an intentional torts claim.

Figure 5.18 Defense of ___ and Necessity

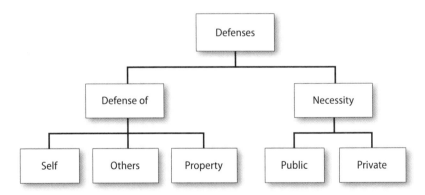

That wraps up our review of Intentional Torts! In the next chapter, we'll explore the most highly tested tort of Negligence.

6

Negligence

Negligence is the most heavily tested area of Tort Law. It differs from Intentional Torts, because Defendant can be held liable for his acts even if he did not act intentionally. Rather, he must have acted negligently. In order to prove a claim for Negligence, Plaintiff must show 1) That Defendant owed her a **duty** (which is established by the appropriate **standard of care**), 2) Defendant **breached** that duty, 3) the breach actually and proximately **caused** plaintiff damages, and 4) Plaintiff suffered **damages** as a result. Finally, don't forget about **defenses!**

Figure 6.1 Negligence

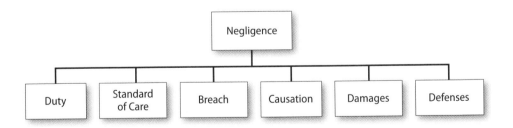

Now let's get into the discussion of each element. Any time Defendant acts, he owes a duty of reasonable care to foreseeable Plaintiffs, unless there is an exception. A duty could also exist where there is an omission to act. There are special rules that apply to bystanders, good Samaritans and those with "special relationships."

Figure 6.2 Duty: Act and Omission to Act

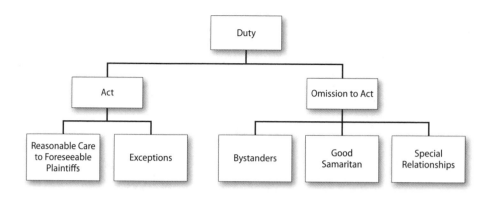

Let's examine duty when a Defendant chooses to act. Again, Defendant owes a duty of reasonable care to all foreseeable Plaintiffs. (Be sure to remember the Cordozo and Andrews views on this topic, as you may come across a "Think-um" question that tests the issue of duty in depth.) The first exception occurs if you find yourself dealing with a Defendant who is a Land Occupier. In that case, the traditional standard of care depended on the status of the Plaintiff as a trespasser, licensee, or invitee. The modern rule is that a duty of reasonable care is owed regardless of Plaintiff's status. This is also the rule in California.

Other exceptions include Emotional Distress and Wrongful Life. There is generally no duty for purely emotional harm, although courts have started to protect Plaintiffs in a few situations.

Figure 6.3 Duty of Reasonable Care and Exceptions

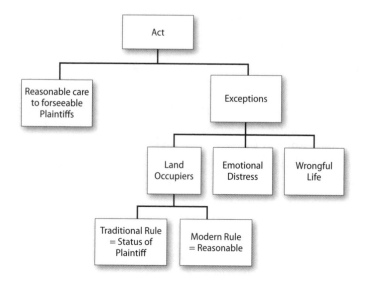

We now have to determine the applicable standard of care in our Negligence analysis. In most situations, the reasonable person standard will be the applicable standard of care. In other words, Defendant must exercise reasonable care under the circumstances.

Standard of care becomes an issue when the facts indicate that some other standard of care should apply. Sometimes the standard of care can be established by statute, wherein the doctrine of Negligence Per Se becomes applicable. Sometimes it can also be established by custom. Other variations on the general standard include the standard of care owed by common carriers, professionals, the mentally ill, and children. Also, keep an eye out for situations where the standard may change due to an emergency.

Figure 6.4 Standard of Care

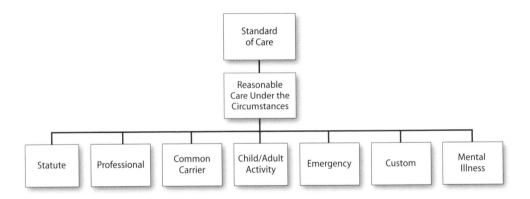

If Defendant's conduct falls below the standard of care, breach is established. However, a little analysis may be needed to establish such a breach. There are three main ways a Plaintiff can prove breach. They include 1) an unexcused violation of a statute (Negligence Per Se) 2) the failure to act reasonably, which may be established by the Learned Hand Test, and 3) Res Ipsa Loquitor.

In order to prove breach using Negligence Per Se, you must show that 1) Plaintiff was in the class of persons the statute was meant to protect, 2) Plaintiff suffered the type of harm the statute was meant to protect against, and 3) Defendant's conduct was not excused.

In order to prove the Defendant acted unreasonably using the Learned Hand Test, you must show that the probability and gravity of the harm outweighed the burden to protect against it, plus the social utility (if any) of Defendant's conduct.

Finally, to prove breach using Res Ipsa Loquitor, Plaintiff must show that there was probably negligence, that it was likely defendant's negligence, and the Plaintiff was not at fault.

One mistake I've seen students make is that they think they need to use all three of these when analyzing a negligence problem. This is not the case. I've included a few practice essays to help illustrate this point.

Figure 6.5 Breach

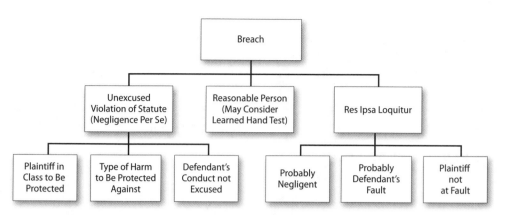

Learned Hand Test: Balance the gravity and likelihood with the burden and utility (B < PL)

Also, remember that no matter how you establish breach, you do not automatically establish a negligence claim. To complete your negligence analysis, you must also prove Causation and Damages.

Now on to Causation! To prove Causation, plaintiff must prove that Defendant's acts were both the actual and proximate cause of Plaintiff's injuries. To avoid any confusion, keep in mind that the term "factual cause" is sometimes used in place of "Actual Cause" and the term "legal cause" is sometimes used in place of "Proximate Cause."

Figure 6.6 Causation

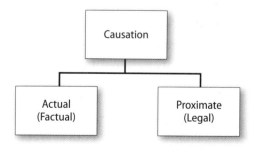

Actual Cause establishes the causal link between the defendant's conduct and the plaintiff's injuries. There are two main tests used to establish Actual Cause: 1) The "But-For" Test, and 2) The Substantial Factor Test. Under the "But-For" Test, the plaintiff must prove that "but for" the defendant's act, the plaintiff would not have been injured. Under the Substantial Factor Test, the plaintiff must prove that the defendant's act was a substantial or material factor which caused the plaintiff's injury. If there is only one cause that you can identify as the cause of the plaintiff's injury, you should apply the "but-for" test. If there's more than one cause, you should apply the "substantial factor" test.

In situations where the plaintiff cannot identify with specificity which among multiple defendants engaging in substantially simultaneous negligent conduct, only one of which injures the plaintiff and causes his harm, the burden shifts to the defendants to prove which one caused the plaintiff's injuries. This principle of alternative liability was established by the California Supreme Court in *Summers v. Tice*, 33 Cal.2d 80, 199 P.2d 1 (1948).

Finally, Market Share Liability may be available when a plaintiff is unable to prove which defendant is responsible for how much of the plaintiff's injuries. In such a case, the court would hold each defendant responsible for the same percentage of the damages as the percentage of market share that defendant has.

Figure 6.7 Actual (Factual) Cause

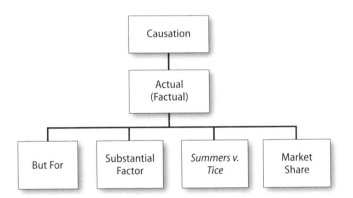

While Actual Cause is concerned with **whether** Defendant's conduct caused Plaintiff's injuries, Proximate Cause examines **how** the injury resulted from Defendant's Conduct. This is a policy limitation wherein there is no liability if Plaintiff's injury was not foreseeable because it was sufficiently unexpected or bizarre. This does not mean that Defendant's conduct was not negligent, rather, it means that the Defendant is not liable for negligence. Liability will not attach unless Proximate Cause is established.

When examining fact patterns for proximate cause issues, we look for an unforeseeable plaintiff, an unforeseeable manner of injury, an unforeseeable type of injury, or unforeseeable events. Noticeably absent is an unforeseeable extent of injury. This is because of the "Eggshell Plaintiff Rule." The Defendant takes the Plaintiff as he finds him and is responsible for whatever damage is caused.

Figure 6.8 Proximate (Legal) Cause

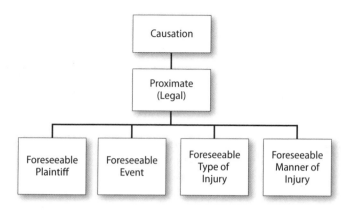

Finally, a Plaintiff must also prove the final element of Damages. If there are no damages, there is no recovery for negligence. We will look at what damages are available when we discuss remedies available for all torts.

Figure 6.9 Damages

Now that we've established Negligence, we need to consider any available defenses. The main defenses available in a Negligence case are Contributory Negligence, Comparative Negligence, and Assumption of the Risk.

Contributory Negligence is the negligence of the plaintiff that contributes to the accident. Its effect is that a plaintiff who is shown to be contributorily negligent is totally barred from recovery. Comparative negligence is the negligence of the plaintiff that contributes to the accident. Its effect is that the plaintiff's recovery is reduced by the percentage of her negligence.

Comparative negligence is now the approach followed by most jurisdictions and is either pure or modified. Under a pure comparative negligence system, damages are always apportioned regardless of the percentages of fault between the parties. Under a modified or partial comparative negligence system, damages are apportioned only if the defendant is more at fault that the plaintiff. If the plaintiff is more at fault than the defendant, the plaintiff is barred from recovery.

Assumption of the Risk exists where there is a voluntary exposure to a known and appreciated risk. The plaintiff must know and appreciate the risk involved, yet voluntarily choose to expose herself to that risk. This assumption can either be express or implied. An Express Assumption of the Risk will completely bar a Plaintiff from recovery. An Implied Assumption of the Risk traditionally had the same effect. However, many jurisdictions have absorbed it into comparative negligence.

Figure 6.10 Defenses

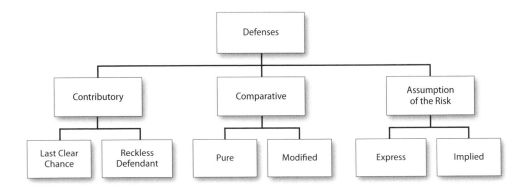

Let's wrap up our discussion of this chapter with a quick look at Negligent Infliction of Emotional Distress ("NIED").

To prove NIED, Plaintiff must show 1) negligent conduct 2) causing emotional distress 3) that manifests itself with physical symptoms or results from physical impact. In many jurisdictions, bystanders can recover, but they generally must be 1) close in time and relationship to the actual victim of the defendant's conduct, 2) be present and aware, and 3) suffer emotional distress.

Figure 6.11 Negligent Infliction of Emotional Distress

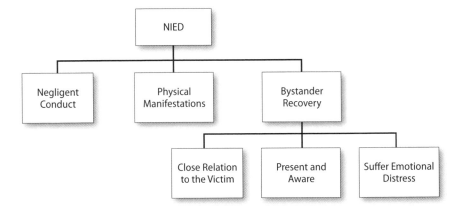

This wraps up our flowcharts for Negligence. If you are uncomfortable with any of the concepts covered, make sure to go back and review the substantive law, as I can guarantee that you will be tested on Negligence at some point in some fashion. Remember, Torts is a three-part hierarchy. Negligence is the most important, Intentional Torts and Strict Liability are second, and Defamation/Privacy/Misrepresentation/Fraud/Nuisance are third in importance. In the next chapter, we'll take a look at Strict Liability in detail.

7

Strict Liability

We now move on from Negligence to a new tort theory: Strict Liability. Strict Liability is different from Negligence and Intentional Torts, because a plaintiff does not need not prove unreasonable or intentional conduct to succeed on a claim of strict liability. Rather, Defendant will be held strictly liable despite the amount of care exercised in certain situations. Strict liability primarily relates to two categories of situations: Defendant's Acts and Strict Liability for Defective Products.

Figure 7.1 Strict Liability

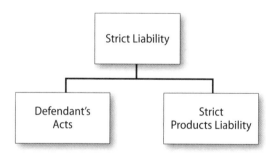

Defendant's Acts has three categories of situations: wild animals, abnormally dangerous activities, and defective products. So, if you see a situation wherein Plaintiff is injured by a wild animal, meaning that it is not generally considered to be domesticated, Defendant can be held strictly labile. The same thing is true is Plaintiff is injured while Defendant is engaged in an abnormally dangerous activity or if Plaintiff is injured by a defective product created by Defendant.

Figure 7.2 Defendant's Acts

When dealing with animals; make sure that you are dealing with a wild animal in order for strict liability to apply. If Plaintiff is injured by a domesticated animal, such as a pet cat or dog, generally negligence will apply. Be on the lookout for facts that indicate that Defendant is keeping a wild animal as a pet. In most instances, even though the wild animal is a pet, strict liability will apply.

Figure 7.3 Animals

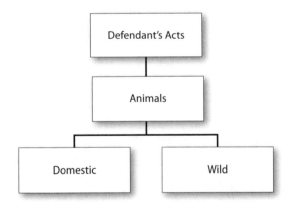

With Abnormally Dangerous Activities, you will look for situations wherein Defendant is engaged in a high-risk activity that is uncommon in the area, wherein Defendant cannot eliminate the risk. Working with dynamite is a good example.

Figure 7.4 Abnormally Dangerous Activities

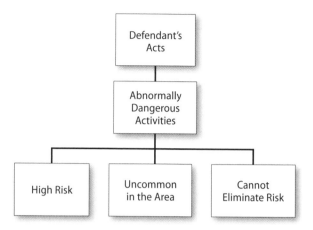

When Plaintiff is injured by a defective product, you may be able to recover under theories of Intentional Tort, Negligence, Strict Liability, or Breach of Implied or Express Warranties. Remember that the applicable implied warranties are the Warranty of Merchantability and the Implied Warranty of Fitness for a Particular Purpose.

Figure 7.5 Defective Products: Defendant Creates Defective Product

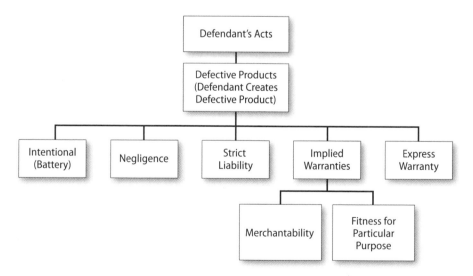

Now let's turn our attention to Strict Products Liability in more detail. When proving a valid strict products liability claim, remember to include the essential elements of Proper Parties, Defective Product, Causation, Damages, and Absence of Defenses.

Figure 7.6 Strict Products Liability

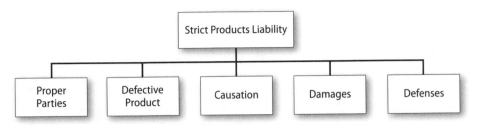

When we break the first two elements down, we note that a Proper Plaintiff can be a Buyer, User, or Bystander. A Proper Defendant can be a Manufacturer, Retailer, Assembler, or Franchisor. The Defective Product element can be shown by proving a Manufacturing Flaw, a Design Defect, or by a Lack of Warning. When considering whether there is a defect in design, most courts use either the Consumer Contemplation Test or the Feasible Alternative Test, where it weighs the danger against the utility of the design.

Figure 7.7 Proper Parties and Defective Product

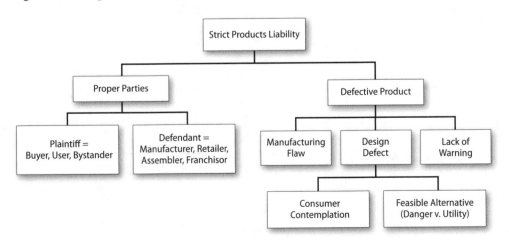

The last three elements include Causation, Damages, and Absence of Defenses. Remember to prove both actual and proximate cause when proving causation. Damages can include Personal Injury, Property Damage, and Economic Loss. Most courts do not allow for recovery of purely economic loss, which includes items such as cost of repairs, cost of replacement and loss of profits.

Finally, when evaluating a Strict Products Liability problem, make sure there is no applicable Defense. The two big ones are Product Misuse and Plaintiff's Fault. Assumption of the risk applies to products liability cases to bar any claim by the plaintiff who knowingly and voluntarily assumed the risk. Although contributory negligence and comparative fault were not defenses under the traditional rule, many jurisdictions now extend comparative fault to strict liability, so that the plaintiff's negligence will reduce her recovery.

Figure 7.8 Causation, Damages, and Defenses

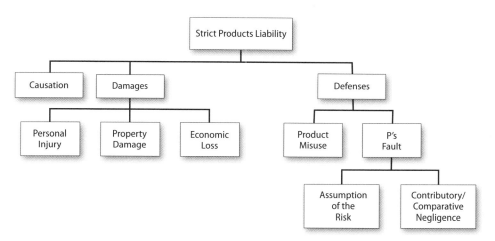

8

Defamation

Defamation, much like Invasion of Privacy and Misrepresentation, addresses harms to interests other than personal or property injury. Defamation redresses harm to a person's reputation and, for our purposes, comes in the form of Libel and Slander.

As we begin, notice that there are four main points of discussion. We need to make sure we know the Common Law, Constitutional Law (First Amendment Applicability), Defenses and Privileges. Also, remember that Invasion of Privacy or IIED or NIED are often partner issues to consider for a defamation claim.

Figure 8.1 Defamation

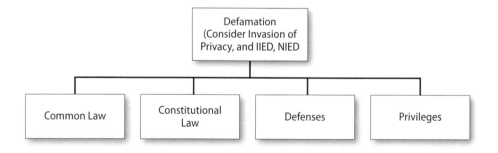

At common law, Defamation first requires proof that Defendant made a defamatory statement of fact that is harmful to Plaintiff's reputation. Remember that statements of fact are susceptible to factual proof, whereas statements of opinion are not actionable. Second, the statement must concern Plaintiff. The statements can be directed towards an individual or small group, and Plaintiff can use extrinsic facts such as inducement, colloquium and innuendo if the words are not defamatory on their face. Note also that Plaintiff must prove that the statement was published (communicated) to a Third Party, and that it was damaging to her.

Figure 8.2 Common Law

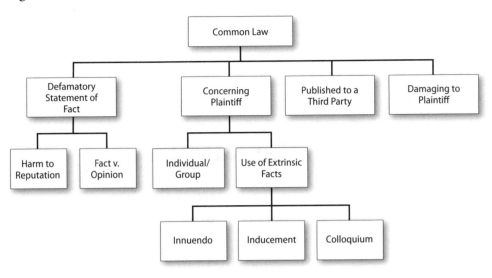

Let's unpack the "Published to a Third Party" element in a little more detail. First, we have to look at Defendant's fault. Defendant has to either intentionally or negligently publish the statement. Strict Liability is not applicable to a defamation claim.

Also, remember that initial publishers, repeaters and disseminators can be responsible for defamation.

Figure 8.3 Published to a Third Party

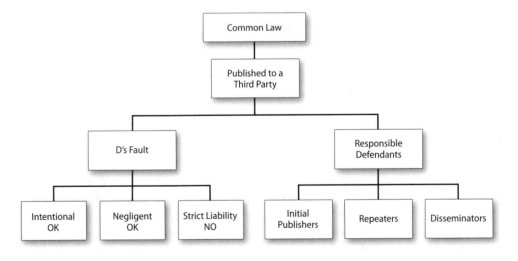

The last element of the common law defamation claim is that the statement must be damaging to Plaintiff. The first thing you have to determine is whether you are dealing with libel or slander. If it is ordinary slander, special damages must be proved. If the statement concerns Plaintiff's business or profession, lack of chastity, or a loathsome disease or guilt of a crime involving moral turpitude, it is defamation per se and no special damages need to be proved.

If it is libel, you need to determine whether it is libel per se or libel per quod. Libel Per Se requires no extrinsic facts to understand the defamatory import, whereas Libel per Quod does. With Libel Per Se, damages are presumed, whereas Libel Per Quod requires proof of special damages.

Figure 8.4 Damaging to Plaintiff

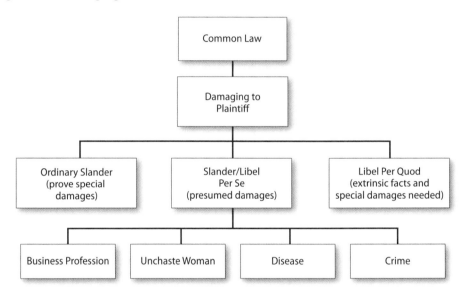

We now must consider Constitutional Law implications in Defamation suits. First, you must determine whether you are dealing with a plaintiff that is a public figure or a plaintiff that is a private person. Then, you have to determine whether the subject matter is a matter of public or private concern. Then you must determine whether the applicable standard was violated.

Figure 8.5 Constitutional Law

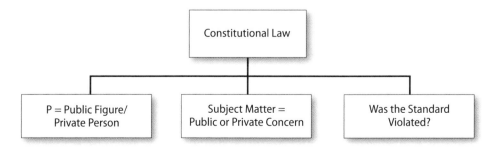

When considering whether the standard was violated, we first have to know what that standard is. If the plaintiff is a public official or public figure, she must prove actual malice, meaning that the publisher of the statement in question knew that the statement was false or acted in reckless disregard of its truth or falsity. When dealing with Private Figure Plaintiffs, proof of Negligence is all that is required, unless you are dealing with Non-Media Defendant in a matter of Public Concern. In that case, proof of malice is required.

Figure 8.6 Constitutional Law Standards

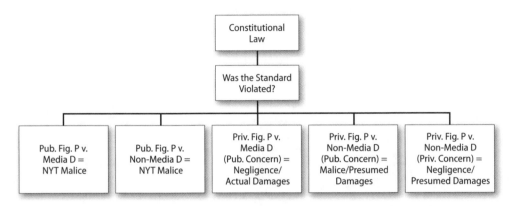

Finally, we can take a look at Defenses and Privileges. A defendant can defend on the basis of truth, consent, and retraction. A defendant may also enjoy an absolute or conditional privilege. Governmental and spousal privileges are absolute, while a statement made for reporting, fair comment or common interest are conditional privileges. Just make sure to keep a lookout for circumstances that may indicate that the qualified privilege has been exceeded.

Figure 8.7 Defenses and Privileges

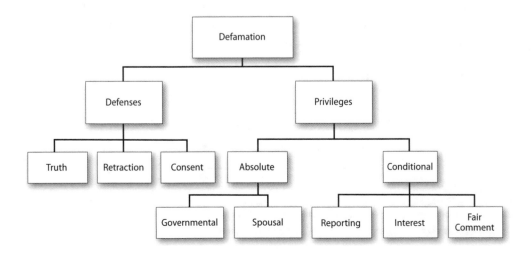

Whew! That wraps up all of the various Torts that can be tested. Make sure you know all of them, including their definitions and/or elements. Using flashcards to drill yourself on the definitions and elements will definitely help. Also, it's worth repeating, memorize these flowcharts in an effort to create a mental checklist for exam day. If you can picture the charts, you will know what issues to look out for as you read the facts.

Now, we have just one more topic to discuss before moving on to Criminal Law. Even though Remedies is a complete course in itself, you need to have a general idea of what types of remedies are available for specific torts.

In a nutshell, there are three types of damages: nominal, compensatory, and punitive. With compensatory damages, a plaintiff suffering personal injury can recover general and special damages, while a plaintiff suffering injury to property can recover compensatory damages when a defendant destroys, damages, or takes the plaintiff's property.

Figure 8.8 Remedies

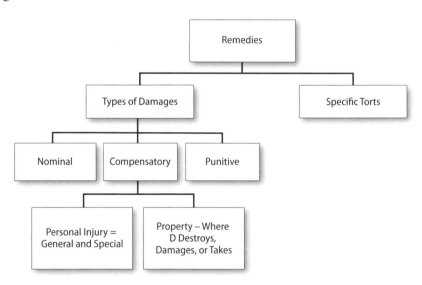

Turning our focus to specific torts, Assault, Battery, False Imprisonment, and Mental Distress, Plaintiff can recover nominal or compensatory damages, as well as punitive damages if Defendant acts with malice.

Victims of Trespass to Property can recover the rental value or the benefit to the Defendant if the trespass results in an ouster. If the trespass results in a severance injury, Plaintiff can recover the diminution in value or the cost of repair.

Figure 8.9 Specific Torts—Assault, Battery, False Imprisonment, Mental Distress, Trespass to Real Property

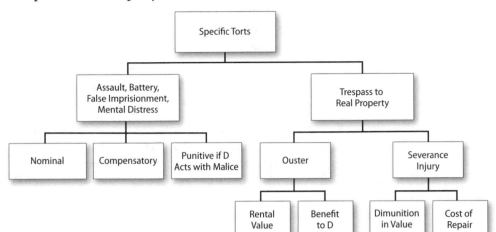

Plaintiffs proving Public Nuisance can recover only if they have a special type of injury, while Plaintiffs proving private nuisance can recover for the loss of use or enjoyment of their property. If the nuisance is permanent, Plaintiff can recover the diminution in value caused by the nuisance.

Plaintiff proving Trespass to Chattel can recover either diminution in value or the cost of repair, depending on the nature and extent of the damage, while Plaintiffs proving Conversion can recover the fair market value.

Figure 8.10 Specific Torts—Nuisance, Trespass to Chattel, Conversion

```
                            Specific Torts
        ┌──────────────────────┼──────────────────────┐
     Nuisance          Trespass to              Conversion
                          Chattel
  ┌────────┴────────┐         │                      │
 Public          Private   Depends on           Fair Market Value
(Private Plaintiff         Nature & Extent
Can Sue if Special         of Damages
Type of Injury)            (Diminution in Value
                           or Cost of Repair)
        ┌──────────┴──────────┐
 Permanent Nuisance =     Loss of Use
 Diminution in Value      or Enjoyment
```

Finally, when considering remedies for Negligence and Strict Liability, look for all loss proximately caused, while remedies available for Products Liability will depend on the theory of recovery.

Figure 8.11 Specific Torts — Negligence, Strict Liability, Products Liability

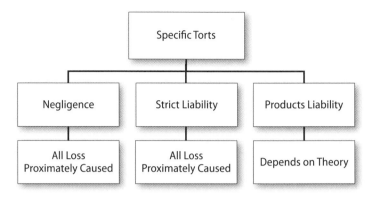

That's it for our Torts flowchart. Now it's time to practice! Be sure to complete all of the practice questions on your own before referring to the sample answers to assess your work. Again, if you find yourself too far off track, review the substantive law and try again. After all, mastery takes lots of practice! Criminal Law is next.

Criminal Law

9

Criminal Law Overview

It's now time to turn our attention to Criminal Law. In a nutshell, in Criminal Law, we address three main areas: Crimes against a Person, Crimes against Property, and Preliminary Crimes.

Figure 9.1 Criminal Law

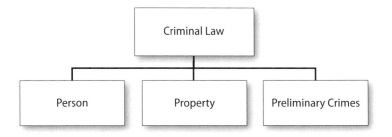

The Crimes Against a Person puzzle begins with Criminal Homicide, which will either result in Murder or Manslaughter. We'll talk about murder in more detail, but for now, just know that it comes in two forms, first and second degree. You'll noticed that there is a (P) next to first degree. This is there to let you know that you may find yourself dealing with Preliminary Crimes when you discuss first degree murder. This will not be an issue with second degree murder or manslaughter. Manslaughter will either be voluntary or involuntary.

Figure 9.2 Crimes against a Person: Criminal Homicide

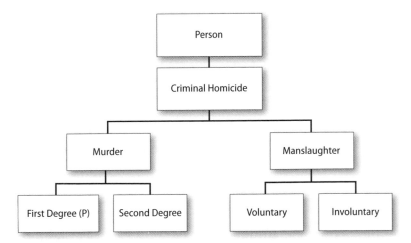

*(P) reminds you to consider Preliminary Crimes:
Solicitation, Attempt, and Conspiracy.

From here, we move to the other crimes against a person. They include Assault, Battery, and False Imprisonment/Kidnapping. Battery includes Rape and Mayhem, and we may have to consider preliminary crimes when discussing Assault, Rape, and False Imprisonment/Kidnapping.

Figure 9.3 Crimes against a Person: Other

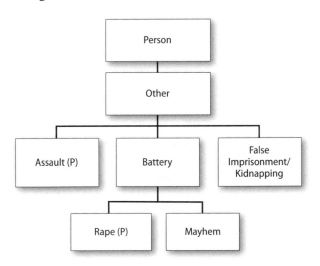

*(P) reminds you to consider Preliminary Crimes:
Solicitation, Attempt, and Conspiracy.

10

Criminal Homicide: Murder & Manslaughter

Let's focus on Criminal Homicide and Murder in more detail. There are three main areas that you must discuss whenever the facts raise a murder issue. They are homicide, malice, and degrees.

Figure 10.1 Murder

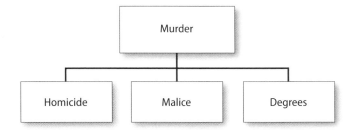

The first element that we must establish is that a homicide occurred, meaning that Defendant caused the death of another. You can establish this by showing that Defendant engaged in an act that directly caused the death of the victim. You may also encounter a situation wherein Defendant's act is an intervening act and is the proximate cause of death or where there is a consequence to Defendant's failure or omission to act. Finally, there are situations where Defendant may be vicariously liable for the death of the victim as an accomplice or under the doctrine of Felony Murder.

Figure 10.2 Homicide

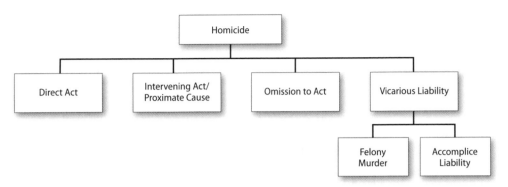

The second element of murder is Malice. You cannot have murder without proving one of the four types of malice. Malice exists if Defendant acts with the intent to kill or intent to cause serious bodily injury. Intent to kill can be inferred by the Deadly Weapon Doctrine if the Defendant uses a deadly weapon in a way that brings about the death of the victim. Malice can also be found if Defendant acts with a depraved heart (a reckless disregard for human life), or if Felony Murder can be established. Felony Murder applies if the prosecution can prove 1) an inherently dangerous felony, 2) that the killing occurred during the perpetration of the felony, and 3) there are no applicable vicarious liability limitations.

Figure 10.3 Malice

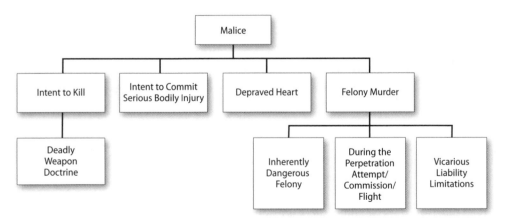

Now, if you are unable to prove any of the four types of malice, or if there is a question as to whether malice may apply, you will need to discuss Involuntary Manslaughter. For example, Defendant's conduct may not rise to the level of depraved heart conduct. In that case, just to cover your bases, you would want to discuss the reckless or grossly negligent conduct form of involuntary manslaughter.

However, if you *do* find that one of these four types of malice exists, you must then discuss the degrees of murder. Most jurisdictions divide murder into either first or second degree. First degree murder applies if Defendant acted with the intent to kill coupled with premeditation and deliberation. Proving Felony Murder will also result in a first-degree murder charge. Second degree murder applies if Defendant intended to kill without premeditation or deliberation or where Defendant acted with a depraved heart or intent to cause serious bodily injury.

Figure 10.4 Degrees

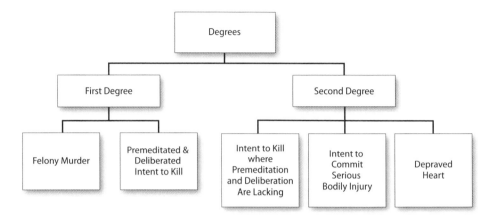

We can't stop there, however. If you have found that one of the for types of malice exist, you must ask yourself if the crime is justified or excused, in which case there is no criminal liability, or if there are mitigating factors that will reduce Murder to Voluntary Manslaughter. (Remember also that if there is no malice, you may have Involuntary Manslaughter.)

Figure 10.5 Effect of Conclusion Regarding Malice

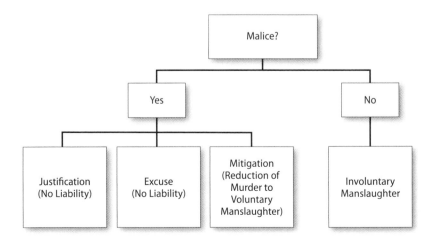

A murder is justified if one of the following defenses apply: 1) Prevention of a Crime or Apprehension of a Fleeing Felon, 2) Defense of Self or Others, or 3) Reasonable Mistake.

Figure 10.6 Defenses: Justification

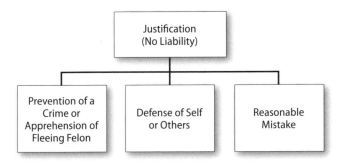

An act with malice can be excused by 1) Youth, 2) Mental Illness, or 3) Intoxication. Intoxication can be either voluntary or involuntary. It can negate an element of a crime and render the defendant not guilty, but it must be involuntary in the majority of states for this defense to work.

When dealing with Mental Illness, you need to know the various tests for insanity. 1) M'Naghten is the traditional rule and requires proof that due to a defect in reasoning caused by a mental disease, Defendant did not know right from wrong or did not know the nature and quality of his actions. 2) The Irresistible Impulse test requires also that the mental disease kept Defendant from controlling her conduct. 3) The Substantial Capacity (MPC) test requires proof that as a result of mental disease or defect, Defendant lacked the substantial capacity to either understand the difference between right and wrong or to conform her conduct to the dictates of the law. Finally, 4) the Durham test, which is the minority view, requires that the crime must be a product of a mental disease.

Figure 10.7 Excuse

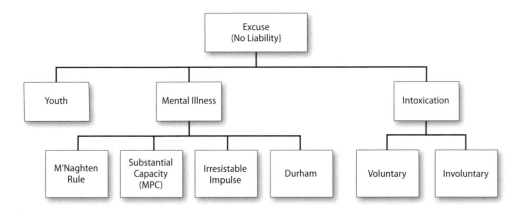

There's one last defense that may apply when you find that malice exists. Always check to see if the murder can be mitigated to Voluntary Manslaughter. An act with malice causing death may be reduced to voluntary manslaughter by one of three mitigating factors: 1) a Good Faith Mistake; 2) Adequate Provocation or Anger; or 3) Coercion or Necessity.

When considering Adequate Provocation, or whether Defendant killed "in the heat of passion," remember to analyze the requirements of reasonableness and "cooling off." Consider whether Defendant was actually provoked and whether she had time to cool off, as well as whether a reasonable person would have been so provoked and would have cooled off.

Figure 10.8 Mitigation: Reduction of Murder to Voluntary Manslaughter

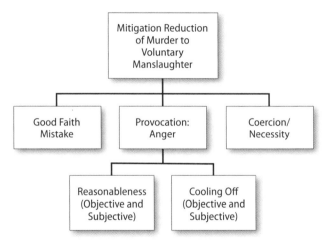

We finally turn our attention to Involuntary Manslaughter. This can result if you find that a homicide has been committed but malice *does not* exist. If you don't find malice, but Defendant's act still causes a death, look to see if Defendant acted with criminal or gross negligence (as opposed to depraved heart conduct required for malice). If so, Defendant should be charged with Involuntary Manslaughter. The same is true if the killing occurred while Defendant was engaged in a misdemeanor which is malum in se (wrong in itself) or while Defendant was engaged in a non-dangerous felony (as opposed to felony murder malice). Finally, Defendant can be found guilty of Involuntary Manslaughter if she only intended slight injury (as opposed to intent to cause extreme bodily injury required for malice).

Figure 10.9 Involuntary Manslaughter

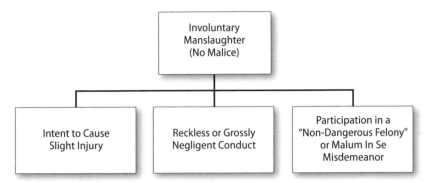

That wraps up crimes that can be committed against a person. We'll continue our Criminal Law Puzzle in the next chapter by examining Crimes against Property and the various Theft Crimes in detail.

11

Crimes against
Property & Theft Crimes

Remember when we took our first look at the Criminal Law puzzle, we saw that the three main areas were crimes against a person, crimes against property and preliminary crimes. We are now turning our focus to crimes against Property, wherein there are two main areas of concerns: Theft and Structures. Theft requires a taking, whereas Structures requires an entering or burning, specifically Burglary or Arson. Theft, Burglary, and Arson may warrant a discussion of Preliminary Crimes, so we have given it the requisite "P" note.

Note that larceny crimes include robbery and extortion, as well as those crimes where Defendant takes delivery of property by means of Embezzlement, Larceny by Trick, or False Pretenses.

Figure 11.1 Crimes against Property

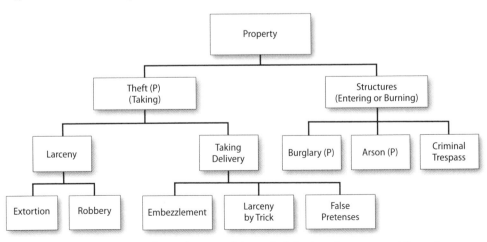

*(P) reminds you to consider Preliminary Crimes: Solicitation, Attempt, and Conspiracy.

Let's focus on Larceny and the other theft crimes in more detail. First, the crime of Larceny requires proof of a trespassory taking and carrying away the personal property of another with the intent to permanently deprive.

Figure 11.2 Theft Crimes: Larceny

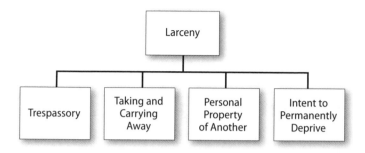

Robbery is very similar in that it requires the same elements as larceny, but adds that the taking must be achieved by means of force or threat of force.

Figure 11.3 Robbery

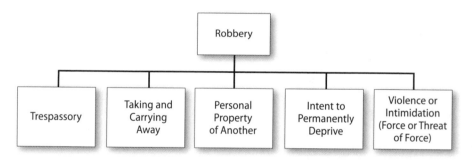

Embezzlement, our first crime that involves taking delivery of property, is accomplished by the fraudulent conversion of the property of another by one who already has lawful possession of it.

Figure 11.4 Embezzlement

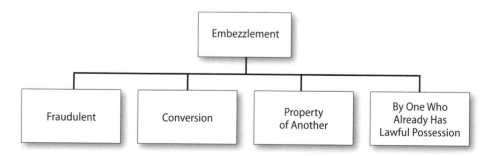

Larceny by Trick requires all of the same elements as larceny but adds that the intent to permanently deprive is formed after obtaining permission by means of written or oral lies or false pretenses.

Figure 11.5 Larceny by Trick

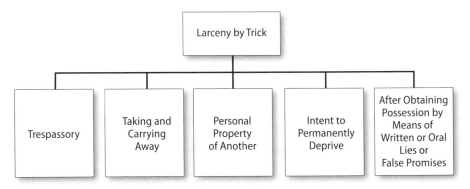

Finally, False Pretenses is a theft crime wherein Defendant makes a false representation of a material present or past fact which causes the victim to pass title to the wrongdoer who knows the representation to be false and intends thereby to defraud the victim.

Figure 11.6 False Pretenses

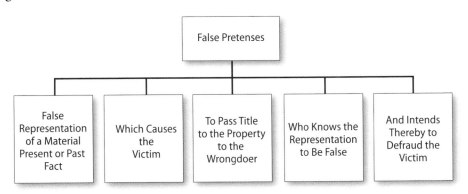

The biggest problem most students have is differentiating between the theft crimes. They know the elements, but when faced with a fact pattern, cannot accurately label the crime tested. The secret is to determine when the intent to steal is formed and whether possession or custody is obtained.

The handy box below may help. If the intent to steal is established *now* (at the time of the act), and *custody* is obtained, the crime is larceny. If the intent to steal is established *later* (after the time of the act), and *custody* is obtained, the crime is also larceny. If the intent to steal is established *now* and *possession* is obtained, the crime is larceny by trick. If the intent to steal is established *later* and *possession* is obtained, the crime is embezzlement. If the intent to steal is *now* and *title* is obtained, the crime is false pretenses. Finally, if the intent to steal is *later*, and the *title* is obtained, there is no crime.

Figure 11.7 Identifying Theft Crimes

Theft Crimes

	NOW	LATER
CUSTODY	Larceny	Larceny
POSSESSION	Larceny by Trick	Embezzlement
TITLE	False Pretenses	No Crime

We're almost done! Remember that we have to consider both theft and structures when dealing with property crimes. While theft involves a taking, structures deal with entering (Burglary) and burning (Arson.) Let's start with Burglary first. It also has a "P" note as a specific intent crime. It requires a trespassory breaking and entering of a protected structure with the intent to commit a felony therein.

Figure 11.8 Structures: Burglary

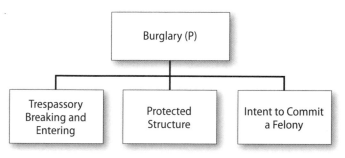

*(P) reminds you to consider Preliminary Crimes:
Solicitation, Attempt, and Conspiracy.

Finally, Arson is also a specific intent crime with a "P" note and requires the burning of a protected structure with malice. Remember that some jurisdictions will also allow for a finding of arson where the burning is reckless or indifferent.

Figure 11.9 Structures: Arson

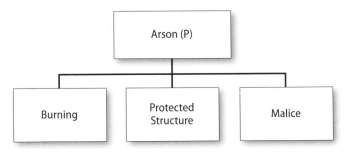

*(P) reminds you to consider Preliminary Crimes:
Solicitation, Attempt, and Conspiracy.

We have one more subject to discuss before wrapping up Criminal Law. Preliminary Crimes are next!

12

Preliminary Crimes

The last piece of the puzzle in Criminal Law concerns Preliminary Crimes. Remember that we put a "P" note on several crimes. Consider all of them "target crimes" that could be the intended result of a preliminary crime. Also, notice that all of them are specific intent crimes.

There are three possible preliminary crimes: Solicitation, Conspiracy, and Attempt. The first step is **solicitation** (someone asks another to commit a crime), the next step is **conspiracy** (the other person asked actually agrees), and the final step is **attempt** (there is an act with the intent to commit the crime which goes beyond mere asking or agreeing, **and** is an act sufficient to qualify as attempt). Therefore, the timeline is Ask/Solicitation — Agree/Conspiracy — Act/Attempt.

Figure 12.1 Preliminary Crimes Timeline

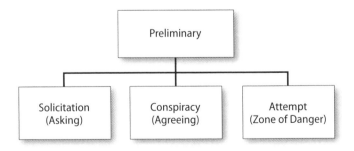

Let's talk about each in a little more detail. Solicitation is the asking of another to commit a crime, coupled with the specific intent that the crime actually be committed. Conspiracy is an agreement for some unlawful purpose. A majority of states now also require an overt act in furtherance. At common law, you needed an actual agreement with two guilty minds. Under the MPC and the unilateral theory, one guilty mind is enough. For Attempt, you must prove that the defendant had the specific intent to commit the crime and also engaged in conduct amounting to a substantial step or dangerously close to commission of that crime. Also, many jurisdictions require that as part of the substantial step/dangerously close analysis that the defendant must perform an overt act in furtherance of the crime.

Figure 12.2 Preliminary Crimes

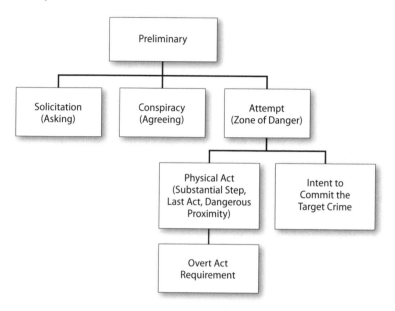

Finally, don't forget to consider any Vicarious Liability issues when discussing preliminary crimes. If the target crime is committed, the perpetrator not guilty of preliminary crimes, but others may be. Solicitation merges into Conspiracy, while a Defendant can be charged with both Conspiracy and the target crime.

Withdrawal can be a defense to both conspiracy and the target crime. Just double check to make sure that the withdrawal was effectively communicated, provided clear renunciation of the crime, and that it was timely enough to thwart the crime. Under common law, withdrawal is too late to negate liability for conspiracy, but timely communication to fellow co-conspirators will negate vicarious liability for future crimes. Finally, Impossibility may be a defense. It comes in two forms: Legal and Factual. Legal Impossibility is a complete defense where the intended act would not constitute a crime. Also, if you are dealing with a specific intent crime, look to see if Defendant actually believed that she was committing a lawful act. If so, she didn't have the specific intent to commit the crime.

Figure 12.3 Vicarious Liability

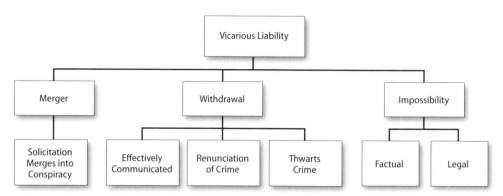

That wraps up our discussion of Criminal Law! Make sure to carefully review the substantive law if you find yourself unfamiliar with anything covered here. Also, remember that practice makes perfect, so be sure to test yourself as much as you can! Good luck on your exams!

Essay Writing

13

Organizational Templates and IRAC

Writing essay answers is not an easy task. As I mentioned, knowing the law and understanding how the pieces fit together is crucial. It will also help if you understand how to use an organizational template and how to write using the IRAC method.

Let's start with the idea of an organizational template. The flowcharts appearing in the previous chapters are an organizational template in themselves, in a sense. You can follow them to help determine what issues need to be addressed as well as the order in which they should be addressed. However, not every issue will be relevant in every essay. To make matters worse, sometimes your conclusion on one issue will cause you to have to consider different issues than if you had reached an opposite conclusion.

So where do you even start? I'll say it again. Start by knowing the law. You must simply know the material cold. Memorize it.

Start by walking through each box of the flowcharts and explain them to someone in a way that would make sense to someone who hasn't learned it yet. Make sure you have memorized all of the definitions and/or elements of every rule that is relevant to each box. Flashcards may help with this task.

Once you have memorized the law, you can begin practicing your essay writing. Having a good organizational template in mind will help guide you through the issues tested.

For example, with Contracts, the big picture tells us that you must first look to see if a contract is properly **Formed**. If it is not, it is not valid and no performance is due. If it is properly formed, then look to see if performance is waived or excused. If it is not waived or excused, then **Performance** is due. If one of the parties fails to perform or performs poorly, then he is in breach of contract. If there is a breach of contract, then you would determine what **Remedies** are available to the non-breaching party in order to compensate him for the breach.

So, let's say you have an essay question that ultimately asks whether a contract to buy widgets has been formed between the parties. You know right away that all of your focus should be on contract formation issues. Luckily, you have a handy dandy flowchart that you can use to help you organize your answer.

First, you know that the answer can vary depending on whether you are dealing with a common law or UCC contract, so that should be the first thing you mention. Write it down on a separate page to outline your general answer.

The next thing you must address is Mutual Assent. Write it down and, under that, write Offer and then Acceptance. Next, you must deal with Consideration. Write that down as well, followed by Defenses to Formation. Now, as you read through the facts of the essay, circle the triggering words that raise an issue and write them in the appropriate space on your outline.

Now, let's say that the facts show that the offeror changed her mind and tried to rescind the offer. This is a triggering fact that begs for a discussion of the mailbox rule to determine if the offer was still open when it was accepted. Therefore, we will write "Offer Still Open?" in our outline between our issues of offer and acceptance.

We may also see facts that suggest detrimental reliance. Therefore, we would add the issue "Promissory Estoppel" to our outline under the Consideration issue. Be sure to include the relevant facts in your outline as well, so you don't forget to include them in your analysis. After all, this is where the bulk of your points will come from!

So far, our Organizational Template/Essay Outline now looks like this:

UCC or Common Law?
Widgets = goods, so UCC controls.

Formation

Mutual Assent

Offer

Offer Still Open?
Offeror called to rescind before checking voicemail. Mailbox rule/merchant's firm offer.

Acceptance
Offeree left voice message accepting offer. Was offer accepted before it was rescinded?

Consideration

Promissory Estoppel
Offeree relied on acceptance. Reliance must be reasonable, foreseeable, and detrimental.

Defenses to Formation

See how that works? Basically, we are just working through the facts to determine what issue they relate to and where they should be discussed. This is how you use an organizational template to outline your answer before you begin to write. When we begin to practice writing your essays, you will see how several different organizational templates are used to help organize each answer.

Now that you know how to approach the overall organization of your essay, you need to understand how to write your essay using the IRAC method. In every law school essay, the facts will give rise to legal issues, and those issues have to be properly identified and analyzed prior to a conclusion being provided. Using "IRAC" means that you will first state the issue ("I"), then the rule ("R"), then apply the rule to the facts ("A"), and, finally, provide a conclusion ("C"). Hopefully you have heard of IRAC before, but just in case you haven't mastered the art of it yet, we'll give it a quick review.

First, know that IRAC is not my personal creation. It has been used since the beginning of time by lawyers, judges, legal educators, and yes, even bar examiners. I tell you this because using IRAC is not optional. You are *expected* to use IRAC in almost all forms of legal writing—especially on essay questions. The good news is that using IRAC also helps you avoid missing issues and allows you to more quickly organize and analyze your essay answers. So, get used to it, because it will be with you for the long haul.

First, let's make it as elementary as possible. Let's say someone presents you with an animal on your desk and asks for your opinion with regard to what type of animal it might be. You suspect that it may be a duck.

- The **Issue** is whether this animal is, in fact, a duck.
- The **Rule** is that ducks have:
    1) webbed feet;
    2) feathers; and
    3) quack.
- The **Analysis** is that the animal on your desk:
    1) has webbed feet just like a duck;
    2) has feathers just like a duck; and
    3) quacks just like a duck.
- The **Conclusion** is that the animal on your desk is a duck.

Now, I truly don't care if the animal on your desk is a duck, a goose, or even a platypus. The conclusion is not nearly as important as a well-reasoned analysis. Note particularly how the analysis section takes each element of the rule and discusses it separately.

Let's address each part of IRAC in a little more detail. After all, it will not always be as simple as our duck example.

First, a legal **Issue** concerns a right or obligation of a party. Issues are legal questions that must be determined by the court or the jury. In a contracts essay, a common issue will be whether the facts indicate that the parties have entered into a valid, legally enforceable, agreement. That broad issue statement will give rise to a discussion of the elements of a contract, including whether there was an offer, acceptance, and consideration, and whether there are any defenses to formation.

Issue spotting is an important skill. As you go through an essay, compare the checklist of possible issues against the facts and include any issue reasonably arguable under the facts of the problem. Doing lots of practice problems will help. The more examples you have of different situations where an issue arose, the easier it will be to spot that issue in the future fact patterns. This is true of cases you've read, as well. They show you sets of facts that raised particular issues. The more problems you do—and remember—the better.

Also, remember "partner" issues. These are issues and facts that usually appear together. For example, if you have an oral contract, you almost always have a Statute of Frauds issue. Remember to consider "nested" issues as well. These are issues within issues. These are the sub-issues you usually need to examine whenever a main issue comes along. For example, in a problem where the Statute of Frauds is an issue, there may also be an exception that should be addressed. That exception may also have certain requirements. This means you will need to identify both the exception and its requirements as sub-issues.

The R in IRAC stands for **Rule**. A rule statement is a discussion of the legal elements raised by the issue. If the issue is whether the contract must be in writing, the rule statement would discuss the Statute of Frauds (certain contracts must be in writing to be enforceable). A sub-issue that the facts may present is whether the contract, even though it is not in writing, falls within an exception to the Statute of Frauds, and the rule statement would describe the relevant exception.

The A in IRAC stands for **Analysis**. Once you have identified the issue and have described the rule, your job is to use the facts to show the reader whether they satisfy the rule. Continuing along with our Statute of Frauds example, your task is to examine the facts to see whether the contract is one that should be in writing, whether there is a sufficient writing, and if not, whether an exception applies. Note that these sub-issues will require their own IRAC analysis.

Finally, you will state a **Conclusion** at the end of each IRAC paragraph. This is simply a short sentence or two that describes how the identified issue should be decided.

Let's look at our Statute of Frauds example using IRAC labels to help identify each part:

Main Issue: Does the contract have to be in writing in order to be enforceable?

Main Rule: According to the Statute of Frauds, certain contracts, including contracts for the sale of any interest in land, must be in writing to be enforceable.

Main Analysis: Since this is a contract for the sale of a farm, which is an interest in land, it must be in writing in order to be enforceable. Because there is no writing, the contract does not satisfy the statute and is unenforceable unless an exception applies.

Sub-Issue: Does an exception to the Statute of Frauds apply?

Sub-Rule: An exception to the Statute of Frauds applies if there has been part performance with regard to the sale of land.

Sub-Rule: Part performance requires that the buyer took possession plus made some payment or made significant improvements.
Sub-Analysis: The buyer made a payment but did not take possession or make any improvements.

Sub-Conclusion: Therefore, the part performance exception does not apply.

Main Conclusion: Because the contract for the sale of land was not in writing and an exception does not apply, the contract is unenforceable.

Now that we have a good handle on organizational templates and IRAC, let's practice writing some essays!

14

Contracts Practice Essays

Now that you know the law and have an attack strategy, you have to practice writing as many essays as you can, covering as many issues as you can. Doing so will help you fill in any gaps in your knowledge, help you better understand how the issues are tested and organized, help you improve your timing, and eventually boost your confidence!

The following pages contain several sample essays. Read the question first and make your best effort to answer it on your own before reading the sample answer and related comments that appear in the next chapter. It should take you about an hour to write an answer to each practice essay.

After writing your answer, compare it to the sample answer and comments to assess your work. Pay careful attention to how the facts raise the issues tested, how the sample answer is organized, how the substance is analyzed, and how the rules are stated. Doing so will help when you find yourself writing an essay on similar topics in the future.

You may also find it helpful to work on the practice essays with a study partner or small study group. Just make sure you make an effort to always write your own answer first before sharing your effort and learning.

Finally, students that feel they need additional guidance as they work through the practice essays can visit PassTheFYLSE.com and submit their essays to a professor for personalized feedback. Students are also able to send specific academic questions or opt for more in-depth tutoring in a group or individual setting.

Contracts Essay 1:
Buyer v. Seller

Buyer wished to purchase a fancy machine recently introduced to the market that was in high demand. Buyer located a seller who would guarantee delivery within six months.

Seller sent Buyer a letter that stated: "Seller can obtain a new machine and hereby offers to sell the machine to Buyer for one million dollars. Seller promises delivery within three months from acceptance. This offer will be held open for one month."

Although Seller deals generally with one of Buyer's subsidiaries, Seller does not sell machines in the normal course of business. However, Seller knew Buyer urgently needed the machine and thought it could increase its goodwill with the sale.

Buyer immediately wrote a letter back to Seller, stating: "We are thrilled that you can deliver the machine in time to fill our needs. We will begin to construct facilities to house the machine immediately, but will continue to shop around. We will hold your offer under advisement for a few weeks as we shop around." Seller responded with a letter stating: "We acknowledge your letter."

Buyer soon became aware that the price of fancy machines had greatly increased, and that none could be purchased for less than $1.5 million, regardless of delivery date. While shopping around, Buyer spent $100,000 on facilities to house the machine.

Buyer decided to accept Seller's offer ten days after receiving the initial letter from Seller. On that same day, Buyer received a letter from Seller stating: "Due to dramatic increase in the market price of the machine, we hereby revoke our offer."

Buyer learned that Seller had obtained the machine and was about to sell the machine to a third company at a higher price.

Does Buyer have an enforceable contract with Seller?

Discuss.

Contracts Essay 2:
Barry v. Realtor

Realtor met Barry through a mutual friend. On Monday, June 30 at 9:00 a.m., Realtor faxed a letter to Barry at his office stating that she had 100 acres of land, located on the corner of First and Main that she would sell to him for $1,000 per acre. Realtor's letter also stated: "Unless I receive your written acceptance by Thursday, July 3 at 5:00 pm, my offer will expire. I will not offer this to anyone else until the offer expires or is rejected, whichever occurs first." Realtor's name, e-mail address, fax and phone numbers were printed at the bottom of the letter.

On July 3 at 1:00 pm, Barry emailed the Realtor a message stating: "I agree to buy your 100 acres for $1,000 per acre." Although Barry's e-mail reached Realtor's e-mailbox less than a minute later, she did not check her e-mail until after 5:00 p.m. on July 3.

Was Realtor's fax an offer to sell Barry 100 acres of undeveloped land for $1,000 per acre?

Assuming Realtor's fax was an offer, was she obligated to offer the land exclusively to Barry until it expired or was rejected, whichever happened first?

Assuming Realtor's fax was an offer, did Barry accept her offer by sending the e-mail on July 3?

Assuming Realtor's fax was an offer, if Barry died before the offer expired and before responding, could his son have accepted Realtor's offer, provided he did so according to its terms?

Suppose Realtor was anxious to sell the land before she left town for the weekend and agreed to sell the land to someone else for more money. Realtor sent a fax to Barry's office revoking her offer at 12:00 pm, by which time Barry and his staff had already left the office for the holiday weekend. No one saw the fax until the following Monday morning.

Was Realtor's revocation effective?

Discuss.

Contracts Essay 3:
Doc v. Patient

Doc is a licensed physician who often volunteered to treat indigent patients. One elderly patient that Doc was treating for Alzheimer's Disease was grateful to have Doc around, because he had no other family to help him. One day, during a routine appointment, Patient said to Doc "I want to pay you back for all you have done for me over the years. If you will care for me for the rest of my life, I will give you my beachfront home. I need to know now that I can depend on you." Doc did not believe that Patient had a beachfront home and continued the exam, saying nothing in response.

Doc eventually forgot about Patient's statement and continued to treat Patient for free as Patient's health declined. Doc's services were worth several thousand dollars.

Doc learned that Patient did in fact own a beachfront home worth a million dollars. Remembering that Patient had offered it to him, Doc wrote a note to Patient stating, "I accept your offer and promise to provide you with all the medical services that you may need for the rest of your life." Doc signed the note and dropped it in the mailbox in front of his home, properly stamped and addressed to Patient's home.

Unfortunately, Patient died in his sleep that night. The letter was delivered by the post office a day later.

Does Doc have an enforceable contract for the transfer of Patient's beachfront home?

Discuss.

Contracts Essay 4:
Marcie, Pete & Friend

In January, Marcie, a country music superstar, contacted Pete via phone in an effort to rent his condo in Hawaii, for December 1, 2, 3, 4, and 5 for the annual songwriter's festival as she does every year for $1000 a night. Pete advised that the condo was not available, but that he could rent her his five-bedroom home for $2000 a night. Marcie told Pete that she only needed one bedroom. She then asked if Pete would consider reducing the rate if she only used one bedroom in the house. Pete agreed that he would only charge her $1500 a night on the condition that she agree to only use one bedroom in the house. Marcie said thank you and instructed him to just send her the bill.

That summer, Marcie's manager booked the dates for her tour and didn't include the Songwriter's Festival in Hawaii in December. Knowing that she wouldn't be able to make it to Hawaii that year, she offered the rental to her friend, who could really use a vacation. Marcie told Friend that the rental was $1500 a night but forgot to mention the one room condition. Friend accepted and agreed to tell Pete to send Marcie the bill.

Friend spent 5 blissful days in the house and, at the end of Friend's stay, Pete sent Marcie a bill for $10,000 ($2000 per night). Marcie has refused to pay the bill, and Friend claims that he is only responsible for $1,500 per day.

What rights, if any, does Pete have against Marcie and/or Friend?

Discuss.

Contracts Essay 5:
CoffeeCo, StarBuzz & BeanCo

CoffeeCo entered into a written contract with Starbuzz to supply Starbuzz with all of Starbuzz's coffee requirements for one year. Under the contract, CoffeeCo was required to deliver on the first day of each month the quantity of coffee that Starbuzz required. The contract price was $5,000 per month, payable upon delivery of each shipment.

CoffeeCo delivered the required quantity each month for the first six months. At the end of the sixth month, CoffeeCo assigned its contract with Starbuzz to BeanCo, which undertook to deliver the requisite quantities for the remainder of the contract term. Starbuzz, having some doubts about BeanCo's reliability, wrote both CoffeeCo and BeanCo a letter in which Starbuzz stated, "We want to be absolutely sure that both CoffeeCo and BeanCo will guarantee that we receive the quantity of coffee that we require each month."

Neither CoffeeCo nor BeanCo responded to the letter. In the seventh and eighth months of the contract, BeanCo made deliveries that were substantially short of the quantity that Starbuzz required and that CoffeeCo had previously delivered. However, Starbuzz accepted and paid for the short shipments.

At the end of the eighth month, Starbuzz entered into a contract with Folger Farms ("Folger") to supply Starbuzz with its requirements for coffee for the remaining four months of the year. The contract price was $7,500 per month, payable upon delivery of each shipment. Starbuzz wrote a letter to CoffeeCo and BeanCo informing them that Starbuzz would no longer accept any coffee shipments from either of them.

Starbuzz then sued both CoffeeCo and BeanCo for breach of contract to recover the difference between the CoffeeCo/BeanCo contract price and the Folger contract price. CoffeeCo defended on the ground that, after its assignment to BeanCo, it was no longer liable to Starbuzz. BeanCo filed a counterclaim for breach of contract against Starbuzz to recover its lost profits.

Which party is likely to prevail in the lawsuit involving:

1. Starbuzz vs. CoffeeCo?

2. Starbuzz vs. BeanCo?

Discuss.

Contracts Essay 6:
Keith v. Toby

Keith owned several music stores that specialized in guitars. Keith entered into a contract with Toby to buy 100 guitars. The terms of the contract were as follows:

> Ten new Taylor guitars made from koa wood were to be delivered to Keith each Friday morning by 10:00 a.m. for the next ten weeks;

> Each guitar was to have original paperwork certifying that it is authentic;

> Payment was due 30 days after delivery; and

> Each guitar costs $400.00.

Keith and Toby signed the agreement.

On the first Friday after the contract was signed, Toby delivered ten Taylor guitars made of koa wood with the required paperwork. Keith accepted delivery, inspected the guitars, and put them on sale. Since Keith was paying $400.00 for each guitar, he had to sell them for $1000.00. Keith only sold four guitars that first week.

On the second Friday, Toby brought ten more guitars. Keith inspected them and found two that were not made of koa wood and two that appeared to be used. Keith rejected all ten guitars. That week, Keith did not sell any guitars, so he still had six in stock.

On the third Friday, Toby brought ten more guitars. Keith inspected them and all were Taylor guitars made of koa wood, but Toby was missing paperwork for two of the guitars. Keith accepted the eight with paperwork and rejected the two without. Keith did not sell any guitars that week, so he had 14 guitars available for sale in his shop.

On Friday of week four, Toby brought ten more Taylor made koa wood guitars, each with paperwork. However, Toby did not arrive at Keith's shop until 1:00 p.m. in the afternoon. Keith rejected all of the guitars and claimed that Toby had breached the contract by delivering non-conforming guitars and being late on delivery. Keith told Toby not to deliver any more guitars. Keith also refused to pay for the guitars that had been delivered.

Did Toby and/or Keith breach the contract? If so, what are their rights?

Discuss.

Contracts Essay 7:
Painter v. Fred

Fred and his wife wanted their house painted and contacted Painter. Painter informed Fred that he would charge $50 an hour and that the paint would cost $20 per gallon. Painter estimated that it would take 40 hours and 20 gallons of premium paint to complete the job. Fred and his wife agreed to pay the $50 an hour but decided to supply their own paint. The parties entered into a valid written contract in which Painter would paint the house in one coat in one week for $2000.00 and Fred would supply all of the premium paint needed. When Fred went to purchase the paint, in an effort to save money, he purchased non-premium paint for $5 a gallon rather than the premium paint at $20 a gallon.

On the first day Painter started to paint the house, he noticed that the non-premium paint was not covering as well as premium paint and informed Fred at the end of the day that he would need more than 20 gallons.

On the second day, Fred's wife told Painter that "Instead of the original color we agreed upon, I'd like to pain the doors red instead." Painter estimated that it would take an extra two hours and a gallon of paint. Fred's wife verbally agreed, and Painter purchased the paint Fred's wife requested for $30.

After painting three sides of the house and the doors as requested by Fred's wife, Painter ran out of paint at the end of the fourth day (32 hours). Fred refused to buy more paint.

Painter packed up his equipment and sent Fred a bill for 32 hours of labor and one gallon of paint.

Fred refused to pay the bill, believing that Painter wasted the paint so that he would not have enough to finish. Fred also hates the red doors and insists that they were not part of the contract.

In his suit against Fred, what are Painter's rights and what damages, if any, will he recover?

Discuss.

Contracts Essay 8:
Pearson & Baker

Pearson, a wheat distributor, sent an offer to sell eight crates of wheat to Baker Supplies, (Baker). The entire offer is contained on a signed form. Pearson's name and address appeared on the front side of the form, along with blank spaces for the description of the goods, quantity, price, and delivery date. The blanks were filled in with the appropriate information. On the bottom of the front side of the form, the following statement appears:

> Any contract resulting from the acceptance of this offer shall consist only of those terms appearing on the front and reverse sides of this document.

The reverse side of Pearson's form has five paragraphs. The fourth paragraph reads:

> Any disputes arising under this agreement shall be resolved through binding arbitration under the rules of the Commercial Arbitration Association.

Baker responded to Pearson's offer with its standard acceptance form. Baker's form contains its name, address, and company logo at the top of the page with the words "Purchase Order" just below. It has blank spaces for the description of the goods, quantity, price, and delivery date, which Baker filled in with information matching the information on Pearson's offer. Baker's Purchase Order form has four paragraphs on the back. Paragraph four states:

> "The laws of the State of California shall govern this agreement and any claims or controversies arising during performance shall be resolved through proceedings in the courts of the State of California."

Baker's Purchase Order form has a signature line at the bottom of the front side, but due to a clerical error, the form sent to Pearson was not signed. Soon after receiving Baker's Purchase Order form, Pearson purchased five crates of wheat from local suppliers for shipment to Baker. The week before any wheat is shipped to Baker, the price of wheat fell sharply.

1. If Baker informs Pearson that it will not accept the five crates of wheat, will Baker be liable to Pearson for breach of contract? Discuss.

2. Assume instead that Pearson delivers the five crates of wheat to Baker, and Baker pays to Pearson the full contract price. If Baker has a complaint about the quality of the wheat it received, must Baker submit its claim to the Commercial Arbitration Association?

Discuss.

Contracts Essay 9:
CompServe v. InfoTech

InfoTech is a data processing company. InfoTech's business depends on the operation of several large computers. InfoTech decided to employ an outside company to provide computer maintenance and service. InfoTech's president met with the president of CompServe to discuss a computer service agreement. The next day, CompServe faxed its standard form contract to InfoTech. The contract reads as follows:

> Client hereby agrees to purchase computer maintenance services from CompServe at a cost of $2,000 per month. CompServe hereby agrees to provide up to ten hours of service per month, with additional hours payable at $300 per hour. CompServe further agrees that it will provide same-day service in response to every service request. This agreement shall expire one year from the date on which it is made. In the event that Client fails to make a payment required under this agreement, 80 per cent of the entire remaining balance under the agreement shall become immediately due and payable.

InfoTech signed and returned the contract and made the first $2,000 payment. During the first month of the agreement, InfoTech made two service requests. Both requests were received by CompServe at 9:00 a.m. In each case, CompServe personnel arrived at InfoTech's offices at noon and quickly fixed the problem. In both instances, InfoTech's president complained about the delay but was told it was an unusually busy day. After the second service call, InfoTech sent a fax to CompServe stating that InfoTech would make no further payments under the contract. (InfoTech later hired a different service company). CompServe then sent a letter to InfoTech demanding $17,600, representing 80 per cent of the remaining balance. When InfoTech refused to pay, CompServe filed a lawsuit.

The president of InfoTech claims that during the initial meeting with CompServe's president, she told him that it was absolutely crucial that CompServe respond to service requests within one hour. She says that CompServe's president told the group, "I understand. If you sign up with us, I promise we'll be there within an hour."

Under what theory or theories might CompServe bring a lawsuit against InfoTech; what defense(s), if any, can InfoTech assert; and which party is likely to prevail?

Discuss.

Contracts Essay 10:
Miranda, Blake, Trisha & Garth

Miranda wanted to have a garage sale. She posted signs in the neighborhood which read: "Giant Garage Sale—One electric guitar: $200, designer clothes, bags, books and more! Sunday, Noon to 4:00 p.m."

On Sunday, Blake was jogging by around noon and saw one of Miranda's signs. He ran over to examine the guitar and told Miranda, "I'll take the guitar for $200, but I need to come back to get it with my car. I'll be back before 4:00 with the money and a car." Before Miranda could respond, he left.

Miranda's friend, Trisha, stopped by at 1:00, and saw a designer jacket. Trisha told Miranda, "I'd love to buy that jacket, but I can't afford it!" Miranda replied, "I had hoped to get $300 for the jacket, Trisha, but you've been such a great neighbor all of these years and I've always wanted to pay you back. So, if I can't sell it for $250 by 3:30, the jacket is yours for free." Trisha thanked Miranda and left.

At 1:30, Garth browsed through the garage sale and found a set of vintage books. "I want to buy these," he told Miranda, "but I don't have any cash with me." "That's O.K.," Miranda replied. "I'll sell you those books for $100. The offer's open until 4:00." "Thanks," Garth answered, "I'll be back as soon as I can."

At 3:30, Trisha called Miranda and asked if anyone had purchased the jacket yet. "Not yet," Miranda replied. "No one's here so I'm going to close up early. It looks like it's yours." "Thanks," Trisha responded. "I am going to run to the store and buy shoes and a purse that match the jacket."

At 3:45, Debbie arrived at the sale and said "I'll buy that jacket for $250, and I'll buy that set of vintage books too." Miranda sold the jacket and books to Debbie.

Garth returned before 4:00, saw Debbie carrying the books and said to Miranda, "You can't sell those books to her! We had a deal!" Although he attempted to give Miranda $100, she refused the money.

Trisha arrived shortly thereafter and showed Miranda the shoes and purse that she had purchased to go with the jacket. Miranda told her the jacket had been sold.

1. Does Blake have an enforceable contract with Miranda?

2. Does Trisha have an enforceable contract with Miranda?

3. Does Garth have an enforceable contract with Miranda?

Discuss.

15

Contracts Essay Answers

Please compare your answer to each of the practice essays to the sample answers that follow, noting the issues you missed, whether your rule statements were included and completely stated, and whether you included the relevant key facts in your analysis of each issue. Also notice how the organization of your answer compares to the sample.

Also, please pay close attention to the comments provided following the model answer. They provide guidance on how to best evaluate your own work and on how to improve when analyzing similar issues in the future.

Contracts Essay Answer 1:
Buyer v. Seller

Formation:

(Ultimate Issue) Was a valid contract formed between Buyer and Seller?

It must be established that a valid contract was formed in order for Buyer to assert a cause of action against Seller. A contract requires mutual assent, which is generally established when one party's offer is met by the other's acceptance, and consideration.

Applicable Law:

(Threshold issue) What is the applicable law?

Contracts for the sale of goods are governed by the UCC, while contracts for everything else are governed by the common law. Because this is a contract for the *sale of goods*, the *UCC*, rather than the common law, will apply.

Offer:

(Contract Formation Issue Element 1) Did Seller make a valid offer to sell the machine to Buyer?

(Rule) An offer is a statement made by one party (the offeror) to the other party (the offeree) which contains the essential terms of a contract and reasonably is intended to create the power of acceptance in the offeree. (Analysis) Here, Seller's letter to Buyer stating that Seller "offers to sell the machine to Buyer for one million dollars ... delivery within three months from acceptance" is a valid offer, because it contains the essential contract terms (e.g., price, quantity, subject matter and time for performance were all stated) and was intended to give Buyer the power to accept the offer. (Conclusion) Therefore, a valid offer was made.

Is the Offer Still Open?

(Sub Issue 1) Was Seller's offer still open for acceptance at the time it was accepted by Buyer?

(Rule) As a general rule, an offer is revocable at any time before acceptance, even where it expressly states that it will remain open for a certain time. Thus, no contract was formed if Seller effectively revoked its offer prior to Buyer's acceptance.

Revocation:

(Sub issue 2) Did Seller revoke its offer before or after Buyer's acceptance?

(Analysis) The facts indicate that ten days after Buyer received the offer, it received another letter from Seller stating, "we hereby revoke our offer." On this same day,

Buyer decided to accept Seller's offer. (Sub rule) According to the general rule, a *revocation is effective upon receipt*. However, an *acceptance is effective upon dispatch* (by reasonable means). (Conclusion) If Buyer had mailed its acceptance prior to receipt of Seller's revocation, then Buyer would have accepted prior to revocation, and a valid contract would have been formed.

Is the Offer Revocable?

(Sub Issue 3) Was Seller's offer irrevocable?

(Rule) If the offeror promises to hold the offer open for a certain period, the promise may render the offer irrevocable if it is a "firm offer" or is supported by consideration or detrimental reliance.

Merchant's Firm Offer:

(Sub Issue 4) Was Seller's offer a "Firm offer"?

Seller stated in its letter that its "offer will be held open for one month." (Rule) U.C.C. § 2-205 provides that when a merchant makes a written, signed offer to buy or sell goods including a promise to hold the offer open, the offer is *irrevocable* for the period stated, not to exceed three months. (Analysis) Thus, Seller's written offer to sell the machine (goods) which it stated would be held open for one month will be irrevocable for that period if Seller signed the letter and Seller is a *"merchant."* Most likely, Seller signed its offer (any mark or stamp of the company will suffice). However, it is doubtful that Seller is a "merchant" with respect to this transaction. (Rule) According to the U.C.C., a "merchant" is one who deals in the kind of goods involved or holds himself out as having special knowledge or skills relating to the goods involved. (Analysis) Seller does not normally sell machines and has dealt with Buyer's subsidiary regularly, but not with Buyer. Thus, it appears that Seller did not deal with machines or hold itself out to Buyer as having special knowledge in the area. (Conclusion) Because Seller was not a "merchant", the offer was not a "firm offer."

Consideration or Detrimental Reliance:

(Sub Issue 5) Was Seller's offer to hold the offer open supported by consideration or detrimental reliance?

Seller's promise to hold its offer open for one month was not supported by consideration. Buyer gave nothing in return but a thank you. However, modern courts will allow that an offer may become irrevocable for a reasonable time if the offeree *reasonably relies* on the offer to his or her *detriment* and such *reliance is reasonably foreseeable* by the offeror. Here, Buyer wrote a letter responding to Seller's offer indicating that it was going to immediately construct facilities to house the machine but would hold off on acceptance for a few weeks in search of a better price. A modern court should rule that Seller had knowledge of facts (it acknowledged receipt of Buyer's letter) which would lead it to reasonably foresee Buyer's detrimental reliance (construction of housing facilities at a cost of $100,000). A modern court could conclude that Seller's offer was irrevocable for a "couple of weeks" as relied upon by Buyer.

Acceptance:

(Contract Formation Element 2 Issue) Did Buyer accept Seller's offer?

A contract cannot be formed absent acceptance by the offeree. The facts state that Buyer decided to accept the offer then received the revocation. On these facts, Buyer never communicated its acceptance to Seller. Silence cannot act as an acceptance unless the offer or the previous conduct of the parties permit acceptance by silence. Moreover, Buyer's letter responding to Seller's offer clearly indicated an unwillingness to be bound — Buyer wanted to shop around for a better price before obligating itself to Seller. Buyer has therefore not communicated an intent to be bound, and there has been no acceptance and therefore no contract.

Consideration:

(Contract Formation Element 3 Issue) Was the contract supported by consideration?

(Rule) A contract must be supported by consideration in order to be valid. Consideration is a *bargained for exchange*. Had the parties reached mutual assent, their promises must have been supported by consideration in order to be enforceable. (Analysis) Here, consideration was present in the form of money in exchange for goods.

(Conclusion) However, because there was no valid acceptance, no contract was formed, and Buyer does not have any rights against Seller.

END OF ANSWER.

Professor's Guidance

So how did you do?

Note first that I used the IRAC and element identifiers in the sample answer in an effort to help those who may still struggle with IRAC organization. These identifiers should not be included in the answer to a formal essay.

Now, most students tend to freeze up when they encounter a contracts essay, because they don't know where to start. Here's a tip: Always remember that Contracts is divided into three main areas: **Formation, Performance, and Remedies.**

Any time you see a contracts problem, you should make sure it is properly **formed.** If it is not, it is not valid and no performance is due.

If it is properly formed, then look to see if performance is waived or excused. If it is not waived or excused, then **performance** is due. If one of the parties fails to perform or performs poorly, then he is in breach of contract.

If there is a breach of contract, then you would determine what **remedies** are available to the non-breaching party in order to compensate him for the breach.

Sounds simple, right? It can get pretty complicated, but having this general structure in your mind will help when you sit down to confront a fact pattern.

For this essay, we are only concerned about contract formation, so this is the only issue on which we need to focus for this essay. Otherwise, to identify what general issue is being tested, **Read the Call of the Question First.**

This should be the very first thing you look for. It is usually at the end of a fact pattern. You decide that this is a Contracts Question. That's an important start, not to be minimized on an exam.

The call of the question here is: "Does Buyer have an enforceable contract with Seller? Discuss."

Many essay questions provide insight through the names of the parties. In this instance, "Buyer" and "Seller" provide the clue of a buyer and seller, so the issue most likely revolves around a purchase contract. After reading the fact pattern, I notice several facts revolving around negotiations, so I know I need to focus on Formation issues. Since I have memorized my Contracts checklist of possible issues, I am able to work through the facts to determine what formation issues need to be discussed as I write this essay. So, let's start!

With any Contracts essay, first determine whether the UCC or common law applies. Remember, the UCC applies to the sale of goods; the common law applies to everything else. Note that some students mess up here, finding that the UCC only applies when both parties are merchants—this is not the case. The UCC applies to the sale of goods whether both parties are merchants or not. However, some UCC provisions will apply only if both parties are merchants.

After determining whether the UCC or common law applies, if you are dealing with a formation issue, as you are here, always look to see if mutual assent has been achieved. Remember to define the rule first: Mutual assent is achieved through the process of offer and acceptance. Be sure to provide definitions of offer and acceptance as well. Then, work through each part of the negotiation to find the offer and acceptance. Sometimes it's pretty easy to find the offer and acceptance. Other times, it is more difficult.

Sometimes, you may find that the first few possible offers may not be valid for whatever reason. Perhaps they do not contain definite terms or are not communicated to an identified offeree. It is your job to work through each possible offer to find where an offer has been made. Do not skip through a discussion to conclude where an offer was made without working through this process if there is more than one possible offer.

Before you discuss acceptance, look to see if the offeror tried to revoke the offer prior to acceptance. If he did, then you'll need to include a discussion of whether the offer was still open at the time it was accepted. If there was no attempt at revocation, there's no need to discuss this issue. However, here, we have a problem that needs to be addressed.

When addressing an issue like this, you'll always want to start with the general rule: An offer is revocable at any time before acceptance. Then, analyze the facts under the rules. Here, because we have fact that demonstrates letters crossing in the mail, we can't analyze the facts unless we understand the mailbox rule. If you missed this discussion, make sure to go back and review when an acceptance and revocation are effective.

We also have to remember that we are dealing with the UCC and we have a special rule that applies to merchants when dealing with revocation issues. We therefore need to analyze whether a firm offer has been made. Because we are keen readers of the facts, we can conclude that both parties are probably not merchants, and we should therefore look to see if we could make an argument that consideration or detrimental reliance could be used to hold the offer open.

If you missed this discussion, it's either because you didn't identify it as a discussable issue when working your way through your mental checklist, or you are not strong on the substantive law in this area. Either way, a review would be worth your time if you found yourself struggling a bit on this discussion!

After analyzing whether an offer has been made and whether it is still open for acceptance, you'll need to discuss acceptance. Again, sometimes this is a pretty straightforward issue. Other times, it can get complicated, so just be sure to memorize the checklist of possible issues that can arise with a possible acceptance and know the applicable rules.

After discussing mutual assent, you must discuss consideration. A contract cannot be validly formed unless it is supported by consideration, so please be sure to **always** discuss consideration if you find yourself analyzing a contracts formation essay. Here, the consideration is money in exchange for a machine. This issue was fairly straight forward! Hint: When consideration is otherwise lacking, remember to look to see if promissory estoppel may serve as a substitute!

Finally, when analyzing a contracts formation essay, don't forget about Defenses to Formation. The two biggest ones are the Statute of Frauds and mistake, so keep an eye out for these issues as you read through your fact patterns! There were no defenses at issue here, so they were not included in the discussion.

Contracts Essay Answer 2:
Barry v. Realtor

1. Was Realtor's fax a valid offer?

Yes. In order for a valid offer to exist, there must be:

1) an objectively expressed intent to be bound;

2) that contains sufficiently definite terms; and

3) is communicated to an identified offeree.

Here, Realtor's fax expressed an *intent to enter into a bargain* and contained definite and certain terms. Her fax even used the term "offer," and a reasonable person in Barry's position would believe an offer was being made. The fax also contained *sufficiently definite terms*. She gave a date and time by which Barry could accept, and included a description of the property, including the location of the property and the price. Although time for performance was not included, a reasonable time could be inferred. The offer was also *communicated* to Barry as the intended offeree, as Realtor sent the fax directly to Barry and gave Barry the power of acceptance.

Therefore, Realtor's fax was a valid offer.

2. Was Realtor's offer to keep the offer open enforceable?

No. An offer can be *revoked* at any time before acceptance, even if there is language in the offer that promises to keep the offer open. An exception to this rule is the *Merchant's Firm Offer* rule, which requires a merchant to hold an offer open. Otherwise, in order for a promise to hold the offer open to be enforceable, it must be supported by separate consideration.

Here, Realtor's offer to keep the offer open was not supported by consideration. Also, she is not a merchant, as merchants deal in the sale of goods and not land, so the Merchant's Firm Offer rule does not apply.

Therefore, even though Realtor promised to keep the offer open, she is not bound to do so and could revoke at any time before acceptance.

3. Did Barry accept Realtor's offer?

Yes. According to the *mailbox rule*, an acceptance is effective upon proper dispatch, and a rejection or revocation is effective upon receipt. When no method of acceptance is required by the offeror, the offeree can accept by any reasonable means.

Here, Barry sent (dispatched) his e-mail acceptance to Realtor at 1:00 on July 3, prior to the stated time of expiration of the offer. The e-mail was properly dispatched and in fact did make it into Realtor's inbox. It does not matter that Realtor did not check her e-mail until after the stated expiration time of 5:00. It was also reasonable for Barry to accept via e-mail, as he received the offer via fax.

Therefore, because Barry's acceptance was effective upon dispatch, before the time had expired, he accepted Realtor's offer.

4. If Barry died before the offer expired, could his son still accept?

No. An offer can only be accepted by the person to whom it is made. The death of an offeree terminates the offer.

Here, since the offer was made to Barry, only Barry could accept. His *death terminated the offer* and Son may not accept on his behalf, even if he proceeds according to the terms specified by Realtor.

Therefore, Son cannot accept the offer.

5. Was Realtor's revocation effective?

Yes. An offer can be revoked at any time before it is accepted. According to the *mailbox rule*, a revocation is effective when it is received. The Restatement provides that a revocation is effective when the offeror deposits it in some place that the offeree has authorized as a place to deposit such communications.

Here, Barry received Realtor's revocation when it arrived by fax in his office, which was an authorized place to receive such communication as he had received the original offer in the same fashion. Because Barry received the revocation at 12:00, before he deposited his attempted acceptance at 1:00, Realtor's revocation was effective.

Therefore, the offer was effectively revoked before Barry accepted.

END OF ANSWER.

Professor's Guidance

Hopefully, you remembered my advice to read the question calls first. This question is a little different than the first one, as it has multiple questions appearing in the call. If you are reading quickly, you see the last question regarding whether the revocation was effective. This alone lets you know that you are dealing with a contract formation question.

If you're reading more closely, you can tell that five different questions are asked. Don't let this overwhelm you. This is a blessing, because it automatically sets up the organization of your answer. Anytime you see multiple questions asked following the fact pattern, you should use each one of those questions as an organizational header in your answer.

You can also use each one of these questions to help you identify the issues being tested, so when you are reading through the fact pattern, you can look for the facts that raise those issues. So, if I were writing an answer to this essay, I would write a quick outline using the issues I find in each question. Below that, I'd add rule elements where warranted. Then I'd read the facts again and write down the ones that should be discussed under each rule.

The start of the outline might look something like this:

<u>Was the fax a valid offer?</u>

    Intent to be bound?

        Used the term "offer"

    Definite terms?

        Location, price, time by which it could be accepted.

    Communicated to an Identified Offeree?

        Sent by fax directly to Barry, whom Realtor knew.

<u>Offer to hold offer open enforceable?</u>

    Consideration needed.

    None provided.

    Merchants firm offer?

    Barry not a merchant.

<u>Offer accepted?</u>

    Mailbox Rule

    E-mail dispatched at 1:00 on July 3.

    Is e-mail appropriate method of acceptance?

    Contact information on offer letter included e-mail address. No specific form of acceptance mentioned.

<u>Can Son accept if Barry dies?</u>

Death terminates offer.

<u>Effective revocation?</u>

Mailbox Rule

Revocation received by fax at 12:00 but not seen until Monday.

Now, you will notice that this outline identifies the rules, includes a few relevant facts and reaches some conclusions. It is very important to note that you will not get full credit on your answer if you simply submit this conclusory outline. Rather, use this outline as a template for your answer and spend time writing your analysis of the facts under each rule in an effort to guide the reader towards your conclusions. Here's a tip: to force yourself to write an analysis, try stating your point and follow it using the word **because**. For example, you can say the offer contained all material terms **because** the price of $1000 per acre was stated, the property, including its location on the corner of First and Main, was described, and the date by which the offer could be accepted was provided. See how that is beefier than the outline? The word **because** forces you to **use** the facts rather than simply repeating them.

You may also notice that this essay is similar to the first one in that it follows the organizational template for Contract Formation. The difference is that the questions break the issues down for you rather than simply asking the general question of whether a contract had been formed. Either way, you may still need to work through your mental checklist of possible issues, but your answers will be more limited. For example, here, the Statute of Frauds would be a discussible issue had the question simply been whether a contract had been formed. However, none of the questions contained in the call of the question raised the issue of defenses to formation. Therefore, the Statute of Frauds was not a discussable issue in this essay.

Let's talk for a minute about discussable vs. non-discussable issues. I keep mentioning "mental checklists" and organizational templates. While these are very important in helping identify issues and organizing your answer, you will not discuss every possible issue on your checklist. You will only discuss those issues that are raised by the facts, meaning they are "discussable." So, if the facts raise the issue of formation, you automatically know that you must discuss mutual assent through the process of offer and acceptance as well as consideration. That is because, in order to show proper formation, those elements must be established. However, even though the issues of whether the offer is still open and revocation are on your mental checklist, if the facts do not indicate that there is an issue with regard to whether the offeree accepted on time, you can safely leave out that discussion.

It is also important to note that while you generally do not lose credit for including non-discussable issues, it does take up valuable time and can lead the grader to believe you may not have a really good handle on what is being tested. Therefore, you should try to avoid throwing in the kitchen sink.

Contracts Essay Answer 3:
Doc v. Patient

Does Doc have an enforceable contract for the transfer of the Patient's Beachfront home?

Applicable law:

The UCC covers contracts for the sale of goods while the Common Law controls contracts for everything else. This is a contract for services. Therefore, the *common law* controls.

Valid contract:

A valid contract requires mutual assent, which is reached through the process of offer and acceptance and must be supported by consideration. Intent is determined by the objective manifestations of the parties, and not their subjective intent.

Offer:

Did Patient make a valid offer to Doc?

A valid offer requires a manifestation of *intent to be bound* to *definite and certain terms*, and must also be *communicated* to an identified offeree. Here Patient said that he would give the beachfront home to Doc in exchange for his services. Patient intended to be bound, even though Doc did not believe that he owned the home. The subject matter was identified as a beachfront home, the terms were clear, and Patient communicated the offer directly to Doc. Therefore Patient made a valid offer to Doc.

Termination of the Offer:

Lapse of time:

Did the offer terminate due to lapse of time?

If an offer is not accepted by the time suggested in the offer, or by a *reasonable time* if no time is suggested, the offer will terminate. Here, Doc did not believe that Patient was serious and was silent when he first made the offer. He did not accept until years later when he realized that Patient actually owned the beachfront home. Therefore, there is an argument to be made that the offer lapsed before Doc accepted. However, because Doc's performance required him to care for Patient for the rest of his life, this may not be considered an unreasonable period of time, depending on Patient's health and age.

Did the offer terminate due to Patient's death?

The death of an offeror terminates the offer. Here, Patient died before receiving the acceptance. However, Doc accepted the offer before Patient died. (Discussed below.) Therefore, the offer did not terminate due to Patient's death.

Was the offer irrevocable?

Offers for unilateral contracts cannot be revoked once the offeree has begun performance. If this is found to be an offer for a unilateral contract, Doc may have an argument that the offer was irrevocable because he continued to care for Patient over the next two years after Patient made the offer. However, there is a question as to whether this is a **unilateral or a bilateral** contract. Most likely, it is a bilateral contract, as the law favors the finding of a bilateral contract when the language of the offer is ambiguous. An offer for a bilateral contract can be revoked at any time before acceptance. Therefore, the issue is whether Doc validly accepted the offer.

Acceptance:
Did Doc accept Patient's offer?

Acceptance occurs when the offeree unequivocally manifests an intent to be bound to the offer.

Silence:

When Patient first made the offer, Doc was silent. He could argue that by continuing to care for Patient, his silence was an acceptance. However, Doc did not believe Patient owned the beachfront home when he made the offer, so it is not likely that his silence amounted to an acceptance.

Mailed Acceptance:

According to the **mailbox rule**, an acceptance is effective upon dispatch while a rejection or revocation is valid upon receipt. If Doc mailed the acceptance prior to Patient's death, the acceptance takes precedence, and a valid contract is formed. The acceptance is not "dispatched" until it is properly stamped, addressed, and deposited in the mail. Doc's act of placing the properly stamped and addressed envelope in the mailbox of his home for the mailman to pick up is enough to consider the acceptance as being properly dispatched. Doc therefore validly accepted Patient's offer.

Consideration:

Was there consideration to support the contract?

A valid contract must be supported by consideration. Consideration is the *bargained for exchange* of promises. Here, Patient is bargaining his beachfront home in exchange for Doc's services. This normally would be valid consideration, but there is an issue with regard to whether the parties had bargained for the exchange. Doc did not believe that Patient owned the beachfront home. Therefore, Patient's promise to give the beachfront home did not induce Doc's promise to care for him at the time he made the promise. Therefore, there was no consideration.

Past Consideration:

Patient's estate could argue lack of consideration because Doc's past consideration cannot support a new contract. Patient wanted to pay Doc for all of the work he had done over the years. Arguably, this was *past consideration*, because Doc had already performed the work. However, because Patient was also bargaining for his continued care, this argument is likely to fail.

However, in the end, it is unlikely that this contract is supported by consideration, because Patient's promise did not induce Doc's promise.

Promissory Estoppel:

Promissory Estoppel can serve as a substitute for consideration when the Plaintiff can show that he *reasonably, foreseeably relied* on the promise of another to his *detriment*. Here, again, because Doc forgot about Patient's promise and the promise did not induce Doc to continue to care for him, there is no justifiable reliance. Therefore, Doc will not be able to rely on the doctrine of promissory estoppel as a substitute for consideration.

Therefore, because there is no consideration, the contract is invalid, and Doc does not have a clam against Patient's estate.

Defenses:

Assuming there is a valid acceptance and consideration, we must also examine whether there are any valid defenses to formation of contract.

Statute of frauds:

Does the Statute of Frauds apply?

According to the Statute of Frauds, certain contracts must be in *writing* in order to be enforceable. This includes contracts that cannot be fully performed within a year by the terms of the contract. Contracts for the sale of land must also be in writing in order to be enforceable.

Land:

Patient promised to give the beachfront home to Doc in exchange for Doc's services. This could fall under the land provision of the Statute of Frauds. Because the contract was not in writing and signed by the party to be charged (Patient), it would be unenforceable, unless Doc can show *payment plus possession or improvements*. Here, Doc arguably made payment because he continued to care for Patient, but since he did not take possession or make improvements, the Statute of Frauds is not satisfied and can be a valid defense to enforcement.

Year:

The terms of the contract do not make it impossible for the contract to be fully performed within a year, because Patient could have died at any time. Therefore, it does not fall under the year provision of the Statute of Frauds.

Incapacity:

Did Patient have the capacity to contract?

If a person is incompetent when he enters into a contract, it is voidable at his option. Patient had Alzheimer's Disease when he made the promise to Doc. Therefore, incapacity may be a valid defense if he did not understand what he was promising due to the disease.

Conclusion:

This is not likely to be an enforceable contract. It is questionable with regard to whether Doc properly accepted Patient's offer, and there is no consideration. Even if there was a contract, it was not in writing and would be barred by the Statute of Frauds.

END OF ANSWER.

Professor's Guidance

Once again, we find ourselves dealing with the issue of contract formation. I included this question because it tests several issues that did not appear in the first two essays. Hopefully, you can now see how many types of formation issues can be raised and can differentiate between discussable versus non-discussable issues.

Notice how some of these issues could not be resolved using a simple IRAC paragraph. Rather they required several "mini-IRAC" paragraphs to reach a conclusion on the larger issue. For example, you can't answer the question of consideration unless you first address past consideration and Promissory Estoppel. Similarly, you would want to provide a mini-IRAC for each provision of the Statue of Frauds that applies.

Notice also how your organizational template can help you here. You know to look for defenses to formation in general, and the Statute of Frauds may have jumped out at you. However, you may have missed the issue of capacity to contract. Had you memorized the flowchart regarding defenses to formation, you would notice that capacity is something you need to look for. That way, if your antennae didn't pick up the issue when you read the facts, you would hopefully scan the to see whether capacity is an issue. Then, you find it: Patient had Alzheimer's Disease. Boom! Just like that, you have earned more points!

Contracts Essay Answer 4:
Marcie, Pete & Friend

Pete v. Marcie

A valid contract requires *mutual assent*, which is reached through the process of offer and acceptance, consideration, and an absence of defenses.

Governing Law

The UCC controls contracts for the sale of goods, while the common law will govern all other contracts. Because this contract is one for the rental of a house, the *common law* controls.

Mutual Assent

An *offer* exists is the offeror has a present *objective intent to be bound* to *definite terms* and *communicates* this intent to an identified offeree. Here, the parties entered into negotiations wherein Marcie would rent a house from Pete. First, Marcie contacted Pete to inquire about a condo. This was an inquiry. Pete responded that a house was available on the dates requested for $2000 per day. This was an offer, as Pete intended to be bound, it contained all terms, and was communicated to Marcie.

An *acceptance* occurs when the offeree manifests an intent to be bound to the terms of the offer. At common law, the acceptance must be the *mirror image* of the offer. Otherwise, if the acceptance contains additional or different terms, it is considered a rejection and possibly a counteroffer. Here, Marcie rejected Pete's offer by stating that she only needed one bedroom and asked if he would consider reducing the price if she only used one bedroom. Because there was no price term mentioned, this was another inquiry. When Pete replied that it would be OK on the condition that she only uses one-bedroom and suggested a price of $1500 per day, Pete made another offer to Marcie. Marcie accepted by saying thank you and instructed Pete to send her a bill.

Consideration

Consideration is a *bargained for exchange*. The parties are bargaining for a room in a house in exchange for money. Therefore, the contract will not fail for lack of consideration.

Assignment and Delegation

An *assignment* is a transfer of a right to performance to a third party. Contracts are generally assignable unless the parties expressly prohibit assignment; or if the non-assigning party is subjected to greater risk or has its duties or burdens materially altered as a result of the assignment. A ***delegation*** of duties is the transfer of obligations under a contract. Here, Marcie could no longer use the house and offered it to Friend, telling Friend to ask Pete to send Marcie the bill. This was a valid assignment and delegation, as it was not prohibited by the parties and did not increase the burden on Pete.

However, Marcie did not tell Friend about the condition of using only one room, and Pete ultimately sent Marcie a bill for $2000 a day. The question then becomes whether Friend is bound by the one room condition and whether Marcie is liable for the $2000 a day. The rule is that no delegation of performance relieves the party delegating of any duty to perform or any liability for breach. Therefore, even though Marcie validly delegated her duties under the contract, Marcie is still liable if Friend failed to properly perform. If Friend used the full house rather than just one room, Marcie is liable to Pete for the full $2000 per day.

Pete v. Friend

Absent a ***novation***, an assignee who accepts an assignment promises to perform the assignor's duties and is liable to both the non-assigning party and the assignor. Therefore, Friend, as the assignee is also liable to Pete. However, an assignee is not obligated to liabilities that are unknown to him. Friend was unaware of the condition that he not use the entire house and only agreed to the assignment of the house for $1500 a night. Therefore, he would only be liable for $1500 a night.

END OF ANSWER.

Professor's Guidance

By now you should be getting the hang of how to analyze contracts formation. Start with the rule for formation and then identify the governing law.

Let's take a closer look at the organization. Here, we have three parties involved. Whenever you have more than one party or claim, you should discuss them separately. For example, here, we divided our essay into two main parts: *Pete v. Marcie* and *Marcie v. Friend*.

Also, notice here that we have some back and forth going on in the conversation between the parties. Anytime you see negotiations, it should trigger the issue of contract formation, and specifically, the mirror image rule (and possibly UCC 2-207 if the UCC applies and the acceptance doesn't mirror the offer). Here's another helpful tip to help you earn a few extra points when a negotiation is included in the fact pattern: Analyze each statement made by each party to determine whether it is an offer, counteroffer, rejection or acceptance. Take a closer look at the sample answer to see how this is done.

Also, never forget to include consideration in your analysis of a contracts formation problem, as it is an element of a valid contract. If it isn't mentioned, you can't state with certainty that the parties have a valid contract. It may not always be a meaty issue, but it should always be noted.

The big issue here is the Assignment and Delegation. Whenever this issue is tested, you should start with whether the assignment or delegation is valid. Some sort of breach will generally follow, and it is your job to determine who is liable. If you missed the boat on this, go back and review the rules for assignment and delegation and make sure to note the rules as they are stated in this answer. When you see the issue of assignment and delegation tested again, you can "recycle" some of the language used here and apply it to the new set of facts. This is why practicing as many of these essays as you can is helpful. It builds confidence, helps you learn the law, and gives you rule statements and organizational structure that can be used on future essays.

Contracts Essay Answer 5:
CoffeeCo, StarBuzz & BeanCo

Starbuzz v. CoffeeCo

What is the governing Law?

The UCC applies to the sale of goods, while the common law controls other types of contracts. Here, we are dealing with coffee, which is a good, so the *UCC* applies.

Was there a valid contract between CoffeeCo and Starbuzz?

A valid contract requires offer, acceptance, and consideration. Here, there does not seem to be an issue with *offer and acceptance*, as it appears the two parties agreed to buy and sell coffee for $5,000 a month, payable upon delivery. The issue is whether there exists consideration to support their promises.

Consideration is a bargained for exchange wherein each party suffers a legal detriment. In this contract, it does not appear that Starbuzz has any legal detriment, as it only agreed to buy as much coffee as it requires. Since that amount could be zero, Starbuzz's promise appears to be illusory, as it is not bound to buy any coffee.

However, this contract can still be enforced as a *requirements contract*. Starbuzz can bargain for all of the coffee it requires as long as the requirements are made in *good faith* and are not *unreasonably disproportionate* to stated estimates or previous orders.

Also, according to the *Statute of Frauds*, certain types of contracts, including those for the *sale of goods over $500*, must be in writing in order to be enforceable. Here, the contract price was for goods totaling $5000 a month. As such, it falls under this rule. Because this contract was in writing, the Statute of Frauds is satisfied. There also does not appear to be any other valid defense to formation.

Therefore, a valid contract exists between CoffeeCo and Starbuzz.

Was the contract validly assigned to BeanCo?

Contracts rights are freely assignable unless they involve special skill, taste, artistry, or if the terms of the contract forbid it. Here, supplying coffee does not require any special skill, taste, or artistry and the terms of the contract did not forbid it, so CoffeeCo was free to assign the contract to BeanCo. Under the UCC, a valid assignment also assumes the delegation of duties. Therefore, BeanCo had the right to collect under the contract but also assumed CoffeeCo's duty to supply the coffee under the contract.

Did CoffeeCo breach the contract?

Under the UCC, a party has the right to *adequate assurance* of performance. If the party has reasonable grounds for insecurity, it may demand adequate assurance from the other party in writing. Here, after CoffeeCo assigned the contract to BeanCo, Starbuzz had concerns about BeanCo's reliability and demanded assurance by sending a letter to both CoffeeCo and BeanCo. Neither responded. Because no adequate assurance was provided within 30 days, the contract has been repudiated. At this point, Starbuzz can suspend its own performance, sue for breach or wait for the time of performance and then sue.

BeanCo had a duty to supply all of the coffee Starbuzz required but made deliveries substantially short of what Starbuzz required. BeanCo therefore breached the contract.

It also does not matter that CoffeeCo assigned the contract to BeanCo. Absent a novation, CoffeeCo remains liable on the contract and can be sued if BeanCo failed to perform or poorly performed. Here, there is no evidence of a novation, so Starbuzz can sue CoffeeCo based on BeanCo's poor performance.

What are the damages?

BeanCo's performance fell short in the seventh and eighth months, and Starbuzz signed a contract with Folger for the delivery of the coffee at the end of the eighth month for the amount of $7,500 per shipment. Therefore, Starbuzz can recover the difference between the CoffeeCo's contract price and the Folger contract price, which is $2500 per month for the two months that remained under the original contract with CoffeeCo. It can also recover any damages it incurred as a result of the prior two substandard shipments.

Starbuzz v. BeanCo

As discussed above, BeanCo breached its duty to supply all of the coffee that Starbuzz required under the contract. Because there was no novation, Starbuzz can sue either CoffeeCo or BeanCo for the breach.

What was the effect of Starbuzz accepting non-conforming goods?

Starbuzz's acceptance of BeanCo's improper delivery of the coffee did not prejudice its right to demand *adequate assurances*. Also, a party that receives non-conforming goods can *accept the whole, reject the whole, or accept part and reject the rest*. Further, Starbuzz's acceptance of BeanCo's improper delivery of the coffee did not prejudice its right to demand adequate assurances. Therefore, it rightfully accepted the short supply of coffee and can sue for the damages it caused. It can also suspend performance and hire another vendor (Folger) to complete performance and sue BeanCo for the $2500 extra a month it must spend as a result.

What will happen to BeanCo's counterclaim against Starbuzz to recover lost profits?

Sometimes, a breaching party is entitled to restitutionary damages, but since Starbuzz paid for the short shipments and has an offset of its own damages as discussed above, BeanCo cannot recover on its counterclaim.

END OF ANSWER.

Professor's Guidance

Notice that the call of the question here asks whether each party will prevail in its lawsuit. This provides the organization for your essay. It will be in two main parts: *Starbuzz v. CoffeeCo* and *Starbuz v. BeanCo.* To answer this question, we have to think about our Contracts Template. In order to prevail, there first must be a valid contract with no defenses. Then, check to make sure any conditions have been satisfied or excused and if there are any legitimate discharge arguments. If all conditions have been satisfied or excused, you then discuss breach and finally damages. Also, keep an eye of for issues involving assignment and delegation and/or Third Party Beneficiaries.

So, the first thing we have to ask is whether a valid contract has been formed. This time, mutual assent is not really a discussable issue. However, since mutual assent is an element of contract formation, we have to address it. You can see that the sample quickly mentions that there are no problems and moves on.

However, Consideration is an issue under these facts because we are dealing with a requirements contract. If you missed this issue, you need to spend a little more time memorizing triggering facts. The triggering fact here is that there is no stated or easily implied quantity. Rather the term "require" is used. Note that had the facts mentioned the word "output" or "all that I produce or make" or something similar, that would trigger a discussion of an outputs contract rather than a requirements contract.

We also should mention that the Statute of Frauds is a discussable issue, because the facts trigger the discussion. We are told that the price of goods was over $500, so we need to tell our reader whether it was in writing before we can conclude that there is a valid contract.

We don't have to address conditions or discharge, because those issues are not raised by the facts.

However, at this point, we do have to discuss the assignment before discussing breach, because we are told that it is the Assignee that failed to deliver as promised. So, just like we did in the last essay, we will first discuss whether the assignment was valid and then discuss performance. Remember my tip about recycling language from the last essay? It definitely helps us speed up our writing here.

We also know that whenever we see both the Assignor and Assignee being sued, we need to look to see if there was a novation that would help the Assignor. Triggering facts also help us out here, because they tell us that CoffeeCo claimed it was no longer liable due to the assignment.

This is where some students start to miss issues because they don't return to the facts. They just know that the contract was not properly performed, conclude that there was a breach and move on. However, if you go back to the facts, you see that Starbuzz wrote a letter asking for a guarantee and received no response. This is a triggering fact that should prompt you to discuss adequate assurances. Remember the important tip I mentioned earlier: *Read the Question!* Almost every sentence will be important in that it may give rise to an issue.

For organizational purposes, after discussing performance, I would go ahead and conclude with a discussion of damages on the first claim against CoffeeCo.

From here, I would start a new section of my essay to discuss the claim against BeanCo. We've already established that the valid contract was breached and that both defendants could be liable, but once again, we need to *return to the facts* to see if there is something we are missing. We are told that Starbuzz accepted the non-conforming goods from BeanCo, so that should be addressed to see what effect, if any, it has on the outcome. Anytime you see the triggering fact of non-conforming goods being accepted, you should discuss Plaintiff's options after the demand of adequate assurances.

Finally, the facts tell us that there is a counterclaim for lost profits, so we need to make sure we've mentioned that along the way as well.

Contracts Essay Answer 6: Keith & Toby

Was there a valid Contract?

Here, the contract is governed by the *UCC*, because we are dealing with the sale of goods. Both parties are also *merchants*. Also, there do not appear to be any problems with *formation*, as there are no issues with offer, acceptance, or consideration. The contract was also for the sale of goods over $500 and is therefore required to be in writing according to the *Statute of Frauds*, which it was. Therefore, there are no defenses to formation, and if one party fails to perform or performs poorly, he will be in breach of contract.

Is the contract divisible?

The contract is also divisible, as it involved 10 separate contracts for 10 guitars to be delivered over the next 10 weeks. Therefore, we will examine each possible breach of contract for weeks one through four separately.

Week 1:

Did Toby breach the contract?

The first week, Toby delivered 10 guitars with paperwork and fully performed under the contract.

Did Keith breach the contract?

The first week, if Keith did not pay for the guitars, he is in breach of contract. It does not matter that Keith was unable to sell all 10 guitars during that week, as that was not a condition of the contract.

Is the breach material or minor?

If the breach is minor, the non-breaching party must continue to perform and can sue for damages. If the breach is material, the non-breaching party can suspend performance and sue for damages.

When examining whether the breach is material or minor, the following factors must be considered:

The extent to which the breaching party has already performed: Keith refuses to pay for any of the guitars that were delivered.

Whether the breach was willful, negligent or the result of purely innocent behavior: Keith's breach is willful, as he refuses to pay for any of the guitars he received during that first week.

The extent of uncertainty that the breaching party will perform the remainder of the contract: Keith has stated that he will not pay for any of the guitars.

The extent to which, despite the breach, the nonbreaching party will obtain (or has obtained) the substantial benefit he bargained for: Toby will not benefit at all because he provided the guitars to Keith and Keith refused to pay for them.

The extent to which the non-breaching party can be adequately compensated for the defective or incomplete performance through his right to damages: Toby can be adequately compensated by damages in the amount of $400 per guitar.

The degree of hardship that would be imposed on the breaching party if it were held that the breach was material and that he therefore had no further rights under the contract. Keith would not suffer a hardship, as he has received the guitars and was able to sell 4 of them for $4000, which is the amount he would owe Toby for the guitars. He can still sell the other guitars as well and has told Toby that he does not want any more guitars.

Therefore, Keith has materially breached the contract in Week 1, and Toby has the right to discontinue his performance under the contract and sue for breach.

Week 2:

Did Toby breach the contract?

In week 2, Toby delivered non-conforming goods because two of the guitars were not made of koa wood and 2 of the guitars appeared to be used. Under the contract, he was supposed to deliver 10 new koa wood guitars with paperwork.

Was the breach material or minor?

When examining whether the breach is material or minor, the following factors must be considered:

The extent to which the breaching party has already performed: Toby delivered 6 conforming guitars.

Whether the breach was willful, negligent or the result of purely innocent behavior: There are no facts to determine whether the breach was intentional, but it was at least negligent, as you can easily notice the type of wood on a guitar or whether it has been used.

The extent of uncertainty that the breaching party will perform the remainder of the contract: Toby has the right to cure the breach under the contract if he chooses to do so.

The extent to which, despite the breach, the nonbreaching party will obtain (or has obtained) the substantial benefit he bargained for: Keith will benefit because he already has the guitars that were delivered in week 1 and will not have to pay for the guitars he does not need.

The extent to which the non-breaching party can be adequately compensated for the defective or incomplete performance through his right to damages: Keith can be adequately compensated in damages in the amount of $400 per guitar.

The degree of hardship that would be imposed on the breaching party if it were held that the breach was material and that he therefore had no further rights under the contract. Toby would have to take all 10 guitars back.

The breach is therefore minor. Keith still has to perform but can sue for damages if Toby chooses not to cure.

Did Keith breach the contract?

Under UCC 2-601, if the goods fail in any respect to conform to the contract, the buyer may reject the whole, accept the whole, or accept any commercial unit and reject the rest. Keith chose to reject all 10 guitars, which he had the right to do. However, Toby has the right to cure, should he choose to do so.

Week 3:
Did Toby breach the contract?

Two of the ten guitars were delivered without paperwork, so Toby is in breach of contract.

Was the breach material or minor?

When examining whether the breach is material or minor, the following factors must be considered:

The extent to which the breaching party has already performed: Toby delivered 8 conforming guitars and has therefore substantially performed.

Whether the breach was willful, negligent or the result of purely innocent behavior: There are no facts to determine whether the breach was intentional, but it was at least negligent, as you can easily check the paperwork.

The extent of uncertainty that the breaching party will perform the remainder of the contract: Toby has the right to cure the breach under the contract if he chooses to do so.

The extent to which, despite the breach, the nonbreaching party will obtain (or has obtained) the substantial benefit he bargained for: Keith will benefit because he accepted the eight conforming guitars along with the original ten that were delivered the first week.

The extent to which the non-breaching party can be adequately compensated for the defective or incomplete performance through his right to damages: Keith can be adequately compensated in damages in the amount of $400 per guitar.

The degree of hardship that would be imposed on the breaching party if it were held that the breach was material and that he therefore had no further rights under the contract: Toby would have to take two guitars back.

The breach is therefore minor. Keith still has to perform, but can sue for damages if Toby chooses not to cure.

Did Keith breach the contract?

Under UCC 2-601, if the goods fail in any respect to conform to the contract, the buyer may reject the whole, accept the whole, or accept any commercial unit and reject the rest. Keith chose to reject two of the guitars, which he had the right to do. However, Toby has the right to cure, should he choose to do so.

Week 4:

Did Toby breach the contract?

In week 4, Toby delivered the guitars 3 hours late. Toby therefore breached the contract.

Was the breach material or minor?

When examining whether the breach is material or minor, the following factors must be considered:

The extent to which the breaching party has already performed: Toby delivered 10 conforming guitars on Friday, as promised, although they were three hours late, and has therefore substantially performed.

Whether the breach was willful, negligent or the result of purely innocent behavior: There are no facts to determine whether the breach was intentional, negligent, or innocent.

The extent of uncertainty that the breaching party will perform the remainder of the contract: Toby has delivered conforming guitars and could continue to do so.

The extent to which, despite the breach, the nonbreaching party will obtain (or has obtained) the substantial benefit he bargained for: Keith will benefit because he accepted the eight conforming guitars along with the original ten that were delivered the first week.

The extent to which the non-breaching party can be adequately compensated for the defective or incomplete performance through his right to damages: Keith can be adequately compensated in damages for the late delivery, although he does not seem to have any damages, as he is unable to sell the guitars he already has.

The degree of hardship that would be imposed on the breaching party if it were held that the breach was material and that he therefore had no further rights under the contract: Toby would not be able to benefit from the remainder of the contract and would not be paid for the conforming guitars already delivered.

The breach is therefore minor, and Keith can sue for damages caused by the late delivery, if any.

Given the above, what are Keith's rights?

As mentioned, Keith has the right to reject any non-conforming goods according to UCC 2-601. Since the breaches were minor, if Toby does not cure, Keith must still perform under the contract and can sue for damages caused by the non-conforming deliveries. Because Toby delivered 6 non-conforming guitars at $400 each, Toby could sue for $2400.00 plus any damages caused by the one late delivery, if he has any. However, Keith's recovery will be offset by the amount he owes to Toby in damages.

Given the above, what are Toby's rights?

As mentioned, Toby has the right to cure the breach for the non-conforming guitar deliveries. However, Keith refuses to pay for any of the guitars, so Toby can suspend performance and does not have to deliver any more guitars. He can then sue for damages this caused, offset by the damages owed to Keith, as discussed above. Keith should have to pay for the 10 guitars he received the first week, the 8 he accepted the third week, and the 10 he improperly rejected the fourth week. Further, he will also have to pay damages caused by failing to perform the remainder of the 10 week contract.

END OF ANSWER.

Professor's Guidance

So, how did you do? My guess is that you took one look at this one and panicked because there was so much going on in the facts and that the thought of having to do math was a little overwhelming. I included this practice essay here because I want to show you how having a good organizational plan can help reduce the panic.

Here, we basically have one big contract wherein both parties have duties to perform each week. We also have two big questions that we have to answer: *1) Did Keith and/ or Toby breach the contract and 2) what are their rights?*

There are several ways we could have gone about organizing this. We could have separated the claims into *Keith v. Toby* and *Toby v. Keith* as we did in our previous answer. We could also use the questions included in the call of the question as topic headers as we have done in other essay answers. However, I think the easiest way to go about this one is to *discuss each contract separately*, as each party was supposed to perform once a week. In order to get to that point, we have to start by noting that a valid contract was formed between the parties and that the contract is divisible.

From here, we can address each week as a separate contract and determine whether the contract was breached as well as whether that breach was material or minor. Determining whether the breach is material or minor is important, because it helps determine the rights of the parties. Then, we can finish up the second question by explaining what those rights are. Go back over the sample answer and see how this is accomplished. You will see that it is very straight forward, that language is recycled, and it is easy to follow. Had we not had a good organizational plan in place, the answer may have been more scattered and harder to follow.

Now, let's talk about substance. Students often make the mistake of concluding that there was a breach without explaining whether the breach is major or minor. Most of the time, unless you have a real race-horse question packed with issues, you will need to discuss whether the breach is major or minor as well as how that affects the rights of the parties. If it is a real think-um question like this one, where breach really is the main issue tested, you will want to carefully and methodically go through each factor using IRAC to help make that determination.

Contracts Essay Answer 7:
Painter v. Fred

In his suit against Fred, what are Painter's rights and what damages, if any, will he recover?

Painter will claim that Fred breached their contract.

Governing Law

The UCC governs contracts for the sale of goods. The common law covers contracts for services. Because Paining a house is a service, the **common law** will govern.

Valid Contract

Did Painter and Fred enter into a valid contract? Contract formation requires **mutual assent** (which is reached through the process of offer and acceptance), **consideration**, and **absence of defenses**.

Preliminary Negotiations: Painter gave Fred an estimate of 40 hours of labor at $50 an hour using 20 gallons of premium paint for $20 a gallon.

Mutual Assent: The two agreed that Painter would provide the labor to paint the house in one week with one coat for $2000 and Fred would supply all of the premium paint Painter needed to complete the job.

Consideration: Consideration is a bargained for exchange wherein each party suffers a legal detriment. Here, consideration exists in the form of money in exchange for painting service. Although Fred's promise to supply all of the premium paint needed may seem illusory because the amount is not clearly stated, a promise to supply all that is required is still enforceable as long as the amount required is requested in good faith and is not unreasonably disproportionate to any stated estimates.

Absence of defenses: Although this contract does not need to be in writing in order to be enforceable according to the Statute of Frauds, it is in writing and appears to have no defenses to formation. Therefore Painter and Fred entered into a valid enforceable contract.

Additional Paint

After Painter began painting, he realized that the cheap paint Fred purchased instead of the premium paint he was supposed to buy would require more than 20 gallons. Painter informed Fred that he would need more paint. At common law, a modification must be supported by consideration in order to be enforceable. Painter had a pre-existing duty to paint the house and was not offering anything additional in order to get more paint. Therefore, it would appear that the modification is unenforceable.

However, although Painter's estimate was for 20 gallons of premium paint, the agreement was for Fred to provide all of the premium paint Painter required. Premium paint covers more than the cheap paint, and is foreseeable that more paint would be required if cheap paint is used. It will also take longer to paint. Therefore, Painter's request for additional paint is enforceable.

Suggestion: It could also be argued that Fred breached the contract by not providing premium paint as promised. Therefore, Painter could recover the amount caused by that breach.

Red Doors

Fred's wife asked Painter to paint eight of the doors red. Painter agreed and said that it would require an additional two hours and another can of paint that he purchased himself for $30. It would appear that the *modification* is enforceable because it is *supported by consideration*. Fred's wife has to pay for an additional two hours of labor, and Painter must do the work. However, in order for a modification to be enforceable, both parties have to agree. The modification was agreed to by Fred's wife and Painter, rather than by Fred and Painter, the original parties to the contract. If Fred did not agree to the modification, he will not have to pay for the additional two hours of labor or reimburse Painter for the $30 gallons of paint.

Breach

Painter left the job after 32 hours, having painted only 3 sides of the house and the eight doors. Because Painter substantially performed, this is a minor breach. Therefore, Fred still must perform and can sue for any damages caused by the breach.

Fred breached the contract by refusing to buy more paint, forcing Painter to stop working, and by refusing to pay the bill. This is a major breach, because Painter substantially performed and has not been paid for any of his work.

Impossibility/Impracticability

The reason Painter stopped performing was because Fred refused to purchase more paint. It was not impossible for Painter to complete the job, as he could have purchased more paint on his own, but he was not likely to be reimbursed for the cost. Therefore, it would be impracticable for him to continue to perform. As such, he may be able to avoid being labeled a breachor.

Fred did not have an excuse for refusing to pay the bill. He has breached the contract.

What are Painter's rights?

Painter can suspend performance and either sue on the contract or in quantum merit for the value of his services. His recovery will be offset by the amount of any damages he caused.

What are Painter's damages?

Painter expected to make $2000 or $50 an hour for 40 hours. He sent a bill to Fred for 32 hours of work at $1600 and one $30 gallon of paint. Because the modification for the red doors was not enforceable, Fred does not have to pay for the two hours it took to paint the doors or for the $30 gallon of paint. Therefore, under the contract, Painter would be entitled to 38 hours of work, amounting to $1900.

If the value of his services is worth more than $50 an hour (perhaps he gave Fred a great deal) then he could choose to sue in quantum merit and recover the value of his services for 30 hours of work (the 32 hours he worked minus the 2 hours for the doors). For example, if the value of his services is worth $75 an hour, he would recover $2400.

END OF ANSWER.

Professor's Guidance

The main issues tested in this essay were Modification, Breach, and Damages. Hopefully by now you are getting good at spotting those red flag facts that trigger issues.

Contract formation is not really at issue here, because the facts state that the parties entered into a valid written contract. It is sufficient to simply say this or to take a little more time to quickly explain that a valid contract exists. Just be aware of your time constraints and avoid spending too much time on issues that can be quickly addressed.

After mentioning formation, we need to look to see if either party attempted to modify the contract. The red flag facts here are that Painter asked Fred to purchase more paint and Fred's wife wanted the doors painted red. We therefore should discuss each attempted modification separately.

Before we move on to breach, here's a juicy tip that may come in handy: Many students confuse the concepts of modification and additional terms in the acceptance. Just know that if you see someone trying to add terms when accepting the offer, the correct issue is additional terms/UCC 2-207. If you see someone trying to change the terms or requesting something more or less than originally agreed for after the contract has been formed, the correct issue is modification.

Once we decide if the attempted modifications are valid, we have to address the concept of breach. Always remember to address whether the breach is material or minor to help you determine whether the non-breaching party must continue to perform.

Next, follow our mental checklist of possible issues and check to see if we can avoid labeling a party a breachor. Ask yourself whether performance can be excused or discharged. Here, we have a reason why Painter stopped performing, so a discussion of Impossibility/Impracticability is warranted.

Finally, when you discuss rights and damages, make sure to consider the various theories under which Plaintiff could recover, what the value of that recovery should be, and do the math if you are provided with dollar figures.

Most of the time, damages will be only a small part of your essay answer. However, every once in a while, you will get a fact pattern that screams for a larger discussion. Don't be afraid should this happen to you. Rather, just take a deep breath, make sure you discuss all of the other issues raised first, and then recall the various remedies on your mental checklist. If you have a good understanding of them, the triggering facts will jump out at you.

Contracts Essay Answer 8: Pearson & Baker

1. If Baker informs Pearson that it will not accept the five crates of wheat, will Baker be liable to Pearson for breach of contract?

In order to determine whether a breach of contract exists, we must first determine the existence of a valid contract and its terms.

Do Pearson and Baker have a valid contract?

In order to have a valid contract, there must be mutual assent, consideration, and absence of defenses.

Governing Law:

The UCC governs the sale of goods, and the common law governs all other contracts. This is a contract for the sale of wheat, which is considered a good. Therefore, the UCC controls.

Mutual Assent:

Mutual assent is reached through the process of offer and acceptance where both parties manifest an intent to be bound to definite, essential terms. Here, Pearson offered to sell and Baker offered to buy five crates of wheat. Pearson's offer was in writing and contained the essential terms of subject matter, quantity, price, and delivery date. Baker accepted by sending a standard acceptance form mirroring the terms regarding subject matter, quantity, price, and delivery date.

The Mirror Image Rule and UCC 2-207:

The two forms contain conflicting provisions with regard to how disputes will be resolved. Pearson's forms states that disputes will be resolved through arbitration, while Baker's states that they will be resolved according to the laws of California. Therefore, there is a question with regard to whether Baker made a valid acceptance.

Under the common law "mirror image" rule, an acceptance, which varies the terms, is treated as a counteroffer and rejects the original offer, but under the UCC, it can still be an acceptance.

When analyzing *UCC 2-207* you must first determine whether there is a definite and seasonable expression of acceptance. Here, there is, as Baker responded to Pearson's offer with a purchase order that mirrored the essential terms of the offer. Then you look to whether the potential acceptance was expressly conditioned on agreement to the additional or different terms. Here, there is no language mentioned that would indicate that this is true. Therefore, according to the statute, a contract arises based on the communication between the parties and a valid acceptance has occurred.

Consideration:

Consideration is a bargained for exchange. Here, the parties are bargaining for crates in exchange for money. Therefore, consideration is present.

Absence of Defenses:

According to the *Statute of Frauds*, certain types of contracts must be in writing in order to be enforceable, including contracts for *the sale of goods over $500*. The writing must contain all essential terms and be signed by the party to be charged. Here, the two offer and acceptance forms comprise the writing. Pearson signed its form, while Baker did not. However, the fact that the acceptance was on a form that had Baker's name, address, and company logo with the words "Purchase Order" on it, along with the hand written terms, is sufficient to constitute a signature for purposes of the Statute of Frauds. Therefore, the Statute of Frauds is not a valid defense.

Therefore, if Baker informs Pearson that it will not accept the five crates of wheat, Baker be liable to Pearson for breach of contract.

2. If Baker has a complaint about the quality of the wheat it received, must Baker submit its claim to the Commercial Arbitration Association?

Again, the two forms contain conflicting provisions with regard to how disputes will be resolved. Pearson's forms states that disputes will be resolved through arbitration, while Baker's states that they will be resolved according to the laws of California. Therefore, there is a question with regard to what happens to the arbitration term.

UCC 2-207(2) controls this situation.

When the parties are both *merchants*, as they are here because they both deal in the sale and distribution of wheat, the additional or different terms automatically become part of the contract unless:

1) The offer expressly limits acceptance to the original terms,

2) The additional or different terms materially alter the contract, or

3) The offeror has already objected to the additional or different terms or objects within a reasonable time after receiving notice of the additional or different terms.

Here, we have an *arbitration clause*, which is almost always seen as material. Therefore, the clauses are treated as proposals for addition to the contract, meaning they will not become part of the contract without assent.

Baker did not assent to the arbitration clause. As such, it does not become part of the contract and Baker does not have to submit its claim to the Commercial Arbitration Association.

END OF ANSWER.

Professor's Guidance

This essay is included to give you an idea of how the battle of the forms can be tested and how UCC 2-207 can be analyzed. I hope you are using the flowcharts and resulting memorized checklists to help you spot and analyze these issues.

Did you start with formation in an effort to determine if the contract was properly formed? By now, you should be getting pretty good at this! Just follow the formation flowchart and work through issues of mutual assent, consideration, and absence of defenses.

The arbitration clause issue forces us to examine something new, specifically, the battle of the forms and UCC 2-207. Again, remember that this is different from the discussion of contract modification discussed in the previous practice essay, because the arbitration clause was an additional term in the offer, not a modification to an existing contract.

To answer the arbitration clause question, we simply follow our flowchart that shows us how to analyze UC 2-207. If you did not recognize this issue or if you reached an incorrect conclusion, make sure to go back and review the substantive law in this area. Also, and I can't stress this enough, **memorize** the flowchart regarding analysis of a UCC 2-207 problem. These fact patterns look more complicated than they actually are.

Contracts Essay Answer 9:
Compserve v. InfoTech

CompServe v. InfoTech

Governing Law:

Contracts for the sale of goods are governed by the UCC; contracts for services are governed by the common law. Because this is a contract for computer services, it is governed by the *common law*.

Is there a valid contract?

Valid contract formation requires mutual assent, which is reached through the process of offer and acceptance, consideration, and the absence of defenses.

Mutual Assent:

Mutual assent is reached through the process of offer and acceptance wherein both parties intend to be bound by essential terms.

Offer:

After some preliminary negotiations, CompServe faxed its standard form contract to InfoTech, offering computer maintenance services for $2000 a month for 10 hours of service each month and $300 for each additional hour required. In this offer, CompServe promised provide same-day service. The offer provided that the agreement would expire one year from the date on which it was made, and if InfoTech failed to make a payment, 80% of the balance was immediately due and payable. The terms, including subject matter, quantity, price, and time for service were clearly stated, and CompServe intended to be bound. Therefore, CompServe made a valid offer.

Acceptance:

InfoTech signed and returned the contract, intending to be bound to its terms. Therefore, there is a valid acceptance.

Consideration:

Consideration is a bargained for exchange. Here, the parties bargained for computer services in exchange for money. Therefore, consideration is present.

Absence of Defenses:

According to the Statute of Frauds, certain contracts, including contracts that cannot be fully performed within a year, must be in writing in order to be enforceable. The writing must be signed by the party to be charged and contain all essential terms. Here, the contract is set to expire a year from the date of execution, so the contract, by its terms, cannot be fully performed within a year and must be in writing. This contract is in writing and is signed by InfoTech. It therefore *satisfies the Statute of Frauds.*

Parol Evidence Rule:

Once a contract has been reduced to writing, it will control. The parol evidence rule prohibits the introduction of any prior or contemporaneous written or oral agreements where it contradicts a term contained in fully integrated contract. CompServe's oral promise that they would provide service within an hour of being called is Parol Evidence. Because there is no *merger clause* in the contract, InfoTech can try to claim that the contract was only partially integrated and that the evidence should be admitted, as it does not contradict CompServe's "same day service" promise. However, the presence of a merger clause does not conclusively resolve the question of whether the contract is fully integrated. Rather, the judge will decide this question.

In making this decision, the court will either employ the Williston "four corners" test or the Corbin "surrounding circumstances" test. Under the Williston test, the court will only look to the four corners of the document to determine whether the parties intended it to be a total integration. Under the Corbin test, the court will consider evidence to determine the actual intent of the parties.

Finally, even if the contract is found to be a *total integration*, the court may still allow the evidence to clarify meaning should it find the term "same day service" to be ambiguous. If the contract is found to be only *a partial integration* or if the "same day service" term is found to be ambiguous, the evidence will be admitted, and InfoTech would have a good argument that CompServe either broke its promise or failed to perform a condition of the contract.

Conditions:

A condition precedent is a future event that creates a duty of performance. If the condition fails, performance is excused. A condition subsequent is an event that, if it occurs, brings performance to an end.

Here, if InfoTech fails to make a payment under the agreement, 80% becomes immediately payable. This is an *express condition subsequent*, as InfoTech's duty to pay 80% is not triggered unless it fails to make a payment under the agreement. This is clearly a condition, because the words "In the event that …" are used in the written contract, evidencing the intent to create a condition, rather than a promise. This is important, because the failure of a condition will excuse performance, whereas the failure of a promise results in a breach, which can be either major or minor, as discussed below.

When InfoTech failed to make payments, it triggered the duty to pay 80% of the balance. However, InfoTech can argue that it is excused from performance, because a condition precedent to its obligation to pay is contingent on CompServe's timely service. If the parol evidence is admitted, the language "If you sign up with us, we will be there within an hour" could be interpreted as an express condition precedent, and InfoTech could be excused from performance.

Anticipatory Repudiation:

When one party unequivocally states that it does not intend to perform before the time performance is due, it is treated as an anticipatory repudiation. When this happens, the other party can suspend performance and sue immediately for breach or wait for the time for performance and then sue.

Here, InfoTech's fax stating that it would not make any further payments under the contract is an anticipatory repudiation allowing CompServe to suspend performance and sue.

Discharge of duty:

If a party can show that his duty to perform is discharged due to impossibility, impracticability, or frustration of purpose, he can avoid being labeled a breachor.

Here, it was not impossible or impractical for InfoTech to perform. However, it could try to argue that the purpose of the contract was frustrated because CompServe's inability to provide service within the hour frustrates the purpose of their agreement. If the parol evidence is admitted and InfoTech is successful in claiming frustration of purpose, it's duty to pay will be discharged.

Breach:

A breach occurs when a party has an absolute duty to perform and either fails to perform or performs poorly. If InfoTech's duty to perform is not discharged by the failure of a condition or by frustration of purpose, it's failure to pay will be considered a breach. A breach can be material or minor. If the breach is major, the non-breaching party can suspend performance and sue for damages. If it is minor, it can sue for damages caused by the breach, but must still perform.

Here, if InfoTech's performance is not excused, it breached the contract by failing to pay under the agreement. It only made two of the twelve payments due under the contract. Therefore, the breach is major, and CompServe does not have to continue to perform as it sues InfoTech for breach.

Damages:

This contract contains a *liquidated damages clause* that InfoTech will pay 80% immediately if it fails to make a payment. These clauses are enforceable as long as the damages are difficult to predict at the time of formation and are not unreasonably disproportionate to stated estimates and are not a penalty.

The court here is not likely to enforce this clause, because damages could be reasonably determined by CompServe's hourly rate. Further, it appears that the 80% balance becoming immediately due and payable is a penalty and would be unconscionable, as CompServe had only provided services for one month.

The court is therefore more likely to award compensatory damages if it finds that InfoTech's performance was not excused.

Conclusion:

CompServe will sue InfoTech for breach of contract. InfoTech will try to admit parol evidence claiming that CompServe promised to provide service within an hour and that its failure to do so amounted to the failure of a condition, which excuses InfoTech form performance. If InfoTech is successful in this defense, it will prevail. If not, CompServe will recover compensatory damages caused by InfoTech's breach.

END OF ANSWER.

Professor's Guidance

Hopefully you are getting better and better the more you practice! If not, you should reach out to your professor or a tutor. Remember, you can always submit your essays for feedback and work with a live tutor at *PassTheFYLSE.com*. Most of the time, students that are still struggling at this point know the law, but just need a little advice to help them to better translate their knowledge and to fill in any holes in their writing approach. I included this essay because it tests conditions and the Parol Evidence Rule. Let's look at those issues in a little more detail.

Did you correctly spot the Parol Evidence Rule as an issue? Here's a big tip: Any time you have a writing, you should examine the facts carefully to see if the Statute of Frauds or the Parol Evidence Rule should be discussed. First, see if it is the type of contract to which the Statute of Frauds applies. If it is, make sure the writing satisfies it. Then, look to see if one of the parties is alleging anything not included in the writing. If so, then you must discuss the Parol Evidence Rule. Remember, the Statute of Frauds protects you when there is no writing or when there is a problem with the writing, while the Parol Evidence Rule protects you after your agreement has been reduced to writing.

Conditions should also be discussed here, because the Parol Evidence that we are attempting to introduce could be considered a condition. When discussing conditions, always identify what type of condition it is and whether it has been satisfied or excused before moving on to your discussion of breach. Also, as we mentioned before, always make sure you look for facts that may help the non-performing party avoid being labeled a breachor.

Finally, damages were an issue here as well. Take a close look at how I analyzed the liquidated damages clause. Anytime you see that such a clause is included in the contract, you should always address it first to decide if it is valid. If it is valid, apply it. If not, or there is a possibility that it is not, you will need to calculate the resulting damages in the usual way.

Contracts Essay Answer 10:
Miranda, Blake, Trisha & Garth

Blake v. Miranda

What law governs?

The UCC governs contracts for the sale of goods, while the common law governs contracts for services. Because this question deals with the sale of goods, the *UCC* controls.

Is there a valid contract between Blake and Miranda?

Valid contract formation requires mutual assent, which is reached through the process of offer and acceptance, and consideration. There must also be an absence of defenses.

Mutual Assent:

Was an offer made?

An offer exists when the offeror manifests an objective intent to be bound to definite terms, including price and quantity under the UCC, and the offeror communicates the offer to the offeree.

Signs:

The first possible offer was made by Miranda when she posted signs for her garage sale. However, the sign is likely just an *advertisement* for her garage sale. Advertisements are generally not considered offers unless they meet all of the requirements of an offer. Because the sign did not mention quantity with regard to the clothes, bags, and books, and because the sign was communicated to the general public, it is an invitation for offers rather than an offer. The only exception may be the guitar.

Even though the sign did contain definite terms with regard to the guitar, it was not specific as to who had the power of acceptance. There was only one guitar available, and the price was clearly stated, but it did not it did not limit acceptance to "first come first served." Had it done so, as discussed below, Blake may have made a valid acceptance by showing up. Otherwise, because acceptance was not limited, there was not an offer made by the sign that could be accepted.

Blake's Statement as an Offer:

Blake arrived at Miranda's home at noon and said he wanted to buy the guitar for $200. He will argue that because there was only one available and the price was clearly stated on the sign, an offer existed that gave him the power of acceptance. He will further argue that he did in fact accept by showing up at noon as required by the sign and telling Miranda that he would buy the guitar. However, as discussed above, it is unlikely that the sign was a valid offer, so Blake's statement that he would buy the guitar for $200 was more likely the first offer made.

Blake identified the subject matter (the guitar,) stated a price ($200) and communicated it to Miranda. He further explained that he wanted to go home to get his car and would be back before 4:00. Blake made a valid offer to Miranda at this point.

Acceptance:

Did Miranda accept Blake's offer?

Subject to certain exceptions not present here, silence does not constitute acceptance. Therefore, Miranda did not accept Blake's offer for the guitar. Absent a valid acceptance, there is no contract.

Additional terms:

If the sign was found to be an offer and Blake's statement was an attempted acceptance, we also must examine additional terms contained in the acceptance.

At common law, the acceptance must *mirror* the offer. When the offeree includes an additional term in the acceptance, as Blake does here by stating that he needs to get a car first, he makes a *counteroffer*. However, *UCC 2-207* will still allow a finding that a contract exists between the communication of the parties. Here, because the parties are not merchants, the additional term would not become part of the contract unless Miranda assents. Therefore, Blake's statement that he needs to get a car does not become part of the contract.

Consideration:

Was consideration present?

Consideration is a bargained for exchange between the parties. Here, the consideration is money ($200) in exchange for goods (the guitar). Therefore consideration exists to support the contract.

Guitar Conclusion:

If the sign created the power of acceptance in Blake and he accepted by showing up at noon, a valid contract was formed between the parties. However, because it is not likely that the sign was an offer that could be accepted, and Miranda did not respond to Blake's verbal offer to buy the guitar, no contract existed.

Trisha v. Miranda

Governing Law:

As discussed above, the UCC governs the contract between Trisha and Miranda.

Mutual Assent:

As discussed above, the sign was not likely an offer, so the first possible offer would be Trisha's statement that she would love to buy the jacket. However, since she followed by stating that she can't afford it, her statement was not an offer.

Miranda's statement that she would give the jacket to Trisha for free if Miranda couldn't sell it for $250 by 3:30 was the next possible offer. Her statement contained a price term (free), subject matter and quantity (one jacket) and was communicated directly to Trisha. There was also a condition placed on the offer, stating that it was only available if the jacket didn't sell by 3:30.

Further, Trisha thanking Miranda before leaving manifests her intent to be bound and is a valid acceptance. At 3:30, Trisha called to see if the condition had been satisfied. Miranda responded that no one had purchased the jacket and that it "looks like the jacket is yours." Although this does not seem to be definite enough to constitute an offer, Miranda's statement, coupled with the earlier conversation, would probably lead to a finding that Miranda had made a valid offer. Again, Trisha accepted by giving her thanks and indicated that she was going to buy a matching purse and shows to go with the jacket.

Therefore, mutual assent exists between the parties.

Consideration:

Are the promises supported by consideration?

Consideration is a bargained for exchange. *Past consideration* cannot support a new promise. Here, because Miranda offered the jacket for free, Trisha has not bargained for the jacket, and there is no consideration to support Miranda's promise. Additionally, Miranda's statement that she wanted to pay Trisha back for being a good neighbor will not support the promises, because it is past consideration. Therefore, there can be no valid contract unless a substitute for consideration exists.

Promissory Estoppel:

The doctrine of promissory estoppel can serve as a substitute for consideration when a party reasonably and foreseeably relies on the promise of another to her detriment. Here, Trisha told Miranda that she was going to buy a matching purse and shoes. It was therefore *foreseeable* to Miranda that Trisha was relying on her promise to give her the jacket. It was also *reasonable* for Trisha to rely on Miranda's promise, because they were friends and Miranda mentioned her desire to do something nice for all that Trisha had done for her in the past. Trisha suffered a *detriment in reliance* on Miranda's promise, because she spent money on the matching purse and shoes. This may be enough for Trisha to establish promissory estoppel and enforce the contract.

Jacket Conclusion:

If Trisha can establish promissory estoppel, she will be able to recover against Miranda.

Garth v. Miranda

Governing Law:

Again, the UCC controls, as this contract is for the sale of goods.

Mutual Assent and Consideration:

Garth's statement that he wants to buy the books but doesn't have any cash is insufficient to constitute a valid offer, because it lacks intent to be bound.

Miranda's statement that she would sell the books for $100 is a valid offer, communicated to Garth and containing the material terms.

Garth's statement that he'll be back as soon as he can with cash and his subsequent return with the money evidences his intent to be bound. Consideration is also present, as both are bargaining for money in exchange for books. The only question that remains is whether Miranda had a responsibility to hold the offer open until he returned with cash.

Option:

Was the offer still open, giving Garth the power of acceptance, or can Miranda revoke the offer before Garth returned?

When neither party is a merchant, an offer to keep an offer open must be supported by additional *consideration* to be enforceable. Here, Garth gave no additional consideration to support the promise. Therefore, Miranda was free to sell the books to Debbie before Garth returned with the money. By selling the books to Debbie, Miranda has effectively revoked her offer to Garth.

Books Conclusion:

Because Miranda's offer to keep the offer open was not supported by consideration, she was free to revoke her offer to Garth and did so by selling the books to Debbie. There was no enforceable contract between Garth and Miranda.

END OF ANSWER.

Professor's Guidance

I hope you had some fun with this last Contracts essay! It contains familiar formation issues and forces you to carefully examine mutual assent and consideration with each conversation.

Hopefully this was a good review for you and helps solidify your confidence when writing an answer to a Contracts Formation problem.

Another point you should take away from this essay is that the UCC always applies when dealing with the sale of goods, even if the parties are not merchants or the goods are worth less than $500. For whatever reason, many students wrongly assume that if the goods are sold by a non-merchant, the common law applies. This is not true. The Statute of Frauds is the only rule triggered by the $500 amount, and only certain provisions of the UCC apply to merchants. Therefore, make sure you know when merchant status matters. You can use this chart to help!

SECTION	TOPIC
2-201(2)	Statute of Frauds — merchant's confirmatory memo rule.
2-205	Merchant's firm offer.
2-207(2)	Additional terms in acceptance or confirmation — "battle of the forms" rule for merchants.
2-209(2)	Agreement excluding modification except by signed writing — form supplied by merchant.
2-312	Warranty against infringement.
2-314	Implied warranty of merchantability.
2-316(2)	Disclaimer of implied warranty of merchantability.
2-403(2)	Entrusting goods to merchant gives her power to transfer rights to buyer in ordinary course.
2-509(3)	Risk of loss in the absence of breach (noncarrier cases) — passes on buyer's receipt if seller is a merchant, otherwise on tender of delivery.

This wraps up our Contracts essay practice! I encourage you to practice on more questions released by your state bar association and to complete the practice multiple choice questions as well if you haven't already done so.

16

Torts Practice Essays

It's time to practice writing some Torts essays! I'm assuming you now know the law and have a good handle on how it all fits together. Use these essays to fill in any gaps in your knowledge, help you better understand how the issues are tested and organized, help you improve your timing, and eventually boost your confidence!

Similar to those you will find in Contracts and Criminal Law, you will find several sample essays on the following pages. Read the question first and make your best effort to answer it on your own before reading the sample answer and related comments that appear in the next chapter. It should take you about an hour to write your answer to a practice essay.

After writing your answer, compare it to the sample answer and comments to assess your work. Pay careful attention to how the facts raise the issues tested, how the sample answer is organized, how the substance is analyzed, and how the rules are stated. Doing so will help when you find yourself writing an essay on similar topics in the future.

You may also find it helpful to work on the practice essays with a study partner or small study group. Just make sure you make an effort to always write your own answer first before sharing your effort and learning!

Finally, for students that feel they need additional guidance as they work through the practice essays, they can visit PassTheFYLSE.com and submit their essays to a professor for personalized feedback. Students are also able to send specific academic questions or opt for more in-depth tutoring in a group or individual setting.

Now let's get down to business!

Torts Essay 1:
Viki v. Don

Don, the principal of a high school, summons Viki, a schoolgirl, to his office, and abruptly accuses her of immoral conduct with various men. Don bullies Viki for an hour and threatens her with prison and with public disgrace for herself and her parents unless she confesses. When Viki refused to confess, Don grabs her backpack off her arm as she runs out the door crying, intending to keep it until she confesses. Viki becomes ill as a result of the incident.

What possible tort claims can Viki assert against Don?

Discuss.

Torts Essay 2:
Sam v. Barb

Barb is a 14-year-old girl living with her mother, Arlene, in a quiet neighborhood. Barb has been diagnosed with schizophrenia, a mental disease that causes her to exhibit delusional and violent behavior. Barb would sometimes attack people in her neighborhood and was prescribed medication to control her behavior. Arlene was aware of Barb's condition and past attacks but was not aware that Barb had stopped taking her medication. The age of majority in the state is 18.

After being off of her medications for about a week, Barb confronted her neighbor, Sam, as he walked along the sidewalk in front of her house. Without provocation, Barb got up close to Sam's face, and gestured as if she was slicing her throat with a fake knife. Barb screamed: "I know you want to kill me, so I'm going to make sure I get to you first!" She then calmly walked away.

A few days later, Barb saw Sam in the street and immediately jumped on her bicycle. She rode as fast as she could directly towards Sam. Sam was afraid Barb was going to hit him and jumped out of the way as Barb swerved to miss him at the last minute. Sam fell on the ground and suffered a severe concussion and a broken nose as a result.

Sam has sued on theories of assault and battery. What is the likelihood of his success?

Discuss.

Torts Essay 3:
Randy v. Travis

It is against the law to text while driving. Travis was texting when she veered out of her lane and hit Randy's car, causing Randy injuries.

Discuss the possible claim Randy has against Travis.

Torts Essay 4:
Parent v. MFR

Parent got into an accident while driving an automobile manufactured by MFR. Child was sitting in the passenger seat, restrained by a seatbelt, and was seriously injured by the airbag when it deployed. MFR was aware that children are often injured by airbags but did not design the automobiles to include a widely used sensor that would turn off the airbags when it detected the presence of a child in the seat. Parent brings suit against MFR on behalf of child for injuries suffered by Child.

On what theories can Parent recover? (Assume Parent has standing to bring suit on behalf of Child.)

Discuss.

Torts Essay 5:
Jenny, Sarah & Courtney v. Restaurant

Jenny spent the evening enjoying drinks at a restaurant with her friends. While going into the restroom at the restaurant, Jenny slipped and fell on a puddle of water that was leaking from a broken pipe under the sink and injured her arm. The restaurant knew the pipe was leaking and had called a plumber in earlier that day to repair it. The plumber could not make the repair until the next day, so the restaurant attempted to turn the water off but was unable to do so. A restaurant employee was therefore sent in to mop the bathroom floor every 10 minutes. However, this did not prevent the floor from being slippery.

After Jenny's fall, an employee stood in front of the restroom to prevent others from entering for the remainder of the night. After closing, the manager placed multiple towels under the sink as well as a sign reading "Do Not Enter. Wet Floor."

Later that night, Pam, a waitress who had keys to the back door, broke into the restaurant to party with her friends, Sarah and Courtney. Pam had been previously convicted of burglary on several occasions, but the restaurant had never conducted a background check on her.

The girls attempted to locate some flashlights to help them see in the dark. All of the restaurant lights had been turned off, including the exit signs that were required by statute to be illuminated at all times. The restaurant had not replaced the bulbs in the signs, because some customers complained that they affected the overall ambiance of the restaurant.

As Pam, Sarah and Courtney worked their way towards the bar, Sarah tripped over a vacuum cord that was stretched across the floor. Brett, an independent cleaning contractor, had left the vacuum plugged in and was napping in the restaurant office. Sarah tripped over the cord, hit her head on the bar, and broke her nose.

Courtney slipped and fell on the wet in the restroom as she was running in to get Sarah some paper towels to stop the bleeding. It was dark, and she did not see the sign. As a result of the fall, Courtney broke her ankle.

Courtney's scream woke Brett, but by the time he made his way to the restroom, the girls were gone. He heard the door slam but decided not to say anything because he had been sleeping on the job.

1. Jenny wishes to sue the restaurant for its failure to maintain the bathroom in a safe condition. On what theory or theories, if any, can Jenny recover from the restaurant?

2. Sarah and Courtney want to sue the restaurant. On what theory or theories, if any, can Sarah and Courtney recover from the restaurant?

Discuss.

Torts Essay 6:
Lance & Richard v. Theater

Richard was so excited to see the latest Galactic Star movie that he spilled his drink on the floor. The spill caused the theater aisle floor lighting to short circuit. Not wanting to miss the beginning of the movie, Richard decided not to tell anyone and moved to another seat after the movie started.

A state statute requires theater aisle floor lighting that allows patrons to exit safely in case of an emergency. The theater was in violation of this statute due to Richard's spill.

Lance stopped at the snack bar to buy some popcorn and a root beer before walking into the theater. He entered the crowded theater just as the movie started and the house lights had been turned down. He noticed an empty aisle seat next to Richard, where Richard had spilled his drink.

As Lance stepped from the aisle to the seat, not noticing the puddle left from the spill, Lance lost his balance, slipped, and broke his ankle.

Lance's root beer flew out of his hand and spilled all over Richard. Richard is allergic to root beer and suffered a severe allergic reaction as a result.

Can Lance and Richard sue the theater for negligence?

Discuss.

Torts Essay 7:
Andrew v. John

Andrew was looking for a job and had applied for work at a fast food restaurant. The employer contacted Andrew's previous employer, John. John said, "Well, Andrew was a pretty good worker, but I wouldn't hire him. I heard the news around town that he is a member of the 'Community Supreme Group.'" (The Community Supreme Group was a well-known and thoroughly disliked radical organization. It had been linked with several violent acts.) Because of those statements, Andrew did not get the job. Andrew was not, nor had he ever been, a member of the Community Supreme Group. Andrew finds out about the statement and sues John.

Upon what theory can Andrew recover? Fully discuss your answer.

Torts Essay 8:
Betty v. Fred

Fred and Betty were coworkers. One night, they both had too much to drink after work, and they shared a romantic moment. Fred asked his friend Barney to videotape Fred and Betty while they were kissing at the bar. Betty was married at the time and regretted the kiss. Fred became quite angry when Betty resisted his future advances. He called Betty at home many times in an attempt to get her to leave her husband. When she continued to refuse, Fred called Betty's husband at home and told him that he and Betty had kissed and were in love. Fred also posted the video that Barney had recorded on the internet. Betty's Boss saw the video and fired both Betty and Fred for violating company policy. Betty's husband also left her as a result of the alleged affair.

Under what theory or theories could Betty recover against Fred?

Discuss.

Torts Essay 9:
SaveCo, Dustin & Kevin

SaveCo is a large discount superstore located in the town of Hillshire. The parking lot is equipped with bright lights to ensure the safety of its customers. The lights are scheduled to turn on automatically during opening hours while it is dark outside. The lights are also set to come on in response to loud noises. The lights come on several times in the middle of the night, waking nearby residents. Several residents complained that the lack of sleep caused by the lights resulted in adverse health effects.

One resident, Dustin, was fed up with losing sleep and drove down to the store just after closing time. He confronted the store manager, Kevin, and began yelling obscenities. During the course of the confrontation, Dustin stormed off and yelled "Your boss is a dope smoking idiot!" The store was mostly empty at the time of the incident, but there were a few employees that witnessed the confrontation.

What tort claims can Kevin raise against Dustin?

What tort claims can the residents of Hillshire bring against SaveCo?

Discuss.

Torts Essay 10:
Andy v. Doctor

Andy was addicted to prescription pain pills. Doctor, Andy's roommate and a licensed pharmacist, routinely prescribed pain pills to Andy, even though he knew Andy was abusing them. Doctor's pharmacy was inspected by the Department of Health and was found to be in violation of statutes related to cleanliness. The sink had dirty sitting water, and open containers of products were near dust pans and brooms. Dead bugs and rodent fecal matter were also observed.

One evening, Andy took three pain pills, which was one more pill than the prescribed amount, and went to bed. Andy woke up suffering from headache, fever, dizziness, and nausea and was rushed to the hospital. Andy was diagnosed with fungal meningitis.

If Andy sues Doctor, under what tort theories can he recover?

Discuss.

17

Torts Practice Essay Answers

Please compare your answer to each of the practice essays to the sample answers that follow, noting the issues you missed, whether your rule statements were included and completely stated, and whether you included the relevant key facts in your analysis of each issue. Also notice how the organization of your answer compares to the sample.

Also, please pay close attention to the comments provided following the model answer. They provide guidance on how to best evaluate your own work and on how to improve when analyzing similar issues in the future.

Torts Essay Answer 1:
Viki v. Don

Viki v. Don

Intentional Infliction of Emotional Distress

Issue: Is Don liable for IIED?

Rule: IIED is shown where plaintiff can prove: 1. Defendant acted intentionally or recklessly; and 2. Defendant's conduct was extreme and outrageous; and 3. Defendant's act is the cause of such distress; and 4. Plaintiff suffers severe emotional distress as a result of defendant's conduct.

Analysis: (Element 1 issue) Did Don act *intentionally or recklessly*? (Element 1 analysis) Don brought Viki to his office with the intent of coercing a confession out of her. (Element 1 conclusion) Don acted intentionally. (Element 2 issue) Was Don's conduct *extreme and outrageous*? (Element 2 analysis) Rather than simply asking Viki whether she engaged in immoral conduct, Don bullied her for an hour, threatening her with prison and public disgrace for herself and her parents. As a principal, he was in a position of authority and knew that Viki, a young school girl, would believe his threats and would submit to his bullying. (Element 1 conclusion) Don's conduct was extreme and outrageous.

(Element 3 issue) Did Don's conduct *cause Viki distress*? (Element 3 analysis) Viki was crying when she ran out of Don's office. She would not have been crying nor would she have become ill had she not been distressed by Don's actions. (Element 3 conclusion) Don's conduct therefore caused Viki distress.

(Element 4 issue) Did Viki *suffer severe emotional distress as a result* of Don's conduct? (Element 4 analysis) Viki cried and became ill as a result of the incident. (Element 4 conclusion) Viki therefore suffered severe emotional distress as a result of Don's conduct.

Conclusion: Don is liable for IIED.

Battery

Issue: Did don commit a battery against Viki when he grabbed her backpack away from her?

Rule: Battery is the intentional, harmful or offensive touching of another without consent.

Analysis: (Element 1 issue) Did don act *intentionally*? (Element 1 Rule) Intent can be shown either by *desire or knowledge to a substantial certainty* that the act undertaken would or may result in touching, harm or offense. (Element 1 Analysis) When Don grabbed Viki's backpack off her arm as she was leaving his office, he intended to yank it off her arm. He at least had knowledge to a substantial certainty that grabbing the backpack, which was closely connected to Viki's body, would result in an offensive, if not harmful, touching.

(Element 2 issue) Was the *touching harmful or offensive?* (Element 2 Analysis) Although the facts do not suggest that Viki was physically harmed by Don's actions in grabbing the backpack, she was most likely offended. It is reasonable to conclude Viki would be offended by Don grabbing the backpack away from her person. (Element 2 conclusion) The touching was offensive.

(Element 3 issue) Was the touching *without consent?* (Element 3 analysis and conclusion) Don grabbed Viki's backpack without her consent.

Conclusion: Don committed a battery against Viki.

Trespass to Chattel/Conversion

Issue: Did Don commit trespass to chattel or conversion by taking Viki's backpack away from her?

Rule: Trespass to chattels or conversion results when defendant intentionally interferes with the personal property of another. Conversion involves a substantial dispossession or damage to the property, whereas trespass to chattels involves less of an interference.

Analysis: (Elements 1 and 2) Don **intended to keep** Viki's backpack, which he knew to be her **personal property**, until she confessed. (Element 1 and 2 conclusion) Therefore, he intentionally interfered with the personal property of another.

(Element 3 issue) Did the *degree of interference* result in trespass to chattel or conversion? (Element 3 rule) *Conversion* involves a *substantial dispossession or damage* to the property, whereas trespass to chattels involves less of an interference. (Element 3 analysis) Don intended to keep the backpack until Viki confessed. Therefore, if he gives the backpack to her, the result will be *trespass to chattel*. If he does not give it back to her or if he keeps it for an amount of time that amounts to a substantial dispossession, the result will be conversion. (Element 3 conclusion) If Don returns the backpack before the school year is over, he has committed trespass to chattel. If he keeps the backpack for longer than that or doesn't return it at all, the result will be conversion.

Conclusion: Don will be liable for either trespass to chattel or conversion depending on how long he keeps the backpack from Viki.

END OF ANSWER.

Professor's Guidance

Wasn't that fun? So, how did you do?

Note first that I used the IRAC and element identifiers in the sample answer in an effort to help those who may still struggle with IRAC organization. They should not be included in the answer to a formal essay.

Let's look at the overall organization first.

Do you notice how I began my answer by identifying the parties: Viki v. Don? It is important to do this, because you may have more than one defendant in a fact pattern. Had Don also had claims he could bring against Viki, we would address those in a separate part of the essay, appropriately labeled Don v. Viki. If we had another defendant involved, we would address that separately as well, identifying that discussion as Viki v. _____ (the other defendant).

Notice also that I separated each possible tort that Don has committed, beginning with the first tort raised by the facts (IIED). I completely analyzed that tort using IRAC before moving on to the next one. I encourage you to use bold, underlines and headings in your essays to help identify to the reader when you are moving on to a new defendant, claim, or element.

Did you recognize IIED as an issue? If not, be sure to read the facts more carefully. The key facts that should have clued you in on this issue include the fact that the principal abruptly accused Viki of immoral conduct, he bullied and threatened her, and that she was upset by this. Anytime you see what may be described as extreme behavior intended to upset another, you should discuss IIED. Issue spotting takes practice. The more cases you read with similar facts, and the more familiar you are with the definitions of each tort, the more likely you are to identify the issue in a similar fact pattern.

Did you fully state the rule regarding IIED before you analyzed the facts to conclude that Don was liable for IIED? Remember, without stating a complete rule first, you will not have a "roadmap" to follow as you analyze the tort. So, anytime you spot an issue, make sure you **completely** state the rule before conducting your analysis of reaching a conclusion. Also, don't forget that sometimes you'll need to define another sub-rule before you continue along with your analysis of one of the elements of the rule that controls the larger issue. (For example, I needed to define intent with regard to battery when I reached the point where I discussed intent as an element of battery.)

Did you take each element of the rule you identified with regard to IIED and provide a separate analysis of each of those elements? Look at how I did this. I noted that there were 4 elements of IIED, and I discussed each one of those elements in a separate paragraph, using the facts to show the reader whether each element could be proven or not. The first element was intent. In your answer, did you simply state that Don acted intentionally, or did you bring up the facts that led you to conclude the Don acted intentionally? If you do not use the facts to support your conclusions, you will lose points. You know that Don brought Viki into his office with a purpose in mind (to use bullying tactics to coerce her into confessing). Tell your reader this. This is what makes his conduct intentional.

Did you notice that extreme and outrageous behavior, causation, and severe emotional distress were also issues that needed to be discussed? If not, you either did not have a full grasp of the rule, or you just assumed that your reader knew this and skipped the analysis. In a court of law, you have to prove every element of the tort. You can never just assume an element exists because it seems clear to you. Therefore, you have to first make sure you know what those elements are and then make sure you address each one, using the facts to prove its existence. If an element really is clear, you don't have to make a big deal out of it, but you still have to mention it. For example, it is clear that the backpack was "the personal property of another" for purposes of the trespass to chattel/conversion analysis. We didn't leave that fact out, but we did simply state that the backpack was personal property that belonged to Viki and moved on to the real discussable issue, which was the degree of interference.

Did you include facts to help you prove each element of IIED? Again, make sure you "show your work" and tell the reader what facts led you to conclude the way you did with regard to each element.

OK, so, now that we've fully discussed IIED, did you recognize battery as an issue? If not, again, you probably did not read the facts carefully. Here's a hint. Make sure you memorize a checklist of all possible issues before writing an essay. We have learned that there are 7 intentional torts. So, as you read through the facts, consider whether each one of those torts could apply. The fact that Don "grabbed" Viki's backpack off her arm should clue you in to the issue of battery. When you see that fact, quickly consider the rule you have memorized for battery. Do the facts lend themselves to a discussion of whether or not there was a touching, whether it was intentional or offensive? If so, you know that is an issue that needs to be discussed. So again, you'll want to state the issue (under a separate heading), state the rule, and then take each element of the rule separately to show your reader which facts relate to that element before reaching your conclusion with regard to each element, and ultimately, your conclusion with regard to the tort claim.

Again, also notice how sometimes you'll have to define and analyze a rule within a rule, as I did here with intent as it relates to battery.

OK, last claim: Did you notice that trespass to chattels/conversion was an issue? This was a little trickier to spot. Again, having a mental checklist of possible issues will help here. The fact that should have led you to discuss this issue was that Don intended to keep her backpack until she confessed. Also, the fact that we don't know when Don returned the backpack should lead you to discuss the possible degree of interference and whether that interference would result in a trespass to chattel or conversion claim. So, it is important not only to notice what facts you have that will help you prove or disprove an element, but it is also important to notice when you are not given facts that relate to an element that needs to be discussed as part of the rule. In those cases, you will find yourself addressing the possibility that the element could be proven if certain facts are shown.

I hope you find this helpful!

Torts Essay Answer 2: Sam v. Barb

Sam v. Barb

Assault

1. Threatening Sam on the Sidewalk

Is Barb liable for assault for threatening Sam on the sidewalk?

Assault is defined as intentionally placing another in reasonable apprehension of an imminent battery.

Here, Barb approached Sam, gestured threateningly and screamed, "I know you want to kill me, so I'm going to make sure I get to you first!" and then calmly walked away. Although Barb *acted intentionally* by threatening Sam, she cannot be liable for assault, because there was no threat of an *imminent battery*. In fact, Barb did not act on her threat until two days later. However, her threat can be used to prove intent for assault and battery when she rode towards Sam on her bicycle.

Barb is therefore not liable for assault for threatening Sam.

2. Riding Bike Towards Sam

Is Barb liable for assault for riding her bike towards Sam?

Assault is defined as intentionally placing another in reasonable apprehension of an imminent battery.

Barb acted *intentionally*, because she believed that Sam was out to kill her and even threatened to get him first. She was aware that Sam was present on the street and intentionally rode her bicycle towards him as fast as she was able. Sam was also *in fear of an imminent battery* because he jumped out of the way, likely believing he would be hit by the bicycle. Sam's *apprehension was also reasonable*, because Barb had previously threatened him and did not swerve to miss him until the last second. Therefore, Barb is liable for Assault.

Battery

Is Barb liable for battery?

Battery is defined as an intentional touching that results in harm or offense. Intent can be established through either actual intent or substantial certainty.

Barb acted *intentionally*, as she believed Sam wanted to kill her and she threatened to get him first. She was aware that Sam was present and intentionally rode her bike towards him as rapidly as she was able. Barb did swerve at the last minute and could claim that she did not intend to hit him and, in fact, did not hit him. However, because she likely *knew to a substantial certainty* that he would *hit the ground* while trying to get out of the way, an *intentional touching* can be established. Harm is also established because Sam suffered injuries as a result of hitting his head on the ground.

Barb is therefore liable for battery.

Defenses

1. Incapacity

Are minor children liable for their intentional torts?

Infants are generally liable for their malicious, intentional, or willful acts or torts. Although infancy is not a defense, a child could escape liability if she was incapable of forming the required intent.

Here, Barb is 14 and lives in a state where the age of majority is 18. Therefore, she is a minor. As a general rule, infants are liable for their own intentional torts. Therefore, it does not matter that Barb is under the age of majority. Further, at age 14, she is capable of forming the requisite intent for assault and battery. As such, Barb can be held liable for her intentional torts.

2. Mentally Disabled

Are the mentally disabled liable for their intentional torts?

The mentally disabled are generally liable for their malicious, intentional, or willful acts or torts.

Because the mentally disabled are generally held liable for their intentional torts, Barb cannot escape liability simply because she has been diagnosed with schizophrenia and can be held liable for her intentional torts.

Sam v. Arlene

Can Arlene be held responsible for Barb's actions?

As a general rule, the common law does not hold a parent liable for the tortious acts of a minor child. However, parents can be held liable when the parent fails to exercise control over a minor child although the parent knows or with due care should know that an injury to another is possible.

Arlene cannot be held liable for Barb's actions simply because of the existence of the parent-child relationship. Also, Arlene will not be held liable even though she knows that Barb has a history of attacking neighbors, because she was unaware that Barb had stopped taking her medication. However, if she reasonably should have known that Barb stopped taking her medications and was a threat to others, she may have some liability in negligence.

Arlene is not responsible for Barb's actions.

END OF ANSWER.

Professor's Guidance

This was another essay testing Intentional Torts.

I've mentioned before that just about every sentence provided in a fact pattern is there for a reason. It either raises an issue or helps you to resolve an issue. Therefore, you must take each sentence and ask yourself why it was included. The fact that Barb is 14 years old and that she has schizophrenia should raise red flags for you to discuss minors and the mentally disabled. Also, the fact that Arlene is included in the fact pattern at all should raise a red flag for you to discuss parental liability.

Moving on to the torts, notice that the call of the question only asked you to consider Assault and Battery. Therefore, you did not need to mention other torts that may apply, such as Intentional Infliction of Emotional Distress or Negligence on the part of Arlene. Again, it is *critical* that you read the call of the question carefully. Sometimes it will help you organize your answer, limit the issues, or provide other valuable information that can save you time and help you earn points.

The only thing to really note in the discussion of assault is to pay attention to the fact that there were two possible assaults here, so we did not lump them together. Rather, we discussed each separately and completely to determine whether an assault had occurred. Also note that we discussed the facts as they related to every element before reaching our conclusion. Failing to do so would most certainly cost you important points on an essay question, as you must prove every element of the tort to prove your case, even if you think it should be obvious to the reader. If an element is missing, there is no tort.

When discussing battery, remember to consider the definition of intent when establishing an intentional touching. If you cannot prove desire, you may be able to prove knowledge to a substantial certainty that a touching would occur, as we did here.

Defenses were definitely worth a lot of points here. If you missed the issue of whether minors are responsible for their intentional torts or whether the mentally disabled are liable for their intentional torts, you may not pass the essay no matter how well you did on your analysis of assault and battery. Remember, just about every fact is given for a reason.

Finally, had the call of the question not limited you to intentional torts, Negligence would most certainly be an issue here, as Arlene failed to control the actions of her child whom she knew to be dangerous. Had you discussed Negligence, you would need to discuss every element, including Duty, Breach, Causation, and Damages. If you are feeling confident, try quickly writing your answer to the negligence issue before moving on!

Torts Essay Answer 3:
Randy v. Travis

Randy v. Travis

Negligence

Negligence is shown when plaintiff can prove the defendant breached a duty of care that caused injury to the plaintiff. The following elements must be established: Duty, Breach, Causation (both actual and proximate), and Damages.

Duty: A duty of reasonable care is owed to all foreseeable plaintiffs.

Standard of Care: Absent a special duty rule, a duty of *reasonable care* is owed. Plaintiff is foreseeable because he is a motorist driving on the same road as defendant. Therefore, defendant owes him a duty of reasonable care, which is to drive safely.

Breach: A breach occurs when defendant fails to exercise the standard of care. Defendant breached her duty or reasonable care to drive safely, because it is not safe, and therefore unreasonable, to engage in a distraction that forces a driver to take her eyes off the road while driving.

****Note to students:** *Depending on the facts, it may be enough to simply state that defendant acted unreasonably as I did above. However, some facts will lend themselves to a complete discussion noting that Breach can be established via the **Learned Hand Test**.*

Breach is can also be established through *Negligence Per Se*. The statute provides the duty and standard of care, and breach will be shown if: a) the plaintiff is within the class of persons the statute was intended to protect; and b) the injury or harm was of the type the statute was designed to protect against; and c) the defendant's violation of the statute was not excused.

The statute at issue here is the *law against texting while driving*. 1) The statute is designed to protect drivers on the road. Plaintiff is a driver on the road, so he is *within the class of plaintiffs* the statute is designed to protect. 2) The statute is designed to protect against car accidents, so the *injury or harm was the type* the statute was designed to protect against. 3) The facts do not suggest that defendant's violation was *excused*. Therefore, breach can be established through negligence per se with regard to the no texting law.

*** Note to students:* *There is a possible second violation here, namely, the failure of defendant to stay within in her own lane. Sometimes, you will need to consider whether defendant's conduct constituted a possible violation of a law, even if the law is not clearly stated.*

Causation: Defendant's breach must be the actual and proximate cause of plaintiff's injuries.

Actual Cause: *But For* defendant's texting, she would not have veered into plaintiff's lane to cause the accident that injured plaintiff.

Proximate Cause: It is *foreseeable* that texting while driving could cause a driver to be distracted and veer into another lane to cause an accident.

Damages: Plaintiff must establish that he suffered damages as a result of defendant's breach. Plaintiff's car was damaged, and he suffered personal injuries from the crash. Therefore, he can establish damages.

END OF ANSWER.

Professor's Guidance

Now let's see how you did. Did you recognize that this was a negligence problem? Any time you see that someone is injured by the non-intentional acts of another (and the question is not asking about crimes), you should always discuss negligence as a possible theory.

Did you spot all of the major elements of negligence: **Duty**, **Breach**, **Causation**, and **Damages**? Remember that each element of negligence must be discussed fully and separately when you analyze a negligence problem.

Did you identify plaintiff as a foreseeable plaintiff to which a duty of reasonable care is owed? When discussing duty, you should always include a discussion of whether a duty is owed, who it is owed to, and what standard of care applies. Note that the general standard is that of reasonable care, but a higher or lower duty may be owed under certain circumstances. Make sure you review those special duty rules.

Did you identify the failure to exercise reasonable care and negligence per se as possible ways to prove breach? When discussing breach, you should always try to establish breach via the failure to exercise reasonable care first. If the facts lend themselves to a discussion of the Learned Hand Test, you will need to apply it to establish unreasonableness. A thorough analysis of the probability, gravity, burden, and utility will need to be included in your analysis for full credit. It is not enough to say that the likelihood and gravity of harm outweigh the burden and utility to act differently. That is a conclusion—remember that your conclusion will be less important than your analysis here.

Don't stop there. Remember that you can establish breach in other ways (Negligence Per Se and Res Ipsa Loquitor). So, look at the facts to determine whether either of these theories apply. Whenever you see a statute or law given in a negligence fact pattern, you should *always* discuss Negligence Per Se. Sometimes the law will be clearly stated, as it is here with the fact that "Texting while driving is against the law." Other times, the statute may be a little more ambiguous as it is here with the failure to stay in your own lane. Use your common sense here. Look to see if the plaintiff does something that may be considered against the law (or something she could be cited for). If so, you'll want to discuss negligence per se. The failure to stay in the lane was a minor issue here, so it wouldn't be that big of a deal if you missed it. However, it could result in a little boost of points if you fall short in other areas.

Also, remember that when you discuss negligence per se, it is *not enough* to simply state that a statute was violated. You *must* thoroughly analyze each factor of the test to prove negligence per se: a) the plaintiff is within the class of persons the statute was intended to protect; and b) the injury or harm was of the type the statute was designed to protect against; and c) the defendant's violation of the statute was not excused.

Although it doesn't apply here, remember that res ipsa is another way of proving breach. When you see something that does not otherwise occur without the negligence of someone—such as a plane falling out of the sky—you will want to fully discuss the res ipsa factors: 1. The harm suffered is most likely caused by negligence of someone; 2. It is more likely that it was defendant's negligence (or defendant had exclusive control of object which caused the harm); and 3. The Plaintiff was not at fault.

The next big issue is Causation. Did you remember to break it up into two issues: Actual cause and proximate cause? Make sure you **always include both** parts every time you discuss causation. Also don't forget that when you have more than one possible cause, you should discuss the substantial factor test. (When you have only one cause, as you do here, you'll use the but-for test.) Also, with proximate cause, look to see if you have supervening events that may break the chain of causation. The key will be to discuss whether each of those supervening causes was foreseeable. In addition to unforeseeable intervening events, if there are facts that raise the issue of (1) an unforeseeable plaintiff; (2) an unforeseeable type of injury; or (3) an unforeseeable manner of injury, you'll need to discuss that issue as well.

Lastly, don't forget about damages. They are usually a given, but since it is an element of negligence, you'll need to quickly address it.

As for defenses, if any defenses were applicable (contributory and comparative negligence or assumption of the risk), you would want to include them after analyzing the prima facie case for negligence. There were no defenses raised by these facts, so they were not included in the discussion.

Finally, although the facts only raised negligence as an issue in this one, remember that you may have more than one claim on an essay. So, just be sure to look for other theories raised by the facts when you see a question grounded in negligence. Perhaps there may be an intentional tort or products liability claim there as well!

Torts Essay Answer 4:
Parent v. MFR

Parent v. MFR

A person injured by a product can base his suit on the following theories: Negligence, Strict Products Liability, Breach of Warranty, or Intentional Tort.

Negligence

Does Child have a Negligence claim against MFR? Negligence requires proof of the following elements: Duty, Breach, Causation, and Damages.

Duty: Does MFR owe a duty to child? A duty of *reasonable care* is owed to all foreseeable plaintiffs. MFR has a duty to provide cars that are designed to protect drivers from harm or injury. Drivers and passengers are foreseeable plaintiffs.

Breach: Did MFR breach its duty to Child? MFR breached this duty by not installing a sensor that would turn off the airbags when it detected the presence of a child in the seat even though MFR was aware that children were often injured by airbags. The *gravity and probability of harm* is great, as children are often seriously injured by airbags. The *burden to take adequate precautions* against the harm is small in proportion to the harm caused. Adding a sensor would not be an unbearable cost.

Further, MFR breached its duty if it did not provide an *adequate warning* that children can be injured by airbags and should not sit in the passenger seat. Again, the cost of having such a warning is small in relation to the gravity and probability of harm. There also appears to be *no social utility* in failing to include a sensor or other mechanism to disable the airbags or to provide a warning.

Actual Cause: Was MFR the actual cause of Child's injuries? *But for* the airbag deploying, Child would not have been injured by the airbag.

Proximate cause: Was MFR the proximate cause of Child's injuries? It is *foreseeable* that children sitting in the passenger seat could be injured if the airbag deploys.

Damages: Did child suffer damages as a result of MFR's breach? Child suffered physical injuries.

Defenses: Does MFR have any available defenses? If a warning was present and parent allowed child to sit in the front passenger seat anyway, recovery will be barred if the case is brought in a jurisdiction that recognizes contributory negligence or will be reduced in a jurisdiction that recognizes comparative negligence. Otherwise, if there was no warning, since Child was wearing a seatbelt, contributory/comparative negligence would not apply.

Because MFR breached its duty of care by failing to include a sensor or to provide a warning and the deployment of the airbag caused injury to Child, Parent will be able to recover on behalf of Child in a cause of action based on negligence.

Strict Products Liability

One who makes, distributes or sells a defective product is strictly liable in tort for damages it causes to a foreseeable user. To prove a claim for strict products liability, a plaintiff must show proper parties, defective product, causation, damages, and absence of defenses.

Proper Parties:

A foreseeable user of a product may recover from parties engaged in the manufacture, distribution or retailing of a defective product. The plaintiff is proper here, because it is foreseeable that Parent would drive with Child in the passenger seat. Also, MFR is a proper defendant, because defendant is engaged in the manufacture of automobiles.

Defective Product:

There are three different ways to prove a defect: 1) Manufacturing defect; 2) Design defect; and 3) Failure to warn.

Manufacturing Defect: A product is defective as manufactured if it departs from its intended design even though all possible care was exercised in the preparation and marketing of the product. Here, since all cars were designed not to include a sensor, there is no evidence of a manufacturing defect.

Design Defect: A design defect exists when a product leaves the manufacturer's facility as intended by design, but the design is defective by one of three tests, tested at the time of the manufacture.

Ordinary Consumer Expectation Test: The product is more dangerous, when used in an intended or reasonably foreseeable manner, than the average consumer/user would expect. Here, airbags are a safety feature that makes automobiles more safe, not less so. However, since the airbag makes the car less safe for children passengers, the inability to disable it when children are in the passenger seat makes the car more dangerous. The design is defective under this test.

Risk/Utility Balancing Test: The risk of harm from using the product outweighs the product's utility. The risk of harm, physical injury to children, outweighs any utility, such as cost savings, in not installing a sensor to disable the airbags. The design is defective under this test.

Feasible Alternative (Restatement 3rd) Test: The foreseeable risks of harm from the product could have been reduced or avoided by the adoption of a reasonable alternative design. The foreseeable risk of injury to a child could have been reduced or avoided had a sensor been installed. The design is defective under this test.

Warning Defect: A product is defective if it lacks an adequate warning about unobvious dangers of using it. A product is unreasonably dangerous if the likelihood and gravity of the harm without a warning outweighs the utility of the product and the burden on the maker or seller to discover the defect and provide an adequate warning. If the car did not contain an adequate warning with regard to the dangers of children sitting in the front seat being injured by airbags, since the probability and gravity of the harm that could be suffered is greater than the burden on MFR to provide such a warning, then the car is defective for failure to warn. Had MFR provided such a warning, the child arguably would have sat in the back seat, avoiding any injury from the airbag.

Causation:

Actual Cause: But for the lack of sensor or warning, the child would not have been hit by the airbag.

Proximate Cause: It is **foreseeable** that children will ride as passengers in the front seat and could be injured if the airbag deploys.

Damages: Child suffered physical injuries as a result of being struck by the airbag.

Absence of Defenses:

Product Misuse and Assumption of the Risk are defenses that will bar a plaintiff's recovery in a products liability action.

Contributory/comparative negligence were not available defenses under the traditional rule, but some jurisdictions now will allow a finding of comparative negligence to reduce a plaintiff's recovery. Product misuse does not apply, since the car was being used in the manner for which it was intended. However, assumption of the risk applies to products liability cases to bar any claim by the plaintiff who knowingly and voluntarily assumed the risk. If a warning was present and parent allowed child to sit in the front passenger seat anyway, knowing that it is dangerous, assumption of the risk may apply. If there was no warning, since Child was wearing a seatbelt, comparative negligence would not apply.

In conclusion, if a products liability claim is raised, Plaintiff will recover unless barred by the defense of assumption of the risk.

Breach of Warranty

Finally, Plaintiff could claim breach of implied warranties. A **Warranty of Merchantability** and **Warranty of Fitness for a Particular Purpose** are implied in every product. A warranty of merchantability warrants that goods are fit for the ordinary purposes for which the goods are used, and the warranty of fitness warrants fitness for a particular, rather than general, purpose. There are no facts to show that the car was not generally safe or not fit to drive. The airbags also deployed as they were supposed to. Therefore, Plaintiff will not succeed on a claim for breach of warranty.

Intentional Tort

MFR could be liable for the intentional tort of battery if MFR knowingly placed a defective product in the marketplace. Since MFR knew that airbags could cause serious injury to children, if MFR did nothing to warn or protect against such an injury, MFR may be liable for intentional tort.

In conclusion, assuming plaintiff did not assume the risk of sitting in the passenger seat, plaintiff may recover under a claim of negligence or strict products liability. Further, if MFR did nothing to warn or protect against such an injury, MFR may be liable for intentional tort.

END OF ANSWER.

Professor's Guidance

So how did you do this time? This one was a real doozie! Look to see what you missed.

Did you spot all four theories under which a plaintiff can recover? Remember to always consider Negligence, Strict Products Liability, Breach of Warranty, and Intentional Tort (if applicable) whenever you see that plaintiff was injured by a product.

Did you remember to go through *all* of the elements of negligence in your discussion of it? Many students forget to do this. Many more forget to do a thorough analysis of the tests for breach. Here, the Learned Hand Test applied. Had there been facts suggesting that a statute had been violated, you would need to perform a full analysis of negligence per se. Had res ipsa been applicable, you would need to discuss the elements of that theory as well.

Did you mention and discuss all of the elements of a strict products liability claim: proper parties, defective product, causation, damages, and absence of defenses? If you missed any of these, go back and look at how each was handled. Notice how they begin with a rule statement followed by an analysis of the rule. **Always** use IRAC. It will help your discussion flow and will help you avoid missing any issues.

Did you mention and discuss the three ways to show defective product: manufacturing defect, design defect, and failure to warn? Always remember to work your way through all three!

As you worked your way through design defect, did you mention and apply the different tests used to determine whether there is a design defect? A complete discussion of those tests is required to earn full credit for that issue.

Once you finish your analysis of defective product, don't forget to complete your analysis by discussing the remaining elements of causation, damages, and absence of defenses!

Many students forget to discuss defenses. You need to memorize which defenses are applicable, along with their rule statements, and scan the facts to see if any defenses are possible.

Did you forget breach of warranty? Many students do, simply because they are worn out or out of time after finishing a full negligence and strict products liability discussion. As you can see, it is usually a pretty short discussion, so do your best to put in what you can!

Did you forget to look to see if an intentional tort claim was possible? You'll want to include this type of discussion when the facts warrant it.

Pay careful attention to how this sample is organized. Rewrite it until you can do it from memory. That way, the template and rules will come to you quickly when you encounter a similar fact pattern on an essay. Once you are comfortable with the organizational flow and the rules, practice, practice, practice!

Torts Essay Answer 5:
Jenny, Sarah & Courtney v. Restaurant

Jenny v. Restaurant

Negligence

Can Jenny sue the restaurant for negligence?

Negligence is shown when Defendant breaches a duty to the Plaintiff that causes damages to the plaintiff.

Duty and Standard of Care

The general rule is that you owe a duty of reasonable care to all foreseeable plaintiffs unless a special duty rule applies. Here, a special landowner duty rule applies. Jenny is an invitee, as she is there for the (commercial) benefit of the restaurant. As an invitee, the restaurant owed Jenny a duty to discover and avoid dangers by either warning of them or making the property safe for its patrons. The restaurant likely breached that duty by allowing water to puddle on the bathroom floor.

Breach

A breach of duty occurs when Defendant fails to meet the standard of care. The restaurant will argue that it met its duty of care, because it attempted to correct the issue by calling a plumber, trying to shut off the water, and sending in an employee to mop every 10 minutes. However, breach is likely to be found, as landowners owe a higher duty of care to invitees. The floor was still slippery despite the mopping. Therefore, since it was unable to make the property safe, it owed a duty to warn of the danger.

Causation

The breach must cause Plaintiff's damages. Here, the restaurant's breach actually and proximately caused Jenny to fall and hurt her arm. But for the restaurant failing to warn or keep the floor dry, Jenny would not have fallen. It is also foreseeable that someone would slip and fall on a wet bathroom floor.

Damages

Jenny suffered damages, as she broke her arm as a result of the fall.

Jenny can therefore recover from the restaurant on a Negligence theory.

Sarah and Courtney v. Restaurant

Negligence

Can Sarah and Courtney sue the restaurant for negligence?

Negligence is shown when Defendant breaches a duty to the Plaintiff that causes damages to the Plaintiff.

Duty

A special duty rule applies here as well. Even though Pam was an employee of the restaurant and let the girls in, they were all trespassers, as they broke in after hours. The restaurant was unaware of Pam's criminal background, and therefore had no reason to anticipate she would trespass (although an argument could be made that the restaurant was negligent in failing to perform a background check). Therefore, the restaurant only owed the girls a duty to refrain from willful or wanton conduct.

Breach

Because the restaurant did not owe a duty of reasonable care to the girls, and the restaurant did not act willfully or wantonly, there is no breach of duty. Further, the fact that the "do not enter sign" was placed at the bathroom door has no effect on the outcome, even though Courtney did not see the sign, because the girls were trespassing.

It also does not matter that Brett may have been negligent in leaving the vacuum out while he napped in the office. While there would otherwise be a question as to whether the restaurant could be liable under the doctrine of respondeat superior, again, because the girls were trespassing, there was no duty of reasonable care owed by either the restaurant or Brett.

Negligence Per Se

The girls could try to argue negligence per se, because the exit signs were not illuminated as required by statute. If Defendant breaches a statute, the doctrine of Negligence Per Se may help Plaintiff establish duty and breach. In order to prove negligence per se, Plaintiff must show that she is within the class of persons the statute was intended to protect; the injury or harm was of the type the statute was designed to protect against; and Defendant's violation of the statute was not excused.

Here, the statute was designed assist customers in safely finding their way to the exits in the dark. The restaurant's conduct was not excused, as taking the bulbs out to enhance the ambiance is not a sufficient reason to violate the statute. There is an argument to be made that the girls were in the class of persons the statute was meant to protect, even though they were trespassing. However, the girls were not patrons trying to find their way to an exit in the case of an emergency and are therefore arguably not within the class of plaintiffs the statute was designed to protect.

Causation and Damages

If the girls can establish negligence per se, they must also establish causation and damages. But for the restaurant's failure to adhere to the statute, they would not have been injured, and it is foreseeable that someone could be injured by fumbling around in the dark. They also suffered damages in the form of Sarah's broken nose and Courtney's broken ankle.

In conclusion, Sarah and Courtney are not likely to recover under a negligence theory.

END OF ANSWER.

Professor's Guidance

Hopefully, you quickly recognized that negligence was the main issue that should be discussed in this essay. The tricky part was that a special standard of care applied to the Plaintiffs as either an invitee or trespasser. However, if you have the issue checklist memorized, you scanned the facts to see if a special duty rule could apply and discovered quickly that you would need to discuss landowner duty. Otherwise, we were able to follow the standard negligence template to determine whether negligence could be proven.

This essay also is a good way to show how you should organize an answer that includes more than one lawsuit. Notice that we treated each separately and completely. Had there been more theories of recovery, we would have addressed those as well for each lawsuit after discussing negligence as we did here.

There were a lot of facts here that needed to be used. Therefore, as you read through each sentence, ask yourself why it is included. Does it raise an issue? For example, why are we told that Brett was an independent contractor sleeping while at work? This fact should have immediately raised a red flag for you to discuss the doctrine of respondeat superior. While it needed to be mentioned, it was not necessary to discuss Brett's status as an independent contractor or whether he was acting in the scope of his employment in detail, because the girls were trespassing. Having said that, if you have time, you may be able to pick up a few points for including a more complete analysis.

This brings up a good point about race horse questions. Race horse questions are long and contain lots of discussable facts and test many issues. Just finishing on time is half the battle. When you find yourself in this situation, it is ok to quickly address each issue as well as you can. This means that your IRAC analysis may not be as formal in structure. You will still need to identify the issue and analyze the rule to reach your conclusion on each issue, but you may not have time to state the issues in the form of a question or to restate long rules before analyzing. Rather, you will make sure you make all of your required arguments for every issue and every element. The discussion of Brett's liability is a perfect example.

Torts Essay Answer 6:
Lance & Richard v. Theater

Lance & Richard v. Theater

Can Lance and Richard sue the restaurant for negligence?

Negligence is shown when Defendant breaches a duty to the Plaintiff that causes damages to the plaintiff.

Duty and Standard of Care

The general rule is that you owe a duty of reasonable care to all foreseeable plaintiffs unless a special duty rule applies. Here, a special landowner duty rule applies. Lance and Richard are invitees, as they are there for the (commercial) benefit of the theater. As invitees, the theater owed both Lance and Richard a duty to discover and avoid dangers by either warning of them or making the property safe for its patrons.

Breach

A breach of duty occurs when Defendant's fails to meet the standard of care. The theater will argue that it did not breach its duty, because the aisle lights were illuminated as required and the floor was clean before the movie started, and Richard had not let them know about the spill. Lance and Richard will argue that a theater employee should have come in to check to make sure the lighting was working when the house lights were turned off. They will argue that the failure to warn of the danger or to make sure the aisles were safe and the floor was clean was a breach of duty.

Negligence Per Se

Lance and Richard could argue *negligence per se*, because the aisle lights were not illuminated as required by statute. If Defendant breaches a statute, the doctrine of negligence per se may help Plaintiff establish duty and breach. In order to prove negligence per se, Plaintiff must show that she is within the class of persons the statute was intended to protect; the injury or harm was of the type the statute was designed to protect against; and the defendant's violation of the statute was not excused.

Here, the statute was designed to ensure that customers could safely walk down the aisles and navigate their way to their seats in the dark. Both Richard and Lance are *within this class*, as they are both movie theater customers in a dark movie theater. The statute was designed to prevent customers from having accidents in the dark. Lance was injured as he attempted to find his seat in the dark, and Richard was injured when Lance slipped. Therefore, it is arguable that the type of harm that occurred is the *type the statute was designed to protect against*. However, there is an argument that the type of injury suffered by Lance was an allergic reaction, rather than a common physical injury one would suffer as a result of having someone spill their drink on them. There is also a strong argument that the theater's *conduct is excused* because the lights were shorted out by the spill, which was an unforeseeable accident. Further, Richard did not bother to tell anyone about the spill or the resulting power outage.

Causation

The breach must actually and proximately cause Plaintiff's damages. *Actual cause* is established, because **but for** the spill not being cleaned up and the lights not being on, Lance would not have slipped and spilled his drink on Richard, causing Lance's broken ankle and Richard's allergic reaction. However, there is an issue with regard to *proximate cause*. The plaintiff, type, and manner of injury must be foreseeable. Foreseeable extent of injury is not at issue, because we must take the Plaintiff as we find him. Both Richard and Lance are *foreseeable plaintiffs*, as they are both patrons in the theater. While it may be unlikely that a spilled drink would cause the lights to short out, it is foreseeable that someone could slip and fall in a dark theater and spill their drink on someone. Therefore, the *manner of injury* may also be found foreseeable. The *type of injury* suffered by Lance is a broken ankle. This is a foreseeable type of injury suffered as a result of a fall. However, the type of injury suffered by Richard, specifically an allergic reaction to root beer, may not be a type of injury that would be considered foreseeable. It may be too bizarre and could cut the chain of causation.

Damages

Both Richard and Lance can prove damages, as Lance suffered a broken ankle, and Richard suffered a severe allergic reaction.

Defenses

Contributory/Comparative Negligence

If a Plaintiff contributes to his own injury, his recovery may be barred under the doctrine of contributory negligence or reduced by his percentage of fault under the doctrine of comparative negligence. Richard's recovery could be barred or reduced depending on his percentage of fault, as he contributed to his own injury by spilling the drink that caused Lance to slip and not notifying a theater employee of the incident.

Conclusion

Breach may be difficult to prove here, and there are also some causation issues. Therefore, it may be difficult for either Lance or Richard to recover from the Theater on a negligence theory.

END OF ANSWER.

Professor's Guidance

Here we are still practicing writing essays on Negligence. As I mentioned, Negligence is the most important Tort and is highly testable. I included this one to show you that sometimes it makes sense to combine your discussion of Plaintiffs that have the same claim against a common defendant rather than treating each Plaintiff's lawsuit separately. Most of the time, you will want to discuss each Plaintiff separately, but here, it makes sense, because both patrons are suing on the same theory and the same alleged breach. The only difference is the type and manner of injury suffered. That is also why we spent so much time discussing causation. This was a real "think-um" question, requiring you to go deeper than usual into your discussion of causation.

I also included this essay to show you how you will often find that you are recycling the same language over and over. Look at how the discussions of duty, breach, and negligence per se in this answer are similar to the previous answer. They contain much of the same language. This is a good thing. If you know how you are going to express a rule or approach a discussion in advance, it will save valuable time. Memorize rules and common discussions so that you can quickly and easily duplicate them when you need to.

Another issue here that we haven't seen before in an essay answer is the defense of contributory or comparative negligence. **Always** make sure to look to see if any defenses apply before concluding. If you find that a plaintiff contributed to her own injury, make sure to discuss *both* contributory and comparative negligence and the effects of each. Also notice that I included the discussion of defenses after I discussed the prima facie case for negligence. Always discuss the applicable tort and all of its elements first before raising any applicable defenses. Also, even though it did not apply here, don't forget to scan the facts of a negligence problem to determine if Assumption of the Risk should be discussed as well.

Torts Essay Answer 7:
Andrew v. John

Andrew v. John

Defamation

Andrew may have a claim for Defamation against John. Defamation is defined as a false statement of facts, of and concerning the Plaintiff, published to a third party, causing damage to Plaintiff's reputation.

In this case, when Andrew's prospective employer called John for a job reference, John said "Well, Andrew was a pretty good worker, but I wouldn't hire him. He is a member of the 'Community Supreme Group.'" Since the statement was oral rather than written, it may be considered slander if it meets the elements required to prove common law defamation.

Did John make a **False and Defamatory Statement of Fact**?

First, John must have made a false and defamatory statement of fact. The first statement "He was a pretty good worker, but I wouldn't hire him" is a statement of opinion rather than a statement of fact. However, the statement "He is a member of the 'Community Supreme Group'" is a statement of fact and may be actionable, if it is also false and defamatory.

At common law, the defamatory statement is presumed false, and the burden is on the defendant to prove the truth of the defamatory statement, as truth is a defense. Here, the statement is false, because we are told that Andrew was not, nor had he ever been, a member of the "Community Supreme Group." It is also defamatory, because the group is a well-known and thoroughly disliked radical organization that been linked with several violent acts. A false statement that someone belongs to the "Community Supreme Group" would harm the reputation of that individual and would subject that person to contempt and ridicule in the community. Therefore, the statement is both false and defamatory.

Was the statement **"of and concerning"** the Plaintiff?

In order to prove defamation, the statement in question must be "of and concerning" the Plaintiff. Here, there is no question that John was talking about Andrew as an individual when he made the statement.

Was the statement **Published to a Third Party**?

In order to be actionable, the false and defamatory statement must be published. Here, the statement was published, because John made the statement to Andrew's prospective employer when asked to provide a job reference. John was at fault because he had "heard the news around town" but didn't bother to investigate before making the statement. John would be responsible whether he was an initial publisher, repeater, or disseminator.

Was the statement **damaging** to Andrew?

The statement must cause damage to Plaintiff. Here, the statement was damaging, because Andrew failed to get the job because of the statement.

Therefore, John will be liable for Defamation unless he has a defense.

Defenses

Does John have any defenses to the slander claim?

Ex-employers have a *qualified privilege* to divulge information about ex-employees, but not if they know it's false or have a bad motive. Here, John is Andrew's ex-employer and has a qualified privilege to divulge information about Andrew, an ex-employee. There is no evidence that John knew the statement was false or whether he had a bad motive.

As long as John can successfully assert this privilege, he will not be liable for defamation.

END OF ANSWER.

Professor's Guidance

So how did you do this time? By now, you should be pretty good at using IRAC to analyze the claims. Did you fully state the issue and rule before analyzing the facts? Did you fully address each element separately before reaching your conclusion?

Finally—remember to **always** check for defenses before making your final conclusion with regard to the claim. As you can see, the privilege defense here was a pretty important issue!

This was a pretty straightforward fact pattern testing the issue of defamation, but it is important to note that anytime you spot defamation as an issue, also consider whether there may be an invasion of privacy claim as well.

Keep practicing!

Torts Essay Answer 8:
Betty v. Fred

Under what theory or theories could Betty recover against Fred?

Invasion of Privacy

Betty may be able to bring an invasion of privacy claim against Fred. There are four types of invasion of privacy. They include 1) Intrusion into Plaintiff's Seclusion, 2) Public Revelation of Private Facts, 3) Commercial Appropriation, and 4) Portraying the Plaintiff in a False Light.

Intrusion into Plaintiff's Seclusion

Intrusion into Seclusion requires proof that Defendant intentionally intruded upon the plaintiff's private affairs, the intrusion would be highly offensive to a reasonable person, Plaintiff had a reasonable expectation of privacy, and the intrusion caused Plaintiff mental anguish or suffering.

Here, by calling Betty's husband at home, Fred *intruded on Betty's private affairs*. Such an intrusion would be *highly offensive to a reasonable person*, as any reasonable person would be horrified if someone called their spouse to reveal the details of an affair. Also, Betty had a *reasonable expectation of privacy* at home and should not reasonably expect Fred to call her husband there. Finally, the intrusion *caused Betty mental anguish and suffering*, as the incident caused her husband to leave her. Therefore, Betty has a claim for the Intrusion into Seclusion form of Invasion of Privacy.

It is arguable that Fred asking Barney to videotape their encounter at the bar was also an Intrusion into Betty's Seclusion. However, Betty did not have a reasonable expectation of privacy at a public bar.

Public Revelation of Private Facts

Public Revelation of Private Facts requires proof that Defendant intentionally publicized (to the public at large) a matter concerning Plaintiff's private life. It also has to be highly offensive to a reasonable person and cannot be a matter of legitimate public concern.

Here, Fred posted the video that Barney recorded to the internet. He did so *intentionally* and, assuming the post was not limited only to a few of Fred's friends and was made public, the internet posting was *publicized to the public at large*. Again, a *reasonable person would be highly offended* by having a video showing them kissing someone other than their husband on the internet. Also, Betty is not a celebrity, so the kiss was *not a matter of public concern*.

Betty can therefore recover for the Public Revelation of Public Facts form of Invasion of Privacy.

Commercial Appropriation

Commercial Appropriation requires Defendant to intentionally misappropriate the name or likeness of another for his own use or benefit. This likely does not apply here, unless Fred made any money off of the video. This form of Invasion of Privacy *does not apply*.

False Light

False light is proved by showing the Defendant gave publicity to a private matter concerning Plaintiff, placing Plaintiff in a publicly false light. That light must be highly offensive to a reasonable person and Defendant must have acted with knowledge or reckless disregard of the falsity of the claim. Again, this form of Invasion of Privacy is not likely to apply, because the incident actually occurred as recorded. As such, there was *no false light*.

Intentional Infliction of Emotional Distress

Intentional Infliction of Emotional Distress, or IIED, occurs when 1) Defendant acts intentionally or recklessly; 2) Defendant's conduct was extreme and outrageous; 3) Defendant's act is the cause of such distress; and 4) Plaintiff suffers severe emotional distress as a result of Defendant's conduct.

Betty should be able to recover under this theory, because the conduct of calling someone's spouse to allege an affair and posting details of the affair to the internet is *extreme and outrageous*. Fred's acts were also *intentional*, as he was angry with Betty for resisting his advances. He likely called Betty's husband and posted the video as an attempt to break up her marriage and to embarrass her. The facts do not state that Betty *suffered severe emotional distress as a result*, but one could argue that the resulting divorce coupled with the loss of her job resulted in severe emotional distress.

END OF ANSWER.

Professor's Guidance

Hopefully you identified Invasion of Privacy and its various forms as issues of discussion for this essay. If not, hopefully including it in this book to practice will help you the next time you encounter similar issues. Students often confuse the various forms of Invasion of Privacy or miss some important elements. Therefore, make absolutely sure you are very familiar with the various forms and their definitions.

Also, don't forget to consider Defamation and Intentional Infliction of Emotional Distress as possible *partner issues* when confronted with a fact pattern that raises Invasion of Privacy issues. Although Defamation was not applicable here, it easily could have been, had we added facts showing that Fred said or wrote something defamatory about Betty.

Torts Essay Answer 9:
SaveCo, Dustin & Kevin

Defamation

Does Kevin have a claim for defamation against Dustin?

Defamation requires that Defendant make a defamatory false statement of fact, of and concerning the plaintiff, published to a third party, causing damage to Plaintiff's reputation. Slander is spoken, while libel is written.

Here, Kevin called Dustin a "dope smoking idiot." Since it was spoken and not written, it could be considered slander. The statement as a whole would be offensive to a reasonable person. The *"dope smoking"* part of the statement is a statement of fact. However, we do not yet know if it is true or false. If it is false, this portion of the statement meets the requirement of being a *false statement of fact*. The *"idiot"* part is more likely an *opinion* rather than a fact, as it is not susceptible to factual proof. Therefore, that part of the statement is not actionable.

Kevin yelled "Your boss is a dope smoking idiot." Because Kevin is the store manager, he is the boss. The statement was therefore *"of and concerning"* Kevin. The statement was also *published to a third party*, because other employees were present and witnessed the event.

There may be an issue with whether the statement caused any harm to Kevin's reputation, as there are no facts that indicate any harm. However, if Kevin can show that smoking marijuana is a crime of moral turpitude, it could be considered *slander per se* and *damages are presumed*. However, this is unlikely. There are also no constitutional issues here, because Dustin is not a public figure, and this was not a matter of public concern.

Kevin is therefore not likely to recover on a claim of defamation.

Trespass to Land

Trespass to Land occurs when Defendant intentionally enters the land of another without permission. The facts state that Dustin came to the store after it closed. We can assume he was on store property when Dustin confronted Kevin. We can also assume that Dustin did not have permission to be there after closing. However, Kevin was not the owner or possessor of the property. While he may have had the right as the store manager to have Dustin removed from the premises, he could not personally sue Dustin for Trespass to Land. SaveCo would have to bring the action against Dustin instead.

Intentional Infliction of Emotional Distress (IIED)

IIED requires Defendant to intentionally engage in extreme and outrageous conduct that causes emotional distress. While confronting someone at their place of work and yelling obscenities at them is extreme and outrageous conduct, there are no facts that indicate that Kevin suffered any emotional distress as a result.

Nuisance

Do the residents of Hillshire have a claim for nuisance against SaveCo?

Nuisance exists if Defendant causes substantial interference with the use and enjoyment of another person's land. Public nuisance exists when is affects a larger group of people, whereas a private nuisance only effects a single person or single family. The lights at SaveCo are a public nuisance because several residents are affected. A *private plaintiff* can't sue for *public nuisance* unless he/she has a unique injury. Therefore, Dustin cannot sue for private nuisance unless he has suffered a unique injury different from the other neighbors. This does not appear to be the case. However, if the action is brought by a government official on behalf of the residents, they do have a claim for public nuisance.

In order to succeed, they must first prove that the interference is substantial. The residents can argue that they suffer sleepless nights and health issues as a result of the lighting, and therefore this element is satisfied. SaveCo could argue that the interference is not substantial, because they can still use and enjoy their property and could simply put up black out curtains to keep the light from waking them at night. It could also argue that the lights are necessary for safety purposes and the inconvenience they cause is slight compared to the benefits of the lighting. This may help them successfully argue that the interference is not substantial.

The residents therefore do not have a nuisance claim against SaveCo if they are unable to prove that the interference is substantial.

END OF ANSWER.

Professor's Guidance

Hopefully, you spotted the issues of defamation and nuisance in this essay question. Make sure to pay special attention to the differences between private and public nuisance, as this distinction is often tested. Also, when answering questions regarding defamation, make sure to determine whether the statement is a fact or an opinion, even if it appears defamatory on its face.

Whenever you can argue both sides, as you could here with regard to whether the interference is substantial, make sure to do so. This will help you gain a few more points from your analysis. Remember, a well-reasoned analysis is more important than a concrete conclusion.

However, when the conclusion is pretty straight forward, as it is here with IIED and trespass to land, you do not have to argue both sides. You can simply explain what element is lacking and move on.

The point is that sometimes you will recognize issues that are not being tested. You obviously needed to fully discuss Defamation and Nuisance to pass this essay, so it would be wise to start with those issues. As I have mentioned before, if you start to run out of time, at least quickly outline the other issues you have spotted so that you can at least get credit for spotting them.

Torts Essay Answer 10:
Andy v. Doctor

Andy v. Doctor

Because Doctor prescribed pills to Andy knowing that he was abusing them and prescribed pills from a contaminated pharmacy, Andy may be able to assert a claim for negligence.

Negligence: Prescribing pills to an addict?

Is Doctor liable for negligence when he prescribed pills to Andy knowing that he was abusing them?

The elements of negligence include:

1) duty of care owed to a foreseeable plaintiff,

2) breach of that duty,

3) causation, including but-for and proximate cause, and

4) damages.

Duty: A duty of *reasonable care* is owed to all *foreseeable plaintiffs*. Doctor at least owed Andy a duty to use reasonable care when prescribing and distributing pills to his patients. As a health care professional, he will be held to the standards of care in accordance with the standards and procedures accepted by the relevant medical community. Andy was a foreseeable plaintiff as a patient purchasing drugs from a pharmacist.

Breach: Doctor breached his duty by prescribing pills to Andy, even though he knew Andy was abusing them. It is not reasonable or acceptable within the relevant medical community to provide drugs to an addict if they are not medically necessary.

Causation: To prove negligence, Defendant must be the *actual and proximate cause* of plaintiff's injuries. *But for* Doctor providing the drugs to Andy, Andy would not have become ill. It is also foreseeable that providing pills to an addict could result in the injury or death of the addict.

However, proximate cause cannot be shown where there is (1) an unforeseeable plaintiff; (2) an unforeseeable intervening event; (3) an unforeseeable type of injury; or (4) an unforeseeable manner of injury. As previously concluded, Andy is a foreseeable plaintiff. There were also no intervening events, and the manner of injury (taking pills) was also foreseeable. However, contracting fungal meningitis was not a foreseeable type of injury that would result from overdosing on pills. Therefore, proximate cause cannot be established.

Damages: Andy suffered damages because he contracted fungal meningitis and had to be rushed to the hospital.

Contributory/Comparative Negligence: If Doctor could prove that Andy was negligent when taking the pills, Andy's recovery may be barred or reduced due to his own negligence in taking more pills than prescribed.

However, because the type of injury was not foreseeable, there is no proximate causation, and Doctor cannot recover on this theory.

Negligence: Providing contaminated pills from a dirty pharmacy?

Is Doctor liable for negligence when he failed to keep his pharmacy clean and provided contaminated pills to Andy?

The elements of negligence include:

1) duty of care owed to a foreseeable plaintiff,

2) breach of that duty,

3) causation, including but-for and proximate cause, and

4) damages.

Duty: Doctor's duty is established above.

Breach: Doctor breached his duty by failing to keep his pharmacy clean and providing contaminated pills to Andy. According to the *Learned Hand Test*, when the *gravity and likelihood of harm outweigh the burden to protect against it*, a breach can be found. It is highly probable that drugs will become contaminated when compounded in an area where dirty water is sitting in the sink, open containers of products are near dust pans and brooms, and bugs, dead bugs and rodent fecal matter are present. The gravity of harm caused by taking contaminated pills is also high, as it could result in injury or death. The burden to protect against it is low, as all Doctor had to do was keep his pharmacy clean and follow established health and safety procedures. Further, no *social utility* has resulted from Doctor's conduct.

Breach can also be proven via the doctrine of *negligence per se.* We are told that Doctor was in violation of statutes related to cleanliness.

Where Defendant's conduct violates a statute, the violation may be negligence per se if:

1) the injury caused by Defendant is the type the statute intended to prevent

2) plaintiff is a member of the class intended to be protected and

3) the Defendant is not excused from compliance

Type: The statutes regarding cleanliness are intended to help prevent contaminated drugs entering the marketplace and injuring patients. Because Andy was injured by taking contaminated drugs, the type of injury is the type of injury the statute intended to prevent.

Class: As a consumer of prescription drugs, Andy was a member of the class intended to be protected by the law.

Excuse: Doctor's conduct was not excused.

Therefore, breach can be shown either through Learned Hand or Negligence Per Se.

Causation: To prove negligence, Defendant must be the *actual and proximate cause* of plaintiff's injuries. *But for* Doctor providing the drugs to Andy, Andy would not have become ill. It is also foreseeable that providing contaminated pills could result in the injury or death of the patient. The type of injury (fungal meningitis) was a foreseeable result of ingesting contaminated pills. Ingesting the pills was a foreseeable manner of injury, and Andy was a foreseeable plaintiff. Proximate cause can therefore be established.

Damages: Andy suffered damages because he contracted fungal meningitis and had to be rushed to the hospital.

Therefore, Andy can recover in an action for negligence against Doctor.

END OF ANSWER.

Professor's Guidance

So how did you do on this last Torts essay? Did you put yourself under timed pressure and finish on time? By now, the negligence essays should start coming pretty easily to you. Hopefully, it is now easy to quickly organize the issues and write the applicable rules so that you can devote the majority of your time to your analysis and thinking through the problem.

I included this essay to show you that sometimes the same theory can be tested more than one way. Here, Negligence is tested twice using two different acts: 1) The Doctor's negligence in prescribing the pills and 2) the Doctor's negligence in failing to keep a clean lab. I also like the fact that the type of injury is unforeseeable under the first negligence theory. Hopefully you are an old pro at spotting these issues by now!

I hope you found these practice essays helpful! For additional practice, I encourage you to visit your State Bar's Website and practice on any actual past bar questions they provide. You'll notice that some can become quite more complex than those we've practiced here, but don't let them scare you. You have the basics down and should be much more comfortable spotting issues, organizing, and writing. Now it's just a matter of making sure you really know the law well enough to help you identify all of the issues that can be tested. Good luck and keep practicing!

18

Criminal Law
Practice Essays

It's time to start practicing your writing on Criminal Law essays. Make sure you have a solid understanding of the concepts covered in the Criminal Law flowcharts and can write out all of the rules quickly.

You'll notice as you work through these essays that there are certain "templates" that are often re-used to discuss certain issues, including Murder. You'll see other templates in both Torts and Contracts. While these are very helpful to help you quickly organize your essay, don't follow them so strictly that it causes you to miss issues and important discussions. Rather, use them as a sample guide as intended. Sometimes your conclusion on one issue will lead you to discuss something else that does not immediately follow in the samples you have practiced.

Trust yourself. As long as you know the law and completely discuss all of the issues raised by the facts, you will earn points. It will not matter that your answer does not exactly mimic the organization of the sample.

Make sure to read the question first and make your best effort to answer it on your own before reading the sample answer and related comments. It should take you about an hour to write your answer to a practice essay.

After writing your answer, compare it to the sample answer and comments to assess your work. Pay careful attention to how the facts raise the issues tested, how the sample answer is organized, how the substance is analyzed, and how the rules are stated. Doing so will help when you find yourselves writing an essay on similar topics in the future!

For students that feel they need additional guidance as they work through the practice essays, they can visit PassTheFYLSE.com and submit their essays to a professor for personalized feedback. Students are also able to send specific academic questions or opt for more in depth tutoring in a group or individual setting.

Criminal Law Essay 1:
State v. Deb

Deb was a teenage mother of a 2-year-old baby named Abby. Deb wanted to go out with her friends but could not find a baby sitter. She was tired of always having to worry about the baby, so she decided to put the baby to sleep and to go out anyway. Concerned that the baby might wake up while she was out, Deb calmly gave Abby a large dose of cold medicine that also contained a sleep aid before she left. Deb ignored a warning on the label that indicated that the cold medicine was not safe for children. When Deb arrived home the next morning, Abby had passed away. An autopsy revealed that the cause of death was related to a cold medicine overdose. Deb was arrested and charged with aggravated child abuse and murder.

Discuss the possible homicide theories upon which Deb could be charged.

Criminal Law Essay 2:
State v. Jeff & Tonya

Tonya asked her husband, Jeff, if he would attack Nancy in an effort to ensure that Nancy could no longer ice skate. Jeff agreed and drove to the rink where Nancy was practicing. Jeff ran onto the ice and struck Nancy in the kneecaps with a baseball bat. Nancy fell, hit her head on the ice, and died as a result.

With what crimes can Tonya and Jeff be charged?

Discuss.

Criminal Law Essay 3:
State v. Don

Don and Victor were hanging out at the lake one day admiring the water skiers going by on fast boats. Determined to try to ski themselves, they walked to a nearby marina and found a boat that had skis and the keys inside. It was obvious that the boat had not been driven in a while, so Don talked Victor into "borrowing" the boat for the summer season.

While out on the water for their first joyride, Victor decided to try skiing, even though Victor had never skied before and Don had never driven a boat. Don was playing around, trying to make Victor fall off the water skies. Don took a turn too fast and Vic, who was skiing behind the boat, crashed into a nearby dock, killing him instantly.

What crimes can Don be charged with based on these facts?

Discuss.

Criminal Law Essay 4:
State v. Joe & Arthur

Joe and Julie were having some marital problems, and Joe moved out of the family home. One night, he drove by Julie's house and saw an unfamiliar car in the driveway.

Later that night, suspecting that Julie had another man at the house, Joe told his friend, Arthur, about the car and suggested that they go check it out. They drove to the house in Arthur's car and parked about a block away. Arthur waited in the car while Joe went to spy through and bedroom window. Joe yelled "How could you?!" as he jumped through the open window into the bedroom.

Joe then went and grabbed a handgun from the dresser drawer, which was locked in its case. Joe chased Carl out of the house, yelling "I'm going to kill you!" Carl tripped, hit his head, and was knocked unconscious.

By the time the police arrived, Joe was on the porch holding the handgun, still locked in its case. Joe told the police that he had chased Carl because he was afraid that his wife was in danger.

1. With what crime or crimes can Joe be charged, and what defenses can he assert?

2. With what crime or crimes, can Arthur be charged, and what defenses can he assert?

Discuss.

Criminal Law Essay 5:
Jason's Bad Day

Jason is a nice guy having a bad day. First, Jason agreed to let his neighbor, Steve, borrow his truck for the week while Steve's car was in the shop. Steve decided to drive to Las Vegas to gamble. While he was there, he learned that he was in a bit of trouble with a mob boss for his gambling debt. In order to pay off his debt, Steve sold Jason's truck to the mob boss.

With no truck, Jason was forced to walk to the store through a bad section of town. On his way back from the store, Derek approached Jason with a knife and threatened to kill Jason if he didn't hand over his wallet. Jason handed the wallet to Derek and then fainted. Derek ran off and discovered that there was no cash or anything of value in Jason's wallet, as Jason had his credit card tucked in his back pocket. As soon as Derek realized this, he threw the wallet into a nearby trash can.

While Jason was unconscious, Gary, a homeless man, noticed Jason's groceries had spilled next to him on the sidewalk. Gary quickly gathered them up. As he saw Jason coming to, Gary put the bag of groceries down and ran away.

It was now dark, so Jason hurried home only to find his ex-wife, Tammy, in his kitchen drinking his wine. Jason had left the door unlocked before he left to go to the store.

Tammy and Jason started talking about Tammy's money problems. During the course of their conversation, Jason promised to loan Tammy $500, and she promised to pay him back at the end of the week. The next day, Tammy decided not to pay Jason back, because he got the house in the divorce.

What criminal charges are Steve, Derek, Gary, and Tammy most likely to face? Discuss any defenses.

Criminal Law Essay 6:
State v. Jim

Jim's wife, Melissa, was much younger than him. She was also very beautiful and attracted the attention of other men. Although Jim was very successful, he was obsessed with the idea that his wife might cheat on him.

One afternoon, Jim came home early from a business trip to surprise Melissa. However, when he got home, he found his wife in bed with his neighbor, Ben.

Jim was furious, but calmly walked out of the house and got into his car. He stayed at a hotel for the next few days.

Three days later, Jim drove to a gun shop and bought a gun. He immediately drove to Ben's house and knocked on the front door. When Ben answered, Jim asked him if he had anything to say. Ben insisted that there was nothing going on with him and Melissa.

Jim became irritated and upset and shot and killed Ben right there in the doorway.

Is Jim guilty of first degree murder or any lesser included offense?

Discuss.

Criminal Law Essay 7:
State v. Jeff

Doug was known around the neighborhood as a shady character. Jeff was a clerk at the neighborhood liquor store. When Jeff saw Doug enter the store, he kept a close eye on him to make sure he didn't steal anything. As Doug walked around the store, Jeff noticed that Doug had a handgun on him. Doug picked up a few bottles of liquor, approached the counter, and handed Jeff a $100 bill. As Doug was about to walk out of the store, Jeff realized that the $100 bill was a fake. Jeff grabbed his pistol from under the counter and screamed at Doug "Stop right there, you thief!" Doug started to run.

Jeff pursued Doug down the street, fired a warning shot in the air, and yelled "You better stop, or I'll shoot you!"

Doug continued to run, so Jeff fired a shot towards Doug. The bullet struck Doug in the back, and Doug died as a result.

What legal justification, if any, did Jeff have for pursuing Doug, and threatening Doug with deadly force?

Discuss.

Criminal Law Essay 8:
State v. Danielle & Julie

Danielle and Julie were out partying at a bar one evening and ran out of money before closing time. They didn't have any credit cards and were completely out of cash. Worried about how they would get home, they asked several patrons for money for a cab but were unsuccessful in their attempts. They became more desperate as the bar closed. They decided to hide out back so that they could approach Philip the bartender as he left for the evening and demand money from him.

Julie became nervous as she watched Philip walk out of the bar and told Danielle "I don't think this is a good idea. We should just walk home." Danielle had a history of mental illness and was exhilarated by the idea of robbing Philip. Julie was shocked when Danielle pulled what Danielle knew to be an unloaded gun out of her purse. Julie was unaware that Danielle was armed and did not know whether the gun was loaded. Julie yelled "That's it, I'm out!" and ran away. Philip heard the commotion and saw Danielle coming towards him with a gun. He pulled out a gun of his own, aimed and shot at Danielle. The bullet struck her in the knee and she fell to the ground. Both Danielle and Julie were arrested.

If Julie and Danielle are charged with conspiracy, attempted robbery and attempted murder, what is the likely outcome? Discuss all applicable charges and defenses.

Criminal Law Essay 9:
State v. Junior

Tony was arrested on felony charges of conspiracy, mail fraud, and racketeering. He was facing 20 years in prison if convicted. Dustin was set to be a key witness in Tony's upcoming trail. A few days before the trail, Tony's son, Junior, tracked down Dustin at his home in the city. Dustin was expecting company that night and left his door unlocked. While he was watching the evening news, he heard a knock at the door and yelled "come in" thinking it was the company he was expecting. Dustin was stunned when he saw that Junior had walked through the door instead and was now standing in front of him with a baseball bat. Junior patted the bat and calmly explained to Dustin that he would "break every bone in his body" if Dustin testified against Tony.

As Junior walked out of Dustin's home, he used the baseball bat to smash a lamp sitting on a table in the entryway and quietly shut the door.

A state statute provides "whoever knowingly and maliciously prevents or dissuades, or who attempts to so prevent or dissuade any witness from attending or giving testimony at any trial, by force or threat of force is guilty of a felony."

With what crimes can Junior be convicted?

Discuss.

Criminal Law Essay 10:
State v. Mike

Jenny wanted to leave her husband, George, but was afraid of losing everything she had in a divorce. She knew that if George died instead, she would receive a large amount of life insurance proceeds. Jenny devised a plan and began having an affair with her married neighbor, Mike. One evening, right after Mike took a sleeping pill, Jenny told Mike that if he didn't kill George that evening, she would tell Mike's wife about the affair.

The sleeping pill made Mike feel a little loopy, and he was terrified that Jenny would follow through on her threat. Mike waited about an hour, climbed through Jenny and George's bedroom window, and fired three shots into George's chest. Mike was unaware that George was already dead, as he had passed away in his sleep earlier in the evening.

Discuss the possible crimes Mike may have committed, as well as any available defenses.

19

Criminal Law Essay Answers

Please compare your answer to each of the practice essays to the sample answers that follow, noting the issues you missed, whether your rule statements were included and completely stated, and whether you included the relevant key facts in your analysis of each issue. Also notice how the organization of your answer compares to the sample.

Also, please pay close attention to the comments provided following the model answer. They provide guidance on how to best evaluate your own work and on how to improve when analyzing similar issues in the future.

Criminal Law Essay Answer 1:
State v. Deb

State v. Deb

(Issue 1) Can Deb be charged with the murder of Abby?

Murder

(Rule) Murder is shown by proving **Homicide** plus **Malice**.

(Element 1 Issue) Did Deb's actions cause Abby's Death, resulting in a homicide?

(Rule) A **Homicide** is the killing of one person by another. (Analysis) As a result of Deb giving Abby cold medicine, Abby overdosed and died. (Conclusion) Deb is the **"but for"** cause of Abby's death.

(Element 2 Issue) Did Deb act with malice?

(Rule) **Malice** can be shown by proving: 1) intent to kill, 2) intent to cause serious bodily injury, 3) depraved heart, or 4) felony murder.

(Malice Issue 1) Did Deb act with the intent to kill?

(Rule) **Intent to Kill:** Malice can be shown by proving that Deb had the intent to kill Abby. (Analysis) Here, Deb's alleged intent was to make Abby sleep while she went out. (Conclusion) Therefore, Deb did not have the requisite intent to prove this type of malice.

(Malice Issue 2) Did Deb act with intent to cause serious bodily injury?

(Rule) **Intent to Cause Serious Bodily Injury:** Malice can be shown by proving that Deb had the intent to cause Abby serious bodily injury. (Analysis) Again, Deb's stated intent was to put the baby to sleep. (Conclusion) It is not likely that malice can be established under this theory.

(Malice Issue 3) Did Deb act with a depraved heart?

(Rule) **Depraved Heart:** If a killing occurs as a result of conduct by the defendant that shows the defendant has acted *with extreme indifference to human life*, then the defendant will be deemed to have acted with the requisite malice for murder. (Analysis) Here, Deb gave a two-year-old a large dose of cold medicine, knowing that it is not safe for children. She also left the child alone after giving the medicine to her. (Conclusion) Therefore, it is possible to find that she acted with extreme indifference to human life.

If Deb's conduct does not rise to the level of extreme indifference to human life, she could still be charged with manslaughter, as discussed in more detail below.

(Malice Issue 4) Did the killing occur during the perpetration of an inherently dangerous felony?

(Rule) **Felony Murder:** A killing during the perpetration of an inherently dangerous felony is considered murder under the felony murder rule. (Analysis) Deb was charged

Professor's Guidance

So how did you do on this essay?

When you encounter a criminal law question on an essay, you will generally be asked to identify the possible crimes and available defenses. Don't freeze up!

First, take a look at how many possible Defendants (bad actors) you have and deal with them one at a time. As you analyze each Defendant, you will discuss each possible crime one at a time, taking your time to IRAC every element of each crime. Remember, you can't convict a Defendant unless you can prove every element beyond a reasonable doubt, so every element **must** be addressed separately. Tip: You can't do this unless you have the crimes and their elements **memorized**. Therefore, flashcards will come in handy when studying.

Finally, whenever you see an essay where the victim dies, you should **always** discuss possible homicide charges, including murder, unless otherwise directed. (Watch out for the situation where Torts, rather than Crimes are being tested!)

Let's start with the organization. There's only one Defendant here, so we used the label **State v. Deb**. Had there been more than one Defendant, you would label and discuss each of them separately. Notice also how we separated each possible charge and each possible theory of malice. We also placed the key issues and rule elements as we analyzed them in bold letters to draw your attention to them.

How did you do on your analysis of murder? Did you remember to discuss homicide and malice separately? Did you clearly define the rules before analyzing the facts? Did you mention all 4 forms of malice and discuss each form in its own individual IRAC paragraph? Did you use the facts to show how each theory of malice can be proven or disproven? (Note that I used the IRAC and element identifiers in the sample answer in an effort to help those who may still struggle with IRAC organization. They should not be included in the answer to a formal essay.)

Did you remember to discuss the degree of murder? After analyzing the crime and deciding what forms of malice apply, you should always address the resulting degree.

Finally, although it may not always be relevant, consider whether a manslaughter charge is appropriate. If you see someone acting tin the heat of passion, you should discuss voluntary manslaughter. Otherwise, if you see that there is an argument that Defendant acted with one of the requisite mental states for involuntary manslaughter, you should discuss it as a possible theory.

When analyzing a criminal law essay, don't forget about Defenses. The most heavily tested ones tend to be self-defense, defense of others, intoxication, and insanity, so be sure to always keep an eye out for possible defenses as you read through your fact patterns. There were no defenses at issue here, so they were not included in the discussion.

If you made any of these mistakes, go back and re-write your answer to address them. Remember, anytime you discuss murder, you should always clearly define it as homicide plus malice. Then you should define homicide and give facts that show whether defendant's actions resulted in the death of the victim. From there, you should define the four types of malice. You may not need to address all of them separately if you find one that obviously doesn't apply (i.e., if there is no underlying felony, you would not need to discuss felony murder). However, for the ones that *do* apply (or are arguable), you **must** discuss each in a separate IRAC paragraph as we have done here.

I hope you found this exercise helpful!

Criminal Law Essay Answer 2:
State v. Jeff & Tonya

State v. Jeff

Conspiracy

Can Jeff be charged with Conspiracy to commit battery?

A conspiracy is an agreement for some unlawful purpose. A majority of states now also require an overt act in furtherance. Tonya asked Jeff to attack Nancy, and Jeff **agreed**. Attacking another person is a battery and is an **unlawful act**. Also, Jeff committed an **overt act in furtherance** of the conspiracy by taking a baseball bat and driving to the skating rink where Nancy was practicing and followed through with the plan. Therefore, because Tonya and Jeff agreed that Jeff would attack Nancy, both Tonya and Jeff can be charged with Conspiracy.

Can Jeff be charged with the murder of Nancy?

Murder

Murder is shown by proving homicide plus malice.

Homicide is the killing of one person by another. As a result of Jeff striking Nancy in the kneecaps with a baseball bat, she fell, hit her head, and died. Therefore, since Nancy died as a result of a chain of events set in motion by Jeff, he is the *"but for" cause* of her death.

Malice can be shown by proving: 1) intent to kill, 2) intent to cause serious bodily injury, 3) depraved heart, or 4) felony murder.

Intent to Kill: Malice can be shown by proving that Jeff had the intent to kill Nancy. Here, Jeff's intent was to attack Nancy to ensure that she could no longer ice skate. Therefore, it is arguable that his intent was to commit a battery, not to kill. However, if the defendant uses a *Deadly Weapon* in a manner suggesting the defendant intended to kill the victim, the law will infer the defendant acted with the intent to kill. Here, Jeff used a *baseball bat*, which could be considered a deadly weapon. However, since he used it to strike at Nancy's legs rather than in a manner suggesting that he intended to kill her, a finding of intent to kill is not likely.

Intent to Cause Serious Bodily Injury: Malice can be shown by proving that Jeff had the intent to cause Nancy serious bodily injury. Since Jeff's intent was to attack Nancy to the degree that she could no longer ice skate and he used a baseball bat to *strike her in the knees*, he intended to cause serious bodily injury. Therefore, malice can be established under this theory.

Depraved Heart: If a killing occurs as a result of conduct by the defendant that shows the defendant has acted with *extreme indifference to human life*, then the defendant will be deemed to have acted with the requisite malice for murder. Here, by attacking Nancy with a baseball bat while she was standing on the ice, Jeff has shown extreme indifference to human life. Depraved Heart murder would result in a *second degree* murder charge for Jeff.

Felony Murder: A killing during the perpetration of an inherently dangerous felony is considered murder under the felony murder rule. Here, Jeff engaged in an aggravated battery, which is an *Inherently Dangerous Felony*, by striking Nancy in the kneecaps with a baseball bat. Nancy fell as a result of the battery, hit her head and died. Therefore, the killing occurred *during the perpetration* of the felony for purposes of the felony murder rule. While there is authority that aggravated battery can serve as the underlying felony for felony murder, some courts treat it as inherent in the act of murder itself and therefore not a predicate felony for a charge of felony murder. If Jeff is prosecuted in a jurisdiction that recognizes aggravated battery as a *proper underlying felony* for felony murder, he can be charged with felony murder, which results in a *first degree* murder charge.

Although the facts do not support intent to kill, Jeff can be charged with murder under the intent to cause serious bodily injury, depraved heart, and felony murder forms of malice.

State v. Tonya

Solicitation

Can Tonya be charged with Solicitation?

Solicitation is an offer, request, or invitation to another to commit a crime with the intent that the person solicited commit the crime. Tonya asked Jeff if he would attack Nancy. This amounts to a *request* for her husband to commit the *crime of battery*. Tonya's desire was to make sure that Nancy could no longer ice skate, so it could be argued that she *intended* for Jeff to commit the crime. Therefore, because Tonya asked Jeff to commit the crime of battery, and it can be argued that she intended him to follow through, she can be charged with solicitation. However, because Jeff agreed, and a conspiracy was formed, the solicitation charge will *merge* into the conspiracy charge.

Conspiracy

Can Tonya be charged with Conspiracy to commit battery? A conspiracy is an agreement for some unlawful purpose. A majority of states now also require an overt act in furtherance. Tonya asked Jeff to attack Nancy, and Jeff *agreed*. Attacking another person is a battery and is an *unlawful act*. Also, Jeff committed an *overt act in furtherance* of the conspiracy by taking a baseball bat and driving to the skating rink where Nancy was practicing and followed through with the plan. Therefore, because Tonya and Jeff agreed that Jeff would attack Nancy, both Tonya and Jeff can be charged with Conspiracy.

Murder

Can Tonya be charged with the Murder of Nancy?

Murder is shown by proving Homicide plus Malice.

A *homicide* is the killing of one person by another. Here. Tonya did not attack Nancy, Jeff did. However, Tonya may be held *vicariously liable* for the acts committed by Jeff.

Under the **Pinkerton Doctrine**, a conspirator may be held liable for criminal offenses committed by a co-conspirator if those offenses are within the scope of the conspiracy, are in furtherance of it, and are reasonably foreseeable as a necessary or natural consequence of the conspiracy. Tonya can be held responsible for the murder of Nancy under this doctrine. As previously discussed, Jeff and Tonya conspired to attack Nancy. Nancy died as a result of that attack. Although the agreement was for Jeff to commit an aggravated battery, it was *foreseeable* that death could result as a consequence of the conspiracy. Therefore, Tonya can be held responsible for the death of Nancy as a *co-conspirator*.

Can Tonya be charged as an accomplice to murder?

Accomplice Liability

One who *encourages* another in the commission of a crime can be liable as an *accomplice* to that crime. Here, Tonya asked Jeff to attack Nancy. Even though she acted with the intent to encourage an aggravated battery and not with the intent to encourage murder, if the commission of the murder by Jeff was a *reasonably foreseeable consequence* of Jeff's actions, Tonya may be liable as an accomplice. Since it is foreseeable that an aggravated battery could result in death, it is proper to charge Tonya as an accomplice.

Note: Because Conspiracy encompasses accomplice liability, with conspiracy having the additional element of agreement, if Tonya is convicted of conspiracy, as discussed above, she cannot also be convicted on an accomplice theory.

END OF ANSWER.

Professor's Guidance

So how did you do on this essay? Take a look at your answer and compare it to the sample as you consider the comments below.

How is your answer organized? Anytime you have more than one defendant, you should discuss each of them separately. Notice how we used the labels **State v. Jeff** and **State v. Tonya** to separate the discussions and to identify which defendant the charges related to. Notice also how we separated each possible charge and each possible theory of malice. We also used bold letters to draw your attention to the claims and elements.

Did you recognize the Conspiracy issue? The key fact that should have triggered your discussion of conspiracy is the word **"agreed."** Also, anytime you have **more than one person acting**, you'll want to consider the preliminary crimes of solicitation, conspiracy and attempt. Look to see if one person asks another to do something. If so, you have solicitation. Then look to see if the person asked actually agrees. If so, you have conspiracy. If the person tries to commit the target crime (battery) but is stopped before he can commit it, you'll need to discuss attempt, our final preliminary crime. Attempt is not an issue here, because Jeff was able to complete the target crime. Therefore, his attempt merges into the target crime.

Did you clearly state the rule? Again, look to see if you had a problem here. It may have been either with your memorization of the rule or because you didn't organize it well enough using the IRAC template.

Did you write a full analysis using the facts to establish every element of the rule? Look again at how we accomplished this. The elements were an **agreement** for an **unlawful purpose**. The agreement was made when Jeff agreed to attack Nancy, and the unlawful purpose was to commit a battery. Note again that this is not a conclusion. Rather, it is an analysis of the facts that leads us to our conclusion: Both Tonya and Jeff can be charged with Conspiracy.

How did you do on your analysis of murder as it relates to Jeff? The most common problems on this essay are 1) the homicide element is not discussed as an element of murder; 2) the rules are not clearly defined before analyzing the facts; 3) all 4 forms of malice are not mentioned; 4) the discussion of malice in all its forms is jumbled together in one big paragraph rather than being separated out into their own individual IRAC paragraphs; 5) individual facts are not applied to show how each theory of malice can be proven or disproven; and 6) missing a discussion of a particular form of malice.

If you made any of these mistakes, go back and re-write your answer to address them. Anytime you discuss murder, you should **always** clearly define it as homicide plus malice. Then you should define homicide and give facts that show whether defendant's actions resulted in the death of the victim. From there, you must **mention all four types of malice**. You may not need to address all of them separately if you find one that obviously doesn't apply (i.e., if there is no underlying felony, you would not need to discuss felony murder). However, for the ones that do apply (or are arguable), you MUST discuss each in a separate IRAC paragraph as I have done here.

Did you miss the possibility of an intent to kill murder charge? If so, it was probably because you did not recognize that it could be argued that the baseball bat is a deadly weapon. Anytime you see a weapon used in causing the death of another, you should discuss the deadly weapon doctrine as it relates to intent to kill.

Did you miss the intent to cause bodily injury murder charge? If so, it was probably because you didn't read the facts carefully. If you have any intent that may arguably fall below the intent to kill level, you should consider intent to cause serious bodily injury.

Did you miss the depraved heart theory? If so, it is probably because you decided that one of the other forms applied and you didn't need to consider it. Here's a hint — anytime you have somebody doing something dangerous, consider whether they are acting with disregard to human life. Tell the reader what they are doing that is dangerous and how it is possible that someone could die as a result.

Did you miss the felony murder theory? If so, it was probably because you didn't recognize that there was an underlying felony. Anytime you have a person dying and the intent was not to kill the victim, look to see if the conduct that the defendant was engaged in when the victim died was an underlying felony. If so (or if it's arguable, as it is here), you should always discuss the possibility of felony murder. Also, don't forget to look for problems with the "during the perpetration" or vicarious liability issues in your analysis of the facts. They will often apply.

Did you miss the fact that aggravated battery may not qualify as a proper underlying felony? If so, you may have missed this fact in your reading. Make sure you have a thorough understanding of the concepts you cover. This was a minor point, but it could pick you up some much-needed points if you recognized it as an issue. The lesson here is to make sure you pay attention to the facts and ask yourself if anything you've learned could throw a wrench in your routine analysis of the issue.

Now let's turn to Tonya's liability. Did you miss the solicitation issue completely? The key fact that should have triggered you to discuss it was the word **"asked."** Anytime you have one person asking another to commit some illegal act, you need to address solicitation.

Did you clearly state the rule? Was it because you jumbled your thoughts together? If so, you may need to work on your IRAC skills and make an effort to clearly separate your rule from your analysis. Did you misstate the rule? If so, you need to work on memorizing the rules. Flashcards will help here. Write the issue on the front: Solicitation and then write the rule on the back: Solicitation is an offer, request, or invitation to another to commit a crime with the intent that the person solicited commit the crime. Make a flashcard for every rule you spot and drill yourself until you have memorized every one of them.

Did you appropriately use the facts in your analysis? Remember, the key to an analysis is to incorporate the facts in order to address every element of the rule. Notice that I put the words REQUEST, CRIME, and INTENDED in bold. These are the elements of our rule. Anytime you encounter a rule that contains elements, you'll want to make sure that you address every element in your analysis by tying a fact to it to show whether the element was met or not.

Did you include an appropriate conclusion? Your analysis should lead your reader to your conclusion. A common mistake made by students is that they will state their conclusion in the analysis portion of their answers, believing that they have analyzed the facts. Take a look at the difference between the analysis and the conclusion. The conclusion answers the question asked in the issue statement, wherein the analysis uses the facts to help lead your reader to the conclusion.

Did you miss Tonya's possible murder charge? Anytime you have more than one defendant and the acts of one defendant result in the death of the victim, ALWAYS consider whether the non-acting defendant can be held vicariously liable for the crime of the other. The theories that may apply are accomplice liability, the felony murder rule's vicarious liability theories, and co-conspirator liability.

Did you miss the homicide element with regard to Tonya's possible murder charge? Just because you covered it when you talked about Jeff, doesn't mean you can skip it now. You have to address the elements of the crime with each defendant. Here, we had an issue with the homicide element, because Tonya wasn't the one swinging the baseball bat. This had to be noted before you discussed why she should be held liable.

Did you miss the possibility of Tonya being held responsible under the Pinkerton Rule (conspirator liability)? Anytime you have identified a conspiracy, you **must** consider whether the co-conspirators can be held liable for the acts of the other co-conspirators. Missing this issue may have also been a result of not knowing the material well enough. Make sure you master each of the concepts you cover before you attempt an essay on it.

Did you miss the accomplice liability issue with regard to Tonya? Whenever you have a person who knowingly, voluntarily, and with common intent unites with another to commit a crime, or in some way advocates or encourages commission of the crime, you should discuss the possibility of accomplice liability. Make sure you know the substance deeply enough to know what crimes merge. For example, here, the solicitation will merge into the conspiracy, as will the accomplice liability. However, the conspiracy will not merge into the target crime.

Finally, another common problem that I see is that many students take the **"Garbage Can Approach"** to these essays. They tell the reader everything they know about a particular issue and give a string of rules that may not be relevant to the facts. There are so many rules out there. Therefore, you must be judicious when deciding which ones to include. Pick and choose among them to decide which ones are raised by the facts and only include those that are raised by the facts. For example, many students discuss withdrawal as a defense to conspiracy. There was no need to talk about withdrawal, because there are no facts that indicated that either defendant had abandoned their plan.

On the opposite end of the spectrum, there are students who write a bunch of conclusions without clearly stating the rules and applying the facts to them. Anytime you identify an issue, you need to clearly state the rule and then choose a fact that coincides with each element of your rule to include in your analysis of it.

Criminal Law Essay Answer 3:
State v. Don

State v. Don

Theft/Larceny

The first crime with which Don could be charged is **Larceny**. Larceny requires the trespassory taking and carrying away the personal property of another with the intent to permanently deprive.

Here, the boat did not belong to Victor or Don. They decided to "borrow" it from a local marina to take a joyride. The boat was therefore *the personal property of another*. The elements of a *trespassory taking and carrying away* are also met here because they took possession, the boat without the permission of the owner and used the keys to drive the boat out into the open water. It does not matter that the keys were left in the boat. The taking was still trespassory.

There may be an issue with the *intent to permanently deprive* element at common law. The facts state that they only intended to "borrow" the boat for the season. They could therefore argue that they intended to return the boat and therefore did not have the intent to permanently deprive the owner of the boat. However, under modern statutes, the intent to keep the property for a substantial period of time long enough to deprive the owner of its use and enjoyment is sufficient.

It is likely that Don could be charged with Larceny.

Murder

Murder is shown by proving **Homicide** plus **Malice**.

A **homicide** is the killing of one person by another. As a result of Don taking a turn too fast in the boat, Victor crashed into a dock and died. Don is the *"but for" cause* of Victor's death.

Malice can be shown by proving: 1) intent to kill, 2) intent to cause serious bodily injury, 3) depraved heart, or 4) felony murder.

Intent to Kill: Malice can be shown by proving that Don had the intent to kill Victor. Don's alleged intent was to make Victor fall off the skies. The facts state that he was "playing around." Therefore, it is unlikely that intent to kill can be proved.

Intent to Cause Serious Bodily Injury: Malice can be shown by proving that Don had the intent to cause Victor serious bodily injury. Again, Don's intent was to cause Victor to fall off the skies. It is more likely that Don intended for Vic to fall into the water than to cause him to crash into the dock. A skier that falls into the water is not likely to suffer serious bodily injury. Therefore, If Don only intended for Victor to fall off the skies into the water, there would be no malice under this theory. Intent to cause serious bodily injury murder would result in a *second degree* murder charge for Don.

Depraved Heart: If a killing occurs as a result of conduct by the defendant that shows the defendant has acted with *extreme indifference to human life*, then the defendant will be deemed to have acted with the requisite malice for murder. Here, Don was speeding in a boat carrying a skier in an area where docks were nearby. Therefore, it is possible to find that he acted with extreme indifference to human life. However, if this conduct does not rise to the level of depraved heart conduct, a better charge would be involuntary manslaughter (discussed below). Depraved Heart murder would result in a *second-degree* murder charge for Don.

Felony Murder: A killing during the perpetration of an inherently dangerous felony is considered murder under the felony murder rule. Don can be charged with *grand theft*, which is a felony. However, it is not likely an inherently dangerous felony by definition. It is also not likely a dangerous felony by manner of commission, because there was no danger in stealing an unattended boat.

However, should there be a finding that the grand theft was an acceptable *underlying felony* for purposes of the felony murder rule, the court would have to consider whether the killing occurred "during the perpetration" of the felony, and whether there are any vicarious liability limitations that should be imposed.

For the purposes of this rule, a felony begins when the felons have gone far enough to be guilty of attempt and ends when they reach a place of apparent safety. Don and Victor had stolen the boat from the marina and were out on the open water enjoying themselves when the killing occurred. It is therefore arguable that the killing did not occur during the commission of the felony. Also, since Don killed Victor, a co-felon, there are *vicarious liability concerns*. Under the traditional view, Don would be liable because Victor's death would be a foreseeable consequence of the felony. Under the modern view, there would be no felony murder liability, because the co-felon willingly participated in the crime.

However, again, it is not likely that the felony murder rule is applicable here because 1) the grand theft does not qualify as an underlying felony, 2) the felons had reached a place of apparent safety, and 3) there would be no vicarious liability imposed under the modern trend.

Involuntary Manslaughter

In the event that the state cannot prove one of the four forms of malice above, it may be able to prove involuntary manslaughter. Involuntary manslaughter requires one of the following mental states:

1. Intent to cause slight injury,

2. Reckless or grossly negligent conduct, or

3. Participation in a "non dangerous felony" crime.

Intent to cause Slight Injury:

Don's intent was to throw Victor off of his skis and into the water. It is arguable that this is equivalent to the intent to cause slight injury. Therefore, Don may be liable for this form of involuntary manslaughter.

Reckless or Grossly Negligent Conduct:

The best argument here is that Don was *grossly negligent or reckless* when he was speeding in an area where docks were present while carrying a skier and took a sharp turn. Therefore, his conduct rises above ordinary negligence. If the jury finds that it does not rise to the level of depraved heart, it can find that it rises to the level of recklessness or gross negligence, which is sufficient to sustain a charge of involuntary manslaughter.

Participation in a "non-dangerous felony" crime:

Finally, if the state is unable to prove felony murder, the state may be able to establish involuntary manslaughter based on the "participation in a non-dangerous felony" theory. Don did engage in grand theft, which is a non-dangerous felony. However, there are still concerns about whether Victor's death occurred "during the commission" of the felony and whether the vicarious liability limitations apply.

In conclusion, since it may be difficult to establish that Don acted with extreme indifference to human life, it is likely that Don will be charged with reckless/grossly negligent manslaughter.

END OF ANSWER.

Professor's Guidance

How did you do? By now, you should be pretty good at analyzing murder and manslaughter. Notice how the organization and rules for murder and manslaughter are recycled from the previous practice essays. Again, this helps with your organization and timing.

The other thing to note here is that when there is a question with regard to whether an element is met, you should discuss both sides for full credit. For example, here, there is a question with regard to whether there is an intent to permanently deprive with regard to the theft crime. There is also a question with regard to whether the underlying crime is a felony that qualifies for the felony murder rule. You'll notice that essay questions are often written with a certain degree of ambiguity to encourage you to argue both sides where warranted.

Criminal Law Essay Answer 4:
Joe & Arthur

State v. Joe

Conspiracy:

Can Joe be charged with Conspiracy?

A conspiracy exists when two or more people make an agreement to commit a crime. Most jurisdictions also require an overt act in furtherance.

Here, Joe and Arthur *agreed* that they would drive to Julie's house. Driving to someone's house just to "check it out" is *not a crime*. Therefore, even though the two made an agreement, they did not agree to commit a crime, even though a crime was ultimately committed. Therefore, Joe cannot be charged with conspiracy. However, if the two are charged with conspiracy, Arthur will be vicariously liable for all crimes committed by Joe in furtherance of the conspiracy.

Burglary:

Can Joe be charged with Burglary?

A burglary is the breaking and entering of the dwelling of another at night with the intent to commit a felony therein. Modern statutes remove the "dwelling" and "at night" elements and will allow for the breaking and entering of any structure at any time of day and will also allow an intent to commit a larceny therein.

Here, Joe entered Julie's home *at night* through an open window. This is arguably a sufficient **breaking and entering**. However, because the window was open, Joe can argue that there was no breaking. More importantly, Joe can argue that there was no *intent to commit a felony or larceny therein*. He will argue that his intent was only to "check the place out" and that the only reason he entered the home was to protect his wife. The prosecution will argue that Joe's intent was to at least commit an assault on Carl, which is a felony. They will argue that the couple was separated, and that Joe knew a man was probably at Julie's home, given the fact that he had seen the car in the driveway. He also yelled "How could you do this?" at Julie upon discovering them together. They will reason that he expected to find a man there and intended to assault him.

The prosecution can also argue that Joe intended to commit a larceny, because he took the gun out of the dresser. However, Joe will argue that he did not intend to permanently deprive Julie of the gun and only intended to use it to scare Carl.

Therefore, Joe could reasonably be charged with burglary, as it is likely that the prosecution can prove that Joe intended to commit an assault on Carl when he entered Julie's home. It also does not matter that the window was open, as modern statutes will allow this as a sufficient breaking and entering, as the entry was unauthorized.

Assault and Battery:

Can Joe be charged with assault and battery?

An assault occurs when Defendant intentionally places another in fear of an imminent battery, whereas a battery occurs when Defendant intentionally or recklessly causes bodily harm to another.

Here, Joe threatened to kill Carl while holding the gun case as he chased him out of the house. Although he did not take the gun out of the case, the fact that Joe chased Carl and made deadly threats is enough to prove that he *intentionally placed Carl in fear of imminent bodily harm.* Carl experienced reasonable apprehension of harm, because he was being chased by the husband of the woman with whom he was sitting in the bedroom after being watched through the window.

Carl also *actually experienced bodily harm* as he fell, hit his head, and was knocked unconscious. Joe will argue that his intent was not to cause harm to Carl, but rather just to chase him out of the house in an effort to protect his wife. However, again, it is not likely that he was acting to "protect his wife," and chasing someone down the stairs while threatening them is reckless behavior, sufficient for the intent required for battery.

Therefore, Joe can be charged with assault and battery.

Attempted Murder:

An attempt occurs when Defendant intends to commit a crime and takes a substantial step towards the commission of the crime. Most jurisdictions also require an overt act.

Here, Joe came to Julie's home, likely expecting to find a man there. He grabbed a gun in its case from the dresser and chased Carl, yelling deadly threats. It is therefore arguable that he acted with the *intent to kill.* However, Joe will argue that he was just trying to scare Carl out of the house and will argue that the fact that he left the left the gun in the case is further evidence of his lack of intent. The prosecution *cannot use recklessness or depraved heart* to establish intent as *attempt is a specific intent crime.*

The *substantial step* requirement is shown when Defendant comes sufficiently close to actually committing the crime to meet the "last act" or "dangerous proximity" tests. Since he did not take the gun out of the case, these tests are probably not met. However, the overt act requirements are met, because Joe took the gun case out of the dresser and chased Carl.

Because Joe did not come close to actually committing the crime of murder, he is not likely to be found guilty of attempted murder.

Larceny:

Did Joe commit a larceny?

Larceny is the trespassory taking the personal property of another with the intent to permanently deprive. Here, Joe took the gun from the dresser without permission. Even though it was his gun, he no longer lived at the home and arguably did not have a right to take it. Therefore, the taking was *trespassory*. Joe was found on the porch with the gun in its case. This is a sufficient *"carrying away,"* as even the slightest movement is enough, but there may be an argument that he *did not intend to permanently deprive* Julie of the gun. Therefore, there is no larceny.

Defenses:

Can Joe claim defense of others as a defense?

Defense of others can serve as an affirmative defense when Defendant acted to protect another. He stands in the shoes of another so that if the other was able to act in self defense, Defendant will be authorized to use reasonable force that is reasonably necessary to protect another. Here, it is arguable whether it was reasonable for Joe to believe that Julie was in danger. After all, the couple was separated, and it would not be unusual for a man to be in Julie's bedroom. Also, as discussed above, he likely knew that she was not in danger. Therefore, this defense is likely to fail.

Can Joe claims consent as a defense?

A defendant's reasonable belief that he has **consent** or permission to enter is a defense to the charge of residential entry. The fact that Joe and Julie are married and that the house may belong to both of them does not matter. Marriage alone is not a defense to burglary. As a matter of law, a defendant has no right to enter the separate residence of an estranged spouse.

Mitigation:

Can Joe argue mitigating circumstances?

Had Carl died, Joe may have been able to mitigate a murder charge to a voluntary manslaughter charge by arguing that he acted in the heat of passion. However, since Carl was only knocked unconscious and did not die, Joe's passion is not a mitigating factor.

State v. Arthur

Conspiracy:

Can Arthur be charged with conspiracy?

A conspiracy exists when two or more people make an agreement to commit a crime. Most jurisdictions also require an overt act in furtherance.

Here, Joe and Arthur agreed that they would drive to Julie's house. Driving to someone's house just to "check it out" is not a crime. Therefore, even though the two made an agreement, they did not agree to commit a crime, even though a crime was ultimately committed. Therefore, Arthur cannot be charged with conspiracy. If he could be charged with conspiracy, he would be liable for all crimes committed by Joe in furtherance of the conspiracy, including all of Joe's crimes as discussed above.

Accomplice Liability

Can Arthur be charged as an accomplice?

One who aids, abets, encourages, or assists another is as guilty as the one who commits the crime. There are different types of accessories: a *principle in the second degree* is the defendant who is present (abets). An *accessory before the fact*, is not present but helps before the crime is committed. An *accessory after the fact*, again, is not present at the time but provides aid after the crime is committed.

Here, Arthur encouraged Joe to "go check it out," and drove Joe to Julie's house. He therefore has helped before the crime was committed and as an accessory before the fact. However, Arthur will argue that the purpose was to just spy on the house rather than to commit a crime. Mere presence at the scene is not enough to convict for accessory liability. However, if the prosecution can prove that Arthur drove Joe to the home knowing there could be a confrontation and encouraged Joe's behavior, he would be vicariously liable for Joe's crimes, as they were arguably a foreseeable consequence of their actions.

END OF ANSWER.

Professor's Guidance

There were a lot of issues in this fact pattern, and it turned into quite the racehorse question. How long did it take you to complete? When dealing with racehorse questions, pay extra attention to your time. Many students spend too much time on the first few issues and end up running out of time and lose points for missing the remaining issues.

Avoid falling into this trap by outlining your answer before you begin. That way, if you at least mention an issue raised, you will get partial credit even if you did not have time to fully analyze it. Also, you may want to prioritize your issues. For example, Attempted Murder and Defense of Others are more important that Larceny in this fact pattern. You should therefore spend more time discussing the most important issues. I highly encourage you to practice writing essays under timed conditions, especially as you get closer to the exam date.

I included this essay mostly because it tests attempt and makes the point that attempt is a specific intent crime. Reinforcing this rule should help you remember to avoid mistaking attempt as a crime when you encounter general intent crimes. Also, anytime you encounter facts indicating the Defendant may have acted with a specific intent to commit a crime and the crime was *not completed*, consider Attempt as an issue. Don't forget that Solicitation and Conspiracy could be easily tested as partner issues as well.

The fact that the essay tests so many different crimes was also attractive, as it gives you a chance to review the rules and to see how the facts can be written to test each crime and defense. Make sure you carefully review and memorize the rules as they are written in the answer. Again, making flashcards will help!

I hope this helps!

Criminal Law Essay Answer 5:
Jason's Bad Day

State v. Steve

Can Steve be charged with Embezzlement?

Embezzlement is the fraudulent conversion of the property of another by one who already has lawful possession of it. Here, Steve obtained lawful possession of Jason's car, as Jason gave Steve permission to drive it for the week. Jason gave Steve possession rather than mere custody of his truck, because Steve could drive the truck wherever he wanted, including to Las Vegas. Steve then converted Jason's car by selling it to the mob boss. Steve did not have the intent to steal the truck at the time he borrowed it and formed the intent after getting into the bind with the mob boss.

Steve may be able to defend on the ground of Necessity or Coercion. This is established when Defendant faces a threat of harm and is coerced into performing an act against his will. It is not likely that this defense will succeed, because the mob boss did not coerce Steve into giving him the truck. Steve chose to sell the truck to the mob boss rather than exploring other options that may have been available.

State v. Derek

Can Derek be charged with Robbery?

Robbery is the trespassory taking and carrying away the property of another with the intent to permanently deprive by means of violence or intimidation (force or threat of force).

Here, Derek threatened Jason with a knife an effort to force Jason to give him his wallet. This is therefore a trespassory taking of the personal property of Jason by means of intimidation or threat of force, as Jason likely believed he would be stabbed if he did not comply. His fear was so intense that he fainted as a result. Derek also did not intend to return the wallet to Jason after taking it, so he acted with the intent to permanently deprive. Derek has therefore committed a robbery.

Derek may try to argue that there was nothing of value in the wallet and that he threw it away. This is irrelevant, because the wallet is still personal property. The value of the property is irrelevant. Also, the fact that Derek threw the wallet away is also irrelevant. It is not necessary for Defendant to keep the property but rather to intend to permanently deprive the owner or to subject the property to a substantial risk of deprivation. This was accomplished by throwing the wallet into a nearby trash can.

Can Derek be charged with Assault?

Assault is intentionally placing another in reasonable apprehension of an imminent battery. Here, Derek threatened Jason with a knife in an effort to steal his wallet. It was reasonable for Jason to believe that he would be stabbed immediately if he didn't comply. Jason was actually in fear of the battery, as he fainted as a result. Derek is therefore liable for assault.

State v. Gary

Can Gary be charged with Larceny?

Larceny is a trespassory taking and carrying away of the personal property of another with the intent to permanently deprive.

Here, Gary gathered up Jason's groceries while Jason was unconscious. The groceries are the personal property of Jason, and gathering them up while Jason was unconscious is a sufficient trespassory taking and carrying away, as the slightest movement is enough. However, there is a question with regard to Gary's intent. Unless he had the intent to permanently deprive Jason of his groceries, there is no larceny. Gary will likely argue that he was just picking up the groceries for Jason, while the prosecution will argue that the only reason Gary put the bag of groceries down was because he abandoned his intent after Jason woke up. This will be difficult to prove.

State v. Tammy

Can Tammy be charged with Burglary?

Burglary at common law was defined as a breaking and entering the dwelling of another at night with the intent to commit a felony therein. Modern statutes remove the at night requirement and allow for the breaking and entering of any structure.

Tammy is Jason's ex-wife and likely does not live at Jason's home, so she entered the dwelling of another. She entered through an unlocked door while Jason was away. This is likely a sufficient breaking and entering under modern statutes. It does not matter that the door was unlocked, as long as she opened the door and entered the property. The facts also state that it was getting dark, so it was likely nighttime, although this is irrelevant under the modern rules.

There may be a problem with the element of intent to commit a felony therein. It is arguable that she committed Larceny, but stealing the wine is likely a misdemeanor, and it is not clear if she had the intent to steal anything of value at the time she entered the home. She is therefore not likely to be charged with Burglary.

Can Tammy be charged with Criminal Trespass?

Criminal Trespass is often the resulting charge when the unlawfully entry does not amount to a burglary. It results when Defendant unlawfully enters into a private property of another person without permission. Tammy did not have permission to enter Jason's home and was likely unwelcome. Therefore, she may be charged with Criminal Trespass.

Can Tammy be charged with Larceny?

Larceny is a trespassory taking and carrying away of the personal property of another with the intent to permanently deprive. Here, Tammy opened Jason's wine and was drinking it when he came home. She took the wine without permission and obviously did not intend to return the wine she drank to Jason. This is a sufficient trespassory taking and carrying away with the intent to permanently deprive as required for the crime of Larceny.

Can Tammy be charged with Larceny by Trick?

Larceny by trick requires that the carrying away be accomplished by oral or written misrepresentation. Tammy did not misrepresent anything to get the money from Jason, and she obtained more than possession of the money. Tammy got title, as Jason never expected to get the exact same bills back.

Can Tammy be charged with False Pretenses?

False Pretenses is a false representation of a material past or present fact which causes the victim to pass title to his property to the wrongdoer, while the defendant knows the representation to be false and intends thereby to defraud the victim.

Even though title was given by Jason, no false representations were made. This is actually conversion, a tort, but there is no criminal liability for failure to repay a loan obtained without false statements being made to obtain the loan.

END OF ANSWER.

Professor's Guidance

I hope you had some fun working through the various theft crimes in this essay! Even if you didn't, hopefully you now have a better handle on the various theft crimes and know how to use the theft crime chart to help you differentiate between the various crimes.

Make sure you review the definitions and have a good handle on how they apply to these facts before attempting another essay testing theft. Again, flash cards will help you memorize the elements.

Also, just because the essay tested mostly theft crimes, there were a few others scattered in there. Assault is often a partner issue to Robbery, and Criminal Trespass may be a partner issue to Burglary.

Also notice how the essay was organized. We treated each defendant separately and discussed all of their possible crimes and defenses separately before moving on to the next defendant. If you outline your answers before writing, as I suggest you should, you could quickly organize your essay as you place each defendant, crime, and defense on your outline. Just remember to always go back and re-read the facts to make sure you don't miss anything rather than relying solely on your outline when writing your answer.

Criminal Law Essay Answer 6: State v. Jim

State v. Jim

Is Jim guilty of first degree murder?

Murder

Murder is defined as homicide plus malice.

Homicide

A homicide occurs when one person causes the death of another. Here, Jim shot and killed Ben. Therefore, homicide can be proven.

Malice

Malice exists when defendant 1) intends to kill, 2) acts with a depraved heart, 3) intends to commit serious bodily injury, or 4) kills someone during the commission of an inherently dangerous felony. Intent to kill accompanied by premeditation and deliberation and felony murder will result in a first degree murder charge. Depraved heart and intent to cause serious bodily injury will result in a second degree charge.

Here, Jim acted with intent to kill, as he was angry with Ben for having an affair with his wife and used a gun to commit the crime. Anytime a dangerous weapon is used in the killing, intent to kill is presumed.

Premeditation and Deliberation

However, this will not result in a first-degree murder charge unless Jim also acted with premeditation and deliberation. Premeditation is thinking it over before acting, and deliberation is acting coolly and calmly, as opposed to suddenly and impulsively. Here, Jim acted with premeditation, as he took the time to drive to the store, buy the weapon, and drive to Ben's home. However, he may not have acted deliberately, as the facts say he became irritated and upset before shooting, so he may have acted impulsively as a result of that frustration. Most likely, however, Jim will have been found to have acted with premeditation and deliberation, which will result in a first-degree murder charge unless it can be mitigated to Voluntary Manslaughter.

Voluntary Manslaughter

A murder charge can be reduced to voluntary manslaughter when defendant can show that the killing was committed during the heat of passion. He must show that he was provoked, that a reasonable person would have been provoked, that he did not cool off, and that a reasonable person would not have cooled off. Here, Jim just found out his wife was having an affair with Ben and was provoked by finding them in bed together. A reasonable person would also be provoked in this situation. There is a question as to whether Jim had cooled off, however. Jim did not act until a few days later, so he arguably had time to cool off, as would a reasonable person.

However, Jim was also arguably provoked again before pulling the trigger, as the facts state that he became irritated and upset when Ben denied the affair. If a reasonable person would also have been provoked and would not cool down, Jim's first-degree murder charge could be reduced to Voluntary Manslaughter.

Conclusion

Jim is likely to be charged with first degree murder. It is arguable that his actions were premeditated and deliberated. Also, it is arguable that Jim cooled down before the killing and was not adequately provoked by his frustration.

END OF ANSWER.

Professor's Guidance

We returned to the issue of murder with this essay. It was fairly simple, with only one defendant and the call of the question limited your discussion to only first-degree murder or lesser included offenses.

The main point I want to make here is to not make what looks like an "easy essay" more difficult than it has to be. You have now practiced enough essays testing Murder that it should almost be second nature to you to write about it. This is a good thing! Therefore, if you read a fact pattern that seems too simple, don't assume it is a trick. Rather, simply read the facts carefully to make sure you haven't missed anything important and be confident in your knowledge. What may seem simple to you may not seem so simple to another student, especially if they haven't practiced. The same advice applies to multiple choice questions.

I assume you did a good job with your analysis of homicide and the Intent to Kill form of malice. There was no need to discuss the other forms of malice, as only intent to kill was applicable, and the call of the question directed you to only consider a first-degree charge. This should have forced you to discuss premeditation and deliberation.

The biggest mistake students often make is that they don't clearly define premeditation and deliberation, or they lump them together believing they are the same thing. They are not. They must be defined separately and analyzed separately as they were in this essay. If you can't prove both, you can't prove first degree.

The call of the question also asked you to consider lesser included offenses. This is a big tip that you should look to see if manslaughter is applicable. Here, the affair, Jim's obsession, anger, and frustration were all red flag facts that should prompt you to discuss Voluntary Manslaughter.

Whenever you discuss Voluntary Manslaughter, you need to always discuss each of the four requirements separately and completely. Address both the objective and subjective provocation factor, as well as the objective and subjective cooling off factor. This issue was worth about 50% of this essay, so it is important that you address it completely.

Criminal Law Essay Answer 7: State v. Jeff

Was Jeff justified in pursuing Doug?

Jeff pursued Doug when Doug ran away after giving Jeff counterfeit money. Forgery and Counterfeiting is a felony in most states. A private person is permitted to apprehend one who has committed a felony in his or her presence, either at the time of its commission or upon immediate pursuit. Since Doug committed a felony in Jeff's presence, Jeff was justified in pursuing Doug in an effort to apprehend him.

Was Jeff justified in threatening Doug with deadly force?

Jeff threatened Doug with deadly force and, after firing a shot in the air, did in fact shoot and kill Doug. While Jeff was justified in pursuing Doug, he was not justified in using deadly force against him.

The use of deadly force to *prevent escape of fleeing felon* is justifiable if the evidence shows that a felony actually occurred, if the fleeing suspect against whom force was used was person who committed the felony, and use of deadly force was *necessary* to ensure apprehension of the felon. The facts show that Doug did in fact commit a felony, however, the amount of force was not necessary. Jeff knew the identity of Doug and could have easily contacted the police so that they could make an arrest themselves.

Further, deadly force in apprehension of a fleeing felon is justifiable only when the citizen has probable cause to believe he or she is threatened with serious bodily harm or the use of deadly force. Jeff was never threatened with serious bodily harm or the use of deadly force. Therefore, he was not justified in using deadly force in *self-defense*.

Jeff could try to argue that he was acting in *defense of others*, as he noticed that Doug had a handgun on his person and he was aware of Doug's "shady" reputation. However, Doug did not use the handgun to rob the store. Rather, he passed counterfeit money, which is not dangerous. It was therefore not reasonable for Jeff to believe that Doug would injure someone else. As such, Jeff did not have the right to use deadly force to stop Doug, because using deadly force was unreasonable under the circumstances.

Finally, when the use of force is not justified, a private citizen may be charged with involuntary manslaughter. Given the facts and the conclusion that Jeff was not justified in using deadly force, he is likely to be charged with voluntary manslaughter.

END OF ANSWER.

Professor's Guidance

This question focused on defenses in an effort to help you better understand the rules regarding those defenses. Had it been an actual FYLSE or bar exam question, it likely would have asked what crimes Jeff could be charged with as well as what charges Doug would face had he lived. A complete answer would then require a full discussion of all crimes as well as the defenses tested here.

This reminds us again that we need to make sure to **pay special attention to the call of the question**. Here, it is very clear that the question intends to limit the discussion only to defenses. If the question seems ambiguous or you are unsure of what is being tested, you should make an effort to discuss all issues raised by the facts.

If you missed any of the rules regarding apprehension of a fleeing felon, self-defense, or defense of others, please be sure to carefully review the substantive law in this area.

Criminal Law Essay Answer 8:
State v. Danielle & Julie

Crimes of Julie and Danielle

Conspiracy

Danielle and Julie can be charged with Conspiracy. A conspiracy is an agreement for an unlawful purpose. Most jurisdictions also require an overt act in furtherance.

Danielle and Julie agreed to rob Philip, which is an *agreement for an unlawful purpose*. The **overt act in furtherance** is Danielle taking a gun out of her purse and approaching Philip. At common law, once the agreement is made, the conspiracy is complete. Unless there is a valid defense, both Danielle and Julie can be convicted of conspiracy.

Attempted Robbery

An attempt occurs when Defendant intends to commit a crime and takes a substantial step towards the commission of the crime.

Both Julie and Danielle can be charged with Attempted Robbery. Robbery occurs when Defendant takes and carries away the personal property of another with the intent to permanently deprive by means of violence or intimidation (force or threat of force). Both Julie and Danielle intended to take and carry away Philip's money without returning it. They both therefore *intended to commit a robbery*.

Danielle used the *threat of force* by approaching Philip with a gun he believed to be loaded. There is also a question with regard to whether Julie intended to use force, since she abandoned their plan after Danielle took out the gun. Although Julie may not have intended to use a gun to threaten Philip, she most likely expected to use some force or threat of force as she planned to rob Philip.

The *substantial step* requirement is shown when Defendant comes sufficiently close to actually committing the crime, to meet the "last act" or "dangerous proximity" tests. Danielle and Julie took a substantial step towards committing the crime, as they waited for the bar to close and began to approach Philip. Unless there is a valid defense, both Julie and Danielle can be convicted of Attempted Robbery.

Attempted Murder

An attempt occurs when Defendant intends to commit a crime and takes a substantial step towards the commission of the crime. Murder is defined as a homicide committed with malice. Attempt is a specific intent crime, so Danielle must have intended to kill Philip to be convicted of Attempted Murder.

Danielle intended to rob Philip but did not likely intend to kill him. Rather, her intent was likely to scare him into giving her his money. Note that this would be an assault, which is defined as intentionally placing another in reasonable fear of an imminent battery. However, Assault is not discussed, as the call of the question limits the charges to Conspiracy, Attempted Robbery, and Attempted Murder. Although Danielle used a deadly weapon, which could raise an inference of intent to kill, Danielle knew that her gun was unloaded when she approached Philip. She is therefore not likely to be convicted of attempted murder.

Julie will likely also be acquitted of this crime. Although she intended to rob Philip, she did not know that Danielle was armed and expressed her dismay as Danielle retrieved the gun from her purse. Neither Danielle or Julie are likely to be convicted of attempted murder.

Defenses of Julie and Danielle

Julie's Defenses

1. Withdrawal

Withdrawal may be a defense to conspiracy and any crimes resulting from the conspiracy. At common law, once the agreement is made, the conspiracy is complete, and withdrawal is not a defense. However, under the MPC and in some states, withdrawal can be a defense to both conspiracy and the target crime. If Defendant renounces and thwarts the crime, there can be no conspiracy or target crime liability.

Here, although Julie renounced her intent to continue to participate in the robbery, she did not thwart the crime. Philip thwarted the crime himself by shooting Danielle in the knee. Therefore, Julie is not likely to escape liability for conspiracy.

2. Abandonment

Julie may try to argue that she should not be convicted or attempted robbery, because she abandoned the plan when she realized that Danielle had a gun. While abandonment can be a defense to attempt, it is not likely to be a good defense in this situation, as the crime was already underway when July expressed her dissent and ran away.

Danielle's Defenses

Insanity

Danielle could try to defend against the charges by arguing that she was insane at the time. Insanity can be proven by four different tests: M'Naughten, Irresistible Impulse, Durham Rule, and the Model Penal Code Substantial Capacity Test.

1. M'Naughten

The M'Naughten test is the majority rule and requires proof that Defendant suffers from a mental disease that causes a defect in reasoning such that she is either unaware of the wrongfulness of her actions or does not understand the nature and quality of her actions. Although the facts indicate that Danielle had a history of mental illness, there are no facts that suggest that she was unaware of the wrongfulness of her conduct or that she did not understand the nature and quality of her actions. Danielle planned to rob Philip in order to get money for a cab ride home. Although she was exhilarated at the time of the act, she is not likely to be able to prove insanity under this test.

2. Substantial Capacity

The MPC Substantial Capacity Test requires Defendant to show that she lacked the capacity to either understand the wrongfulness of her actions or to conform her conduct to the law. Much like the M'Naughten test, it is unlikely that this defense will work. Danielle understood what she was doing and likely knew that it was wrong. She could have decided to get money in another way, as evidenced by the fact that they attempted to ask other patrons for money.

3. Irresistible Impulse

The Irresistible Impulse test requires Defendant to show that, due to a mental disease or defect, she is unable to control her actions or conform her conduct to the law. Danielle could try to argue that her exhilaration prompted by the idea of robbing Philip resulted in her being unable to control herself. If Danielle is successful in this argument, she could be found not guilty by reason of insanity under this test.

4. Durham

Under the Durham test, Defendant must prove that the crime is a product of a mental disease. There is no evidence showing that Danielle acted as a result of her disease. Rather, she acted in an effort to get money for a cab ride home.

END OF ANSWER.

Professor's Guidance

The call of the question is particularly important here, as it limits your discussion to only Conspiracy, Attempted Robbery, and Attempted Murder liability for Danielle and Julie. Some students include a complete discussion of assault as well as a complete discussion of Philip's possible battery charge and applicable defenses. This takes up valuable time and may indicate to the grader that you do not pay attention to directions.

When you are unsure about whether to include an issue, go ahead and mention it, but do not take up much time discussing it. You'll notice how the sample answer here does this with the assault issue. Just be sure to avoid throwing in the kitchen sink, as it will distract the grader and may indicate that you really don't know the law well enough to focus only on the issues tested.

Notice also that I organized this answer by crime rather than by defendant. It wouldn't be wrong to organize it by defendant, but because the same facts applied to each crime, it was easier to just discuss each crime and then discuss the defenses separately, as each defendant could raise different defenses.

Another point of note here is to notice that I discussed each test for insanity separately and completely. This is usually required for full credit. It is not enough to simply state that Danielle had a history of mental illness and may be able to claim insanity. Make sure to memorize these tests and know how to apply the facts to each.

Finally, the issues of withdrawal and abandonment can get complicated, so be sure you know the rules and what is required to avoid liability for the conspiracy, the target crime, and future crimes of co-conspirators.

Criminal Law Essay Answer 9:
State v. Junior

State v. Junior

Witness Tampering

The fist crime for which Junior could be found guilty is Witness Tampering in violation of the state statute.

The statute provides that "whoever knowingly and maliciously prevents or dissuades, or who attempts to so prevent or dissuade any witness from attending or giving testimony at any trial, by force or threat of force is guilty of a felony."

Here, Junior acted *knowingly and maliciously*, because he tracked Dustin down in an effort to *dissuade him from testifying* against Tony. Junior acted maliciously in that his objective was to try to intimidate the key witness into compliance, knowing that Dustin's testimony could alter the outcome of the trial. Junior attempted to dissuade Dustin from testifying at the trial by threatening to "break every bone in his body" if Dustin testified. This statement, coupled with the fact that Junior was carrying a bat and came into Dustin's home uninvited, will meet the requirement for the **threat of force** required by the statute.

Junior will be found guilty of witness tampering.

Assault

Criminal assault occurs when Defendant intentionally places another in reasonable apprehension of an imminent battery.

Here, Junior entered Dustin's home with the intent to dissuade him from testifying. He threatened to "break every bone in Dustin's body" while holding a baseball bat. Junior therefore acted intentionally. Anyone confronted by a man threatening them with a baseball bat would be *reasonably apprehensive* that he could be hit with the bat. However, Junior did not threaten Dustin with an *imminent battery*, but rather threatened a *future battery* if Dustin did not do as requested. Therefore, because Junior did not threaten Dustin with an imminent battery, he will not be guilty of assault.

Making Criminal Threats

The crime of *making a criminal threat* occurs when a person threatens to commit any *crime of violence* against another person.

Here, although Junior may not be guilty of assault, he may be guilty of making a criminal threat. Battery is a crime of violence, and Junior threatened Dustin that he would commit a battery by "breaking every bone in his body" if Dustin testified.

Burglary

Burglary is defined as breaking and entering the dwelling of another at night with the intent to commit a felony therein.

Here, Dustin's door was unlocked and he yelled "come in" when Junior knocked at his door. Junior will try to argue that there was therefore no ***breaking and entering***. However, Dustin was not expecting Junior and would not have allowed him to come in had he not been mistaken as to who was knocking at the door. Junior was uninvited and unwelcome and chose to walk into Dustin's apartment anyway. Under the modern rules, this is likely to qualify as a breaking and entering.

Junior also entered ***the dwelling of another at night***. The facts state that the incident occurred at Dustin's home, which is the dwelling of another, and that it occurred while Dustin was watching the evening news, so it was likely nighttime. Note that modern rules no longer contain the common law "dwelling" and "nighttime" requirements.

Finally, Junior acted with the ***intent to commit a felony therein***, because his intent was to commit the felony of tampering with a witness while in Dustin's home.

Therefore, Junior is guilty of burglary.

Criminal Conversion

A person who knowingly or intentionally exerts unauthorized control over property of another person commits the crime of criminal conversion.

Here, when Junior smashed Dustin's lamp with a baseball bat, he did so ***intentionally*** in an effort to convey his threat to Dustin and was certainly ***not authorized*** to do so. Junior therefore committed the crime of conversion.

END OF ANSWER.

Professor's Guidance

Did you spot all of the possible crimes in your answer? I included this question in an effort to show how the call of the question differs from Question 8 and how that will affect your approach. In Question 8, the call of the question limited the discussion to certain crimes, while Question 9 is more open ended, requiring you to discuss all possible crimes. Most of the time, the crimes will jump out at you and will be very familiar. Other times, they may not be as obvious, especially if you have not covered them in class. This is where your common sense comes in.

I've mentioned before that you should never assume facts not in the question, but if you can see that a crime has been committed under the facts given, you should discuss that crime, even if it is not one of the "biggies" covered in class. Missing the issue of making terroristic threats here probably would not cause you to fail the essay, but you could certainly gain some points if you recognize and discuss it as a possibility—even if it wasn't meant to be tested. So, if the call of the question is open ended and you notice that you can argue another crime under the facts, make sure to include it.

Also, don't forget to consider torts that may also be crimes. Usually, the definitions for the tort and crime will be very similar, as they are here for conversion and assault. Do your best to analyze it, even if you haven't memorized a criminal definition. Missing conversion here would have cost you a lot of points, as the facts are clearly raising this issue by making a point to note that Junior smashed a lamp on his way out.

Finally, whenever you see the language of a criminal statute used in the facts, break it into elements and discuss it just like any other rule you have memorized in an effort to earn full credit. Consider the fact that the test writers gave you the language as a gift!

Criminal Law Essay Answer 10:
State v. Mike

Mike could be charged with conspiracy, murder, attempted murder, and burglary. However, he may be able to escape liability by arguing duress and/or intoxication.

Conspiracy

A conspiracy is an agreement for an unlawful purpose. Conspiracy also requires an overt act in furtherance. Jenny asked Mike to kill George, and Mike **agreed**. Mike also broke into George's bedroom and shot him. Therefore, Mike could be charged with conspiracy.

Mike will argue that there was no true agreement, because Jenny forced him into agreeing, because Jenny threatened to tell Mike's wife about the affair. This is not likely to be a good defense, because the threat of revealing an affair is not the same as threatening someone's life. Mike could have refused Jenny's request and is not likely to be able to successfully argue duress as a defense.

Murder

Defendant is guilty of murder when he commits a homicide plus malice. A **homicide** is shown when Defendant causes the death of another human being. **Malice** can be established by showing intent to kill, depraved heart conduct, intent to cause serious bodily injury, or felony murder.

Here, although Mike acted with the *intent to kill* George by shooting him in the chest with a gun, there is *no homicide* because Mike's acts did not cause George's death. George had already passed away in his sleep earlier that evening. Therefore, Mike cannot be guilty of murder.

Attempted Murder

Defendant commits the crime of attempted murder when he acts with the specific intent to commit a crime and takes a substantial step towards the commission of the crime that goes beyond mere preparation.

Here, Mike acted with the *specific intent to kill* George and *took the steps necessary* to achieve that goal, including shooting George in the chest. Therefore, Mike will be guilty of attempted murder unless he has a valid defense.

Duress

Duress can negate the intent required for the targeted offense and generally involves an imminent threat of serious injury or death. As mentioned, the threat here was the threat of revealing an affair, which is insufficient to trigger the defense. Additionally, duress is not a defense to intentional murder. Therefore, Mike will not be able to defend himself on the grounds of duress.

Impossibility

Mike could try to argue Impossibility as a defense. However, in order for impossibility to apply to attempt, it must be a legal impossibility rather than a factual impossibility. Here, George was already dead when Mike shot him. Therefore, it is *factually impossible* for Mike to murder him. It is not a legal impossibility because it is illegal to commit a murder. Had the facts been as Mike believed them to be, he would have committed the crime of murder. Therefore, impossibility is not a viable defense to the attempted murder charge.

Intoxication

Mike may try to argue that he was *involuntarily intoxicated* at the time of the crime. He would have to show that he did not know or have reason to know that the sleeping pill would make him "loopy" and that he was unaware of what he was doing. However, it is unlikely that Mike didn't know that sleeping pills would make him loopy, as they are meant to help you fall asleep. *Voluntary intoxication* is not a defense, but it may help show that Mike had *diminished capacity* and mitigate the charge to a lesser offense.

The intoxication defense is not likely to work for Mike as he did shoot George three times, because he didn't want Jenny to reveal the affair. It is therefore likely that he understood what he was doing regardless of having taken the sleeping pill. Mike is therefore guilty of attempted murder.

Burglary

Defendant commits a burglary when he breaks and enters into the dwelling of another at night with the intent to commit a felony therein. The facts state that Mike *broke and entered* into George's bedroom *at night* while he was sleeping with *the intent to kill* him. Therefore, all of the elements of burglary are established. Mike cannot use the defenses of duress, or intoxication for the same reasons he could not use them to defend against the attempted murder charge.

There is a question as to whether Mike can claim that he had Jenny's consent to enter the home as a defense. Mike can be found guilty of burglary even though he entered with Jenny's consent and knowledge of his felonious intent. Mike did not have an unconditional possessory right to enter for any purpose, especially the purpose of injuring George, who did not know of or endorse Mike's intent.

George is therefore likely to be found guilty of burglary.

END OF ANSWER.

Professor's Guidance

You should be quite familiar with how to spot and discuss the issues of attempt, murder, conspiracy, and burglary, now that you have done it one last time! This essay should also teach you how to spot and discuss some of the various defenses that have not yet been practiced. Make sure you are just as familiar with these defenses. Although they are tested less regularly, you may very well see them come up again in an essay question or in a multiple-choice question.

Notice also how this essay answer is organized. It does not follow a strict template, but it does flow and refers back to important concepts in a way that is not distracting to the reader. As I mentioned earlier, organizational templates can help you save time and should be followed when it makes sense to do so, but you can use some creativity when organizing your answer when needed. Here, it would have taken too much time to follow the murder template to the letter—especially since there was no homicide.

I hope you found these practice essays helpful! I encourage you to visit the state bar's website to practice on any question it may have released. Finally, if you find that you are still struggling in any area, now is a good time to ask for help!

Multiple Choice Testing

20

Multiple Choice Testing
Strategy & Practice

Now that you have a good idea of how the subjects are tested using essay questions, let's spend a little time discussing multiple choice testing.

First and foremost, as I mentioned earlier, you have to *know* the law. If you worked through the flowcharts provided and do not have any questions with regard to the issues contained in each box, that's great! If, however, you find that something doesn't look familiar to you or that you don't understand how the issues fit together, you need to go back and review those topics in your course materials and outlines.

If you are sure you know the law but still have trouble with multiple choice testing, you need to spend some time memorizing the "triggering" facts that appear in multiple choice fact patterns. This will help you with your essay writing as well.

Try associating facts that trigger the discussion on an issue with each box on the flowchart. For example, on the Formation chart, Promissory Estoppel could be triggered by facts that describe one party relying on the promise of another. Perhaps a worker quit a good paying job and moved across the country in reliance on an employer's offer to hire him. These facts would trigger you to think of promissory estoppel. Or perhaps you have facts that state a contract was oral. This triggers the Statute of Frauds issue.

Remembering the facts of cases you covered throughout your courses will also help. The facts of each case gave rise to issues that were decided by the court. If you can remember that a party was joking about buying a farm in one of your cases and that the court ordered the sale of the farm anyway because of the objective theory of contract, you will know to look for an objective intent to be bound when analyzing facts wherein one party claims that he was joking.

Assuming that you know the law and have a good handle on the triggering facts that raise issues, we now need a strategy of how to best approach a multiple-choice question.

If you remember nothing else that I tell you about multiple-choice testing, remember this: ***Read the question!*** I know this sounds silly, but this is the number one reason students answer questions incorrectly. They fail to read the facts or the call of the question carefully and rush to pick the answer choice that generally relates to the fact pattern without really analyzing how each choice answers the call of the question.

Here's a tip: Read the call of the question first and briefly look over each answer choice before reading the fact pattern. Doing so will help set your focus on the issues being tested. Then, when you read the fact pattern, you do so with those issues in mind and can pay attention to the facts that relate to that issue, noticing any problems that may need to be addressed. The correct answer choice will generally be the one that highlights or solves the problem.

Let's try it. Here's a call of a question:

Which of the following statements most correctly describes the obligations set forth in the writing signed by Adam and Bob?

From this, we know that we are dealing with a written contract and must look at the obligations of each party. Now let's quickly scan each answer choice:

(A) Payment by Adam of the initial $300 is a condition precedent to Bob's obligation to repair the car, and Bob's repairing of the car is a condition precedent to Adam's obligation to pay the additional $400.

(B) Payment by Adam of the initial $300 is a condition precedent in form and substance to Bob's obligation to repair the car, and Bob's repairing of the car is a condition precedent in form, but subsequent in substance, to Adam's obligation to pay the additional $400.

(C) Payment by Adam and repair of the car by Bob are concurrent conditions.

(D) Neither party's obligation to perform is conditioned upon performance by the other party.

By skimming each choice, we know that the answer has something to do with conditions. Therefore, we will now read the fact pattern, paying careful attention to flag any possible conditions:

Adam was in a car accident and contacted Bob's custom Body Shop about having the car repaired. Bob said that he would repair the car for $700, and would sell Adam a new bumper for an additional $150. Using an order form purchased at a stationery store, Bob wrote out all the terms of their agreement. On a printed line marked, "PAYMENT" he wrote, "Repair job—$700, payable $300 in advance and $400 on completion. Bumper—$150 payable on delivery." Both Bob and Adam signed at the bottom of the form.

Which of the following statements most correctly describes the obligations set forth in the writing signed by Adam and Bob?

Now, we know the law and can determine that the triggering facts here raise the issue of whether the payment terms are conditions. Hopefully, you can figure this out pretty quickly based on your knowledge of the law.

If not, think through the rules. Don't just assume a condition exists. Instead, decide whether the language amounts to a promise or a condition. If you decide that a condition exists, then you can determine what kind of condition it is in order to determine the specific obligations of each party.

Here's the rule regarding promises and conditions: If a promise is broken, the breaching party will have to pay damages to put the non-breaching party in the same position he would have been had the contract been properly performed. A condition is a fact that must exist (or not exist) that will either trigger or terminate the duty of performance.

Under these facts, the failure to pay or to make the repairs amounts to a breach of contract. The payment terms simply outline how payment will be made rather than condition the performance of either party. Therefore, **Answer Choice D correctly describes the obligations of each party. Neither party's obligation to perform is conditioned upon performance by the other party.**

My next best tip is to *never assume facts not included in the question.* Even if you are a police officer, medical doctor, or real estate agent and know everything there is to know about crime, medicine, and/or real estate, you have to assume you know nothing but the law you have learned with regard to the topic tested.

Don't fight with the question. In other words, check yourself if you find yourself thinking "Well, if this were true …" or "The defendant was just probably trying to …" or even "This fact pattern is stupid because this would never happen!" Rather, just take the question at face value, making the obvious or very reasonable inferences suggested by the facts, and choose the best answer. Sometimes, you will find the assumption you need to answer the question in the correct answer choice. Just make sure you don't pick an incorrect choice because you made a factual leap not suggested by the facts.

This goes hand in hand with the next tip: *Test each answer choice as a "True or False" question.* In other words, for each answer choice, ask yourself whether the choice is TRUE or FALSE under the facts given. The correct answer will be true 100% of the time under those facts. If you find that you have to assume a fact to make an answer choice true, it is the wrong answer. You will also find that some statements will not be "true" statements of the law. Some will not be "true" responses to the question, even if they are correct statements of the law. Some will include subparts which do not "truthfully" relate to each other.

Let's try it. Remember to try and read the answer choices and call of the question first as well.

After arson fires had damaged several city buildings, the City Council of the City of Snellville voted to offer a reward to aid in apprehension of the arsonists. Signs were posted in various locations throughout the city that read: "$5,000 REWARD is hereby offered by the City of Snellville to any person furnishing information leading to the conviction of persons responsible for setting fire to said buildings." Randy, a police officer employed by the City of Snellville, saw the posters and resolved to make a special effort to catch the arsonists even though he was not assigned to the case.

He told fellow police officers as well as his usual underworld informants that he was especially interested in the case. As a result, Mark, a police officer, and Steve, an underworld informant, passed information to Randy, which they thought might relate to the arson crimes. The tip which Randy received from Mark proved to be of no assistance, but that which he received from Steve led him to conduct a further investigation. His efforts eventually resulted in the arrest of two men who pleaded guilty to setting fires in public buildings. Randy demanded that the City Council pay him $5,000, but the Council refused.

If Randy institutes a lawsuit against the City of Snellville for the $5,000 reward offered in the signs, which of the following would be the City's most effective argument in defense?

(A) The reward should go to Steve, since it was his information which eventually led to the arrest of the arsonists.

(B) The reward was not accepted, since the arsonists were not convicted but pleaded guilty.

(C) Randy gave no consideration for the City's promise to pay a reward, since he was already obligated to attempt the apprehension of the arsonists.

(D) There was no enforceable promise by the City, since the offer was for a gratuitous cash award.

Now that we have read the fact pattern and call of the question, let's look at each answer choice separately.

Choice (A) reads: **The reward should go to Steve, since it was his information which eventually led to the arrest of the arsonists.** Is this a true statement? In other words, is it 100% true that the city's best defense is that Randy is not entitled to the reward because Steve's information led to the arrest? The answer is no. This is not a true statement, because even though Steve gave the information, there is no evidence that Steve knew about the reward and would otherwise be entitled to it. Remember — *Do not assume facts that are not included in the fact pattern.* There is also a better reason why Randy is not entitled to the reward.

Choice (B) reads: **The reward was not accepted, since the arsonists were not convicted but pleaded guilty.** Is this a true statement under the facts as given? The answer again is no. The offer for the reward was properly accepted, because information was provided that will lead to the conviction of the arsonists. Pleading guilty is just a procedural stage in the legal process that ultimately leads to a conviction.

Choice (C) reads: **Randy gave no consideration for the City's promise to pay a reward, since he was already obligated to attempt the apprehension of the arsonists.** Is this a true statement under the facts? The answer this time is yes. As a police officer, Robert was already obligated to attempt the apprehension of the arsonists. A pre-existing duty cannot serve as valid consideration. If there is no consideration, there is no contract. Therefore, this is a pretty darn good defense for the City. But just in case, let's look at answer choice (D) as well.

Choice (D) reads: **There was no enforceable promise by the City, since the offer was for a gratuitous cash award.** Is this a true statement under the facts? This is false. The facts tell us that the reward was offered in exchange for information. This is not a gratuitous promise, so answer choice D is incorrect.

Now wasn't that fun? I promise you that if you read the question carefully, avoid assuming facts, and apply the true/false method that you will find that you make fewer "stupid" mistakes and are more likely to choose the right answer on these types of multiple choice questions.

I can offer a few more suggestions of a general nature that will also help with this type of testing.

Try *"pre-phrasing."* In other words, before you fully contemplate each answer, try answering the question in your head without consideration of the answer choices. If you know the law, the correct answer will often be the one that most closely matches your "pre-phrasing."

Do not change your initial answer unless you are positive that it is wrong. For example, let's say you have pre-phrased your answer and have chosen the answer choice that is most similar and then apply the *True/False* method we covered and determine that it cannot be true under the facts. It's ok to change your answer. However, if you are picking between two answers that you feel are correct, go with your gut.

If you think you have encountered a trick question, you haven't. Although some questions may be harder than others, very few are intentionally deceptive. If you think a question is a trick question, you are probably reading too much into it and should take it at face value.

Pay attention to the *language* used in the answer choices. Incorrect options may not be grammatically correct when read in conjunction with the question presented. Also, answer choices that include qualifiers such as "generally" or "often" may be better answers than the choices that do not.

If you don't know the answer to a question, try to eliminate any answer choices that you know are wrong and then guess. You have at least a 25% chance of getting it right. Just make sure to answer all of the questions.

Try some of these strategies when answering the practice multiple choice questions that follow. Make sure to try to answer each one on your own before looking at the answers and guidance provided.

21

Multiple Choice Practice Questions

Question 1

Jeff asked his neighbor Don to keep an eye on his house while he was away on vacation. While Jeff was away, Don's car broke down. Needing to get to work, he entered Jeff's garage using the keys that Don had given him. The keys to Jeff's car were on the same keychain. Don started Jeff's car and proceeded to drive it to work. On his way to work, Don ran a red light and crashed into a car driven by an elderly couple. The elderly driver suffered broken bones as a result of the crash. Jeff mistakenly believed that he was responsible for the damages, even though Don was driving at the time of the accident. Jeff told the elderly driver that he promised to pay for her medical bills and property damage.

If the driver sues Jeff in an effort to collect on the promise to pay for medical expenses and property damage, she will:

(A) Succeed if Jeff's promise was also supported by consideration.

(B) Not succeed because Jeff was mistaken with regard to his responsibility to pay for the damage caused by the accident.

(C) Succeed if the contract is in writing and otherwise satisfies the statute of frauds.

(D) Not succeed because Don engaged in criminal activity by stealing the car.

Question 2

Dan and Paul were friends spending an afternoon boating on the lake. Dan drove the boat while Paul skied behind it. Dan made a fast, sharp turn with the boat, causing Paul to slam into a nearby dock. Paul sustained severe injuries. Dan and Paul would often try to scare each other by driving the boat erratically while the other skied. If Paul sues Don, what theory would provide him with the greatest amount of recovery?

(A) Assault, Battery, or Negligence.

(B) Assault, Battery, or Recklessness.

(C) Assault or Battery.

(D) Negligence or Recklessness.

Question 3

Marla thought she was happily married until she learned that her close friend, Jane, was having an affair with Marla's husband, Brad. Marla invited Jane to a "friendly" lunch to confront her about the affair. When Jane arrived, Marla pulled out a chair at the table so that Jane could sit. As Jane sat, Marla leaned over and placed her face very close to Jane's ear and whispered, "If you ever go near my husband again, I'll break every bone in your body." Jane was visibly frightened and felt that she could not safely leave the table. If Jane brings an action for assault against Marla, will she prevail?

(A) Yes, if Jane reasonably believed that Marla would do what she said.

(B) Yes, if Marla intended to frighten Jane.

(C) No, if there was no immediate danger.

(D) No, because Marla did not actually make harmful or offensive contact with Jane.

Question 4

Sarah lived in a quiet, upscale neighborhood and was upset when she learned that a drug and alcohol rehabilitation facility was opening near her home and accepting new patients. She believed that it would bring crime to the neighborhood and reduce her property value, so she did everything she could to try to keep the facility from being opened, including voicing her concerns at city council meetings. When her efforts to stop the facility from opening failed, Sarah would sit on the sidewalk day after day, waiting for patients to walk outside. When they did, she would taunt them and take their pictures. As a result, the patients were nervous and fearful of going outside. Several of them sued Sarah for invasion of privacy.

Will the patients prevail in their action?

(A) Yes, if Sarah acted with malice.

(B) No, if Sarah did not publish the pictures.

(C) Yes, because Sarah intruded on the patients' seclusion.

(D) No, because Sarah didn't show the patients in a false light.

Question 5

Brian suffered from a life-threatening disease and was only surviving with the help of a life support machine at the local hospital. He was in severe pain and begged Nurse to unplug the machine for him so that he could die peacefully. Nurse felt very sorry for Brian. Later that night, Nurse unplugged the machine for Brian when she was sure no one else was watching. Brian died shortly after Nurse unplugged the machine.

Of which crime is Nurse guilty?

(A) Murder.

(B) Nurse is not guilty of any crime.

(C) Involuntary Manslaughter.

(D) Voluntary Manslaughter.

Question 6

Marion, an elderly woman, owned a beautiful and valuable piece of property on an island in Hawaii. Her neighbor Tim tried for years to convince Marion to sell it to him, but she refused. After an earthquake shook the island, Tim told her that he heard that there was a 75% chance that the earthquake would cause the nearby volcano to erupt and that Marion's property would be in the danger zone. He offered to help her by buying her property and offered considerably less than market value. In reality, the volcano was dormant and there was no eruption imminent. Marion was so concerned about Tim's made up story that she sold her property to him.

Tim can be found guilty of which crime, if any?

(A) No crime; the value of the property is irrelevant, as parties are free to contract as they wish.

(B) False pretenses.

(C) Larceny by trick.

(D) Larceny.

Question 7

Tracy owned a commercial strip mall. She placed an advertisement in the local paper advertising the that the space was available to rent. Zach, a businessman running a smoke shop in another city, responded to Tracy's advertisement believing it would be a good site to open his second store. Zach did not mention what type of shop he planned to open. Tracy and Zach then entered into a valid lease agreement to begin on May 1, with Zach set to move in on June 1. On May 15, the city passed an ordinance prohibiting the sale of cigarettes, cigars, and smoking paraphernalia in the area where the strip mall was located. Zach telephoned Tracy and told her that he was no longer interested. Tracy sued Zach for breach of contract.

What is the likely result?

(A) Zach will prevail because the purpose of the contract has been frustrated.

(B) Zach will prevail because government action made the operation of the shop unlawful.

(C) Zach will prevail because he had not yet opened the store.

(D) Tracy will prevail because performance was not rendered impossible.

Question 8

Landlord had no notice that Owen owned a dog that had a history of vicious behavior. Sally, another tenant living in the same building as Owen, was entertaining some friends visiting from out of town. As Sally and her friends gathered in the courtyard of the apartment building for a barbeque lunch, Owen's dog darted out of his apartment and bit one of Sally's friends. Sally's friend sued the landlord for damages suffered.

Will Sally's friend prevail in her action against the landlord?

(A) No, because the landlord did not have notice of the dog's history.

(B) No, because a landlord does not owe a duty to a tenant's invited guests.

(C) Yes, because the landlord is strictly liable.

(D) Yes, because the landlord owes a duty to protect a tenant's guests from dangerous conditions.

Question 9

Philip contracted with a local painting company, PaintPlus, to paint his house. When the time for performance arrived, the local painting company assigned the contract to another company. There was no prohibition against assignments in the contract between Philip and PaintPlus. The new paint company began painting but walked off the job before the work had been completed.

Which of the following is true?

(A) Philip must first recover from PaintPlus in order to be able to recover from the second company.

(B) Philip only has a cause of action against PaintPlus.

(C) Philip cannot recover from PaintPlus because he allowed the second company to start painting.

(D) Philip can pursue recovery from either paint company.

Question 10

Andy decided to play a joke on his friend Jack. One night, while Jack was working late at the grocery store, Andy arrived dressed in black and wearing a ski mask. Andy shouted, "This is a robbery!" as he ran through the front door with a fake gun. Jack was actually asleep behind the service counter and was unaware that Andy had entered the store. However, there was a woman shopping for candy in the grocery store at the time the incident occurred.

If Andy is arrested for assault, what will be the outcome?

(A) Guilty, unless a reasonable person would not have been frightened.

(B) Not guilty, because Jack was not aware of Andy's conduct.

(C) Not guilty, because Andy's intent was to play a joke on Jack and not to actually rob the store.

(D) Guilty, because there was a woman shopping for candy in the grocery store at the time of the incident.

Question 11

Dave, Paul, and Dan were business partners and decided to open a pizza shop. As they were just starting out, they needed to purchase equipment, including an industrial pizza oven, a dishwasher, and washer and dryer. They also need to purchase tables and chairs. The partners reached out to a local bank for a loan. In an effort to secure the loan, Paul told the banker that he would personally guarantee the loan on behalf of the partnership and was offered a $100,000 loan to purchase the equipment they required.

If the partnership defaults on the loan, which of the following is the best answer?

(A) Paul's oral promise to guarantee the loan is unenforceable.

(B) Paul's oral promise to guarantee the loan is enforceable.

(C) Paul's oral promise to guarantee the loan is enforceable, because he is a business creditor.

(D) Paul's oral promise to guarantee the loan is enforceable because the "main purpose" rule applies.

Question 12

Dan owned a building downtown. He planned to renovate it but was forced to wait a few years after buying the building in an effort to save enough money to make the renovations. The building sat empty for years and became a popular place for the homeless population in the area to sleep. The building was covered in graffiti, and the unauthorized use of the building resulted in the need for even more renovations. Dan also worried that he would be liable if one of the homeless was injured while camping out in the building. Dan posted several "No Trespassing" signs around the building and set up a tall electric fence around the building that would shock anyone who touched it. Dan also posted a warning sign on the fence.

One evening, Joe, a homeless man, tried to scale the electric fence in an effort to camp inside the building. He was shocked as he tried to climb the fence. Unfortunately, Joe had a condition that caused him to suffer severe brain injury as a result of the shock.

If Joe sues Dan for damages, he will most likely:

(A) Recover because of the eggshell plaintiff rule.

(B) Not recover because Joe was a trespasser.

(C) Recover because a homeowner cannot use force to protect his property.

(D) Not recover because Dan used reasonable force to protect his property.

Question 13

Over the past several years, many people had been hurt by fireworks. In response, the state legislature enacted a statute making it a crime for a private person or business to "shoot any firework from a mortar tube." A local seaside restaurant wanted to attract customers and decided it would be a good idea to promote weekly fireworks shows on Friday nights. The restaurant obtained a permit for its first fireworks display and contacted the local fire department to seek clarification on the law. The fire chief mistakenly advised the restaurant owner that Skylighters were legal, when in fact they were prohibited by the state statute.

The restaurant owner purchased and fired several Skylighters during their first show.

If the restaurant owner is charged with violating the law, he is likely to be:

(A) Convicted because shooting fireworks is a dangerous activity for which defendants are held strictly liable.

(B) Convicted because the erroneous legal advice did not come from an attorney.

(C) Not convicted because the restaurant owner relied on the interpretation of the law provided by the fire chief.

(D) Not convicted because the restaurant owner did not intend to violate the law.

Question 14

When Sally and Adam got divorced, the court awarded Sally the family home. Sally was not able to afford the mortgage payments on her own, so she approached the local bank in an attempt to refinance her mortgage. Later that evening, Sally went to a local restaurant with a friend. She noticed that the loan officer was at the next table over. During the course of the evening, she overheard the loan officer telling his friend that Sally was having trouble making her mortgage payments.

If Sally sues the loan officer for invasion of privacy, she will likely:

(A) Prevail because the loan officer disclosed private facts about Sally.

(B) Not prevail because the Loan officer shared the information only with his friend.

(C) Prevail because the statement was published.

(D) Not prevail because the statement was true.

Question 15

Becky and Gary were engaged to be married. They spent over a year planning the wedding. Becky always wanted to have her wedding at the local Botanical Gardens, so the couple contracted with the venue to secure their wedding date as early as possible. One week before the wedding, Gary became violently ill and was admitted to the hospital. Becky sought to cancel the contract with the Botanical Gardens.

Which of the following is correct?

(A) The contract is likely to be discharged due to frustration of purpose.

(B) The contract is not likely to be discharged because performance is not impossible.

(C) The contract is not likely to be discharged because the couple bore the risk.

(D) The contract is likely to be discharged because the frustration was not substantial.

Question 16

In which of the following circumstances is Defendant most likely to be convicted of Common Law Arson?

(A) A tenant in an apartment building lights a firepit on his first-floor patio. Even though the tenant knows that there is a risk to the balcony of the apartment above him, while the fire is blazing, the tenant goes to the store, leaving the fire burning. The patio furniture on the balcony upstairs catches fire. A neighbor puts the fire out.

(B) Husband's wife was angry after learning that he was having an affair. She quickly gathered all of his belongings out on the front lawn and set them on fire.

(C) Husband plans a romantic evening for his wife. Husband lights candles in their kitchen and waits for her to arrive. Realizing he forgot flowers, he runs outside to pick some from their garden. While he is outside, the pet cat knocks over one of the candles, setting the couch on fire and charring the floor.

(D) An employee was angry that her coworker was promoted over her. She drove over to her boss' home with the intention of confronting him about his poor decision. When she arrived, she noticed that her coworker's car was parked in her boss' garage. She opened the car door, set fire to the front seat, and left. The car exploded as the garage caught on fire.

Question 17

Stacy owed $3000 to a creditor. She did not realize that any claim the creditor may have had against her was barred by the Statute of Limitations. Stacey called the creditor and said "I promise to pay you $500 if you will write off my debt." The creditor agreed.

Is Stacey's promise to pay the creditor $500 enforceable?

(A) No, if Stacy did not also promise not to give up her defense of the Statute of Limitations.

(B) No, because the promise is not supported by consideration.

(C) Yes, because a promise to pay the debt that is otherwise barred by the Statute of Limitations is enforceable without consideration.

(D) Yes, because the promise benefits the creditor.

Question 18

Larry, a clerk at the local grocery store, needed money to pay for his gambling debts. He approached his co-worker, George, and asked if he would be willing to help him rob the store. George knew that Larry was often in trouble with the law but never got caught. He decided this would be a good opportunity to help the police catch Larry in the act, so he agreed to help. Later that night, after the store closed, George drove Larry to the store and sat outside to "keep watch" while Larry went inside to break into the cash registers. While Larry was in the store, George called the police. The police arrived just in time to catch Larry in the act.

Of what crime can George be convicted at common law?

(A) No crime.

(B) Conspiracy.

(C) Attempted Burglary.

(D) Burglary and Conspiracy.

Question 19

Max trained police dogs for a living and kept the dogs in a fenced in yard at his home. Several of the dogs were being trained to attack on command. Because they had not yet fully trained and could be unpredictable, Max posted a sign on the fence that read "Beware of Dogs." His neighbor, Pete, was aware that Max trained the dogs and was also aware that some of the dogs could be quite dangerous. One day, Pete entered Max's fence without Max's permission to retrieve some tools that Pete had borrowed from him some time before. One of the dogs attacked Pete and caused serious injury.

If Pete sues Max to recover damages for his injuries, which of the following statements are true?

(A) Pete will recover because Max was engaged in an abnormally dangerous activity.

(B) Pete will not recover because he was trespassing at the time he was injured.

(C) Pete will recover because the tools he attempted to recover were not "the property of another."

(D) Pete will not recover because he was aware that some of the dogs in Max's yard could be dangerous.

Question 20

Jenny and Sue entered into a written two-year lease agreement wherein Jenny agreed to pay $1500 a month for Sue's rental apartment. The lease stipulated that water, garbage, phone and internet services were included. After the first month, Time Direct, one of the state's biggest internet companies declared bankruptcy and ceased doing business in the state, leaving only one internet company to serve the state's residents. The cost of the phone and internet service doubled to over $200 a month as a result. Jenny and Sue orally agreed to split the difference so that Jenny would now pay an additional $100 a month to compensate for the increase in internet costs.

Is Jenny legally obligated to pay Sue the additional $100 a month?

(A) No, unless the parties reduced the modification to writing.

(B) No, because there was no consideration to support the modification.

(C) Yes, because Sue requested the modification in good faith.

(D) Yes, because the cost increase was not within the control of either party.

Question 21

Larry was a bully and constantly tormented Ed's friend, Doug. Ed told Doug about his plan to confront Larry and "beat him senseless." Doug was excited about the idea and told Ed that he could find Larry at the bus stop the next morning. Ed arrived at the bus stop the next day and assaulted Larry in front of Stacy, Ed's little sister. Stacy stood by and watched the entire incident and did nothing to stop it, as she was pleased that Larry was finally getting "what he deserved."

If Stacy is charged as an accomplice to battery, her best defense will be:

(A) Stacy did not have intent to commit a crime.

(B) Stacy was too scared to help Larry.

(C) Stacy owed no duty to rescue Larry.

(D) Stacy did not take any action to assist Ed.

Question 22

Greg hated his boss, Larry, and was aware that Larry had a serious heart disease. Greg was also aware that Larry had suffered several heart attacks in the past. One day, Greg decided that he would try to scare Larry into having another heart attack. Greg hid in the back seat of Larry's car and waited for Larry to get off work. As Larry was getting in his car at the end of the work day, Greg jumped out of the back seat and screamed "You're a complete loser!" Greg wasn't sure this would kill Larry, but he hoped it would. Larry was so frightened that he had a heart attack and died instantly.

The jurisdiction defines first degree murder as "the premeditated and deliberate killing of a human being." It defines second degree murder with "any unlawful killing of a human being with malice aforethought, except for a killing which constitutes first degree murder."

Which of the following is the most serious crime of which Greg can be convicted?

(A) First degree murder.

(B) Second degree murder.

(C) Involuntary manslaughter.

(D) Voluntary manslaughter.

Question 23

Rob was a very wealthy man and owned several homes. Wishing to provide some income for his adult daughter, Nancy, who had a family of her own, Rob sold one of his homes to Beverly. Rob and Beverly entered into a purchase agreement wherein Beverly would pay $3000 a month over the next thirty years to Nancy. Both Rob and Beverly signed the contract. Nancy did not. If Beverly stops making her monthly payments after the first year, does Nancy have any rights?

(A) Nancy can sue Beverly as a creditor beneficiary.

(B) Nancy can sue Beverly as a donee beneficiary.

(C) Nancy cannot sue Beverly because she is a donee beneficiary.

(D) Nancy cannot sue Beverly unless she also sues Rob.

Questions 24, 25, and 26 are based on the following facts:

Billy needed to make some repairs on his roof. After getting several estimates from roofing contractors, he decided that he could do the work himself for a much lower price. Billy went to the local hardware store, Home Spot, to buy the materials he needed. While he was there, he noticed a 20-foot aluminum ladder in the corner with a big yellow "Clearance 50% Off" sign taped to it. Billy approached Ed, who had been working at the hardware store for over 20 years. Billy asked Ed why the ladder was on sale. Ed told Billy that someone had purchased the ladder a few days ago and had returned it. When Billy asked why the ladder had been returned, Ed said "I'm not really sure. There isn't anything wrong with it." Satisfied by Ed's words, Billy purchased the ladder and took it home.

Billy organized all of his tools and read the directions on how to use the ladder. He also carefully read the warnings. The directions contained a sentence advising users to always have someone else present to hold the ladder when climbing it. However, this was not included in the product warnings.

Billy asked his daughter, Becky, to hold the ladder for him as he climbed up to the roof. Becky lightly placed one hand on the ladder and held her phone in the other hand. Becky was not paying attention to Billy as he climbed the ladder, because she was too busy texting. When Billy reached the fifth rung, the rung broke and caused Billy to lose his balance. As Billy fell, he landed on Becky, causing her to break her arm. Billy also broke his ankle as a result of the fall.

Question 24

If Billy sues Home Spot on a theory of Strict Liability, he will most likely:

(A) Not succeed, because Ed assured Billy that there was nothing wrong with the ladder.

(B) Succeed, if Billy can prove that the ladder was defective.

(C) Succeed, because both manufacturers and retailers can be strictly liable for selling defective products.

(D) Not succeed, unless Home Spot manufactured the ladder.

Question 25

If Becky sues Home Spot on a theory of Strict Liability, she will most likely:

(A) Succeed, if Becky can prove that the ladder was defective.

(B) Not succeed because Becky is not a proper Plaintiff.

(C) Not succeed because Becky contributed to her own injuries by texting while holding the ladder.

(D) Succeed, because Becky's injury was foreseeable.

Question 26

If Billy sues Home Spot on a Negligence theory, he will most likely:

(A) Succeed, if Billy can establish Res Ipsa Loquitor.

(B) Not succeed, if Billy cannot establish that the product is defective.

(C) Not succeed, if Ed was off duty when he assured Billy that there was nothing wrong with the ladder.

(D) Succeed, because Ed did not warn Billy of the danger.

Question 27

Buyer contracted with Seller to purchase one thousand units of turnip twirlers for $3000. The contract was in writing and signed by both parties. The contract provided that Seller would deliver the units by June 1. Seller did not deliver the units until June 10.

Which of the following statements is true?

(A) Buyer must pay for the units.

(B) Buyer can avoid performance if the June 1 date was a promise.

(C) Buyer can avoid performance if the June 1 date was an express condition precedent.

(D) Buyer cannot avoid performance if the June 1 date was an express condition subsequent.

Question 28

Molly was an aspiring comedian who was quickly gaining popularity and notoriety. Ted opened a local comedy club and, in hopes of making it immediately popular, contracted with Molly to perform once a month over the next two years. The contract contained a liquidated damages clause that provided that in the event of a total or partial breach, damages would be calculated in the amount of $500,000. After performing for the first year and a half, Molly was offered an important role in an upcoming movie that would be filmed overseas. Molly told Ted that she could no longer perform at his comedy club.

If Ted sues Molly for breach of contract, he will likely:

(A) Collect money damages in the amount of $500,000.

(B) Obtain specific performance from Molly.

(C) Collect money damages in excess of the cost for Ted to hire another comedian.

(D) Collect both actual and consequential damages as a result of Molly's breach.

Questions 29 and 30 are based on the following facts:

Years ago, Andrew was convicted of being an accessory to a crime, which was a felony, but was only sentenced to probation. Andrew is now working as a security guard at the local university and carries a gun supplied by the university. The jurisdiction has a statute that makes it unlawful for a convicted felon to buy, own, or possess a firearm. Andrew believed that his previous conviction was a misdemeanor and not a felony and did not properly disclose the conviction to the university. While patrolling the streets one night, Andrew spotted some students loitering in a parking lot. One of the students, Larry, appeared to have a weapon, so Andrew drew his gun upon approach. As Andrew approached, he tripped over a curb, causing the gun to fire. The bullet struck Larry in the foot.

Question 29

If Andrew is charged with possession of a firearm in violation of the state statute, he will most likely be:

(A) Convicted.

(B) Not convicted because Andrew lacked mens rea.

(C) Convicted, if Andrew's belief that his crime was a misdemeanor was unreasonable.

(D) Not convicted if Andrew's belief that his crime was a misdemeanor was honest and reasonable, satisfying an objective and subjective standard.

Question 30

If Larry sues the University under a Negligence theory, which of the following is true:

(A) The University cannot be held liable because Andrew's criminal act breaks the chain of causation.

(B) If Larry had a weapon, the University can defend on the grounds of self-defense because it stands in Andrew's shoes.

(C) The University is not liable if it conducted a thorough background investigation before hiring Andrew.

(D) The University is liable if Andrew was negligent in approaching the students with a gun.

Questions 31–50 are actual past FYLSE questions provided by the California Bar Association.

Questions 31 and 32 are based on the following facts:

Joe was a first-year biology student. He told Mary that he was a licensed medical doctor. Joe convinced Mary that she needed a physical examination. Mary agreed to have Joe make such an examination, and a date was set for it. Two days prior to the date for the examination, a mutual friend told Mary that Joe was not a doctor, and that Joe had boasted about how he had persuaded Mary to submit to a physical examination. Mary canceled the examination. The realization that Joe is not a doctor and the fact that he had boasted about his scheme to examine her upset Mary, made her nervous, and caused her to avoid people who know her.

Question 31

If Mary asserted a claim against Joe based on assault, the likely result is that Mary will:

(A) Recover because Joe intended to touch her body.

(B) Recover because Joe perpetrated a fraud on her.

(C) Not recover because she had consented to Joe making an examination.

(D) Not recover because she learned of Joe's deception before the date for the proposed examination.

Question 32

If Mary had not learned of Joe's deception and examination had taken place, the likely result is that Mary could:

(A) Recover damages for battery.

(B) Recover damages for fraud and misrepresentation.

(C) Not recover damages for battery because she consented the examination.

(D) Not recover damages on any theory and less she suffered some physical harm.

Questions 33, 34, 35, and 36 are based on the following facts:

On December 31, Buyer and Seller entered into a written contract under which Seller agreed to sell and Buyer to purchase all of Buyer's monthly requirements of heating fuel during the following year. The contract was identical with those entered into by them for each of the past five years. Although the contracts in previous years made no provision for advanced payment, Buyer had always paid on the first of each month the estimated cost of his orders for the coming month.

Question 33

Assume that on January 5, buyer ordered 5000 gallons of fuel. Seller, who had not yet received any advance payment for January, told Buyer that he would make no deliveries without advanced payment. Buyer refused to pay in advance, bought the fuel elsewhere at a higher price, and sued seller for the difference. The court will most likely hold for:

(A) Seller, because of their past course of dealing.

(B) Buyer, because the writing was a complete and exclusive statement of the agreement.

(C) Buyer, because delivery by Seller was a condition precedent to Buyer's duty to pay.

(D) Seller, because payment in advance is an implied condition to Seller's duty to deliver regardless of their prior course of dealing.

Question 34

Assume that in the last five years, Buyer had never ordered fuel oil for August delivery. On August 1, anticipating an energy shortage, Buyer ordered 5000 gallons of fuel oil for August delivery and tendered payment in advance. Although Seller had a sufficient supply on hand, he refused to deliver. Does Buyer have a cause of action against Seller?

(A) No, because Buyer's promise to buy his August requirements was illusory.

(B) Yes, because Seller had a supply sufficient to fill the order.

(C) Yes, because the agreement set no express limit on the amount buyer could order.

(D) No, because Buyer's order was disproportionate to his normal requirements.

Question 35

Assume that in the last five years, Buyer had never ordered fuel oil for September delivery. Because of an unusual cold spell in early September, buyer bought 3500 gallons of fuel oil from X at a price lower than that specified in the contract with Seller. In a suit by Seller against Buyer for the lost profit on 3,500 gallons, Buyer's best argument is that:

(A) Seller's promise to supply Buyer's requirements was illusory.

(B) The decline in the market price frustrated Buyer's purpose for entering into the requirements contract.

(C) Buyer was not obligated to purchase from Seller any amount in excess of his monthly requirement, and his normal September requirement was zero.

(D) The courts do not favor this type of agreement, because it interferes with the ability of the parties to contract with others.

Question 36

Assume that in November, an agency of Federal Government issued a valid regulation prohibiting heating fuel suppliers from delivering to customers in any month more than 50% of the amount of fuel delivered during the same month of the previous year. On December 1, Buyer ordered from Seller, for December delivery, 5,000 gallons—the same amount he had received from Seller the previous December. Seller, who had only 2,500 gallons available, delivered only that amount. In a suit by Buyer for breach of contract, Seller's best defense is:

(A) That it was impossible for him to fill the order, because he had only 2,500 gallons available.

(B) That the contract was illegal.

(C) That the parties to a contract are presumed to know the law.

(D) That Seller's duty to deliver more than 2,500 gallons was excused.

Question 37

Boss, who was head of an underworld syndicate, ordered Hit to execute M, a merchant who had refused to comply with syndicate demands. Hit had been chosen because he owed Boss a favor. Hit refused to carry out the order. Learning of Hit's refusal, Boss forced Hit at gunpoint to M's store. To save his own life, hit shot and killed M.

If Hit is charged with criminal homicide, does he have a complete defense on the grounds of duress?

(A) Yes, because Hit reasonably feared for his own life.

(B) Yes, because Boss' conduct constituted a threat of immediate and serious bodily harm.

(C) No, because duress does not excuse killing of an innocent person.

(D) No, because duress does not excuse the commission of any felony.

Question 38

S, a supplier of florescent lamps, had for years accepted oral orders for lamps from C, a customer. C phoned S and ordered 1,200 lamps to be delivered at the rate of 100 per month beginning June 1. The lamps were priced at $1 each. S delivered 100 lamps on June 1. With his check in payment for this delivery, C sent S a note saying "$1 per lamp is too high. I will not take the other 1100 lamps. (Signed) C."

S sues, alleging that C breached a contract to take 1,200 lamps. C pleads the Statute of Frauds. What is the result on this issue?

(A) C prevails, because the note sent with C's check was a repudiation, rather than a memorandum, of the oral agreement.

(B) C prevails, because the note sent with C's check is not specific enough to satisfy the Statute of Frauds.

(C) S prevails, because part of the goods had been received and accepted.

(D) S prevails, because the note sent with C's check constitutes a writing sufficient to satisfy the Statute of Frauds.

Questions 39 and 40 are based on the following facts:

South was driving his car in a southerly direction. Prudence and North were each driving their respective cars on the same highway in a northerly direction. All three were driving within the speed limit. North was following unreasonably close behind Prudence. Suddenly, because of South failing to pay attention, his car crossed the center line and came to rest on the shoulder of the northbound lanes. When Prudence saw South's car coming across the highway in front of her, she applied her breaks. Her car did not strike South's car, but North, because he had been following unreasonably close, hit the rear of Prudence's car. Prudence suffered bodily harm and property damage.

Question 39

If Prudence asserts a claim against North and South the likely result is:

(A) South, but not North, will be liable for the full amount of her damages.

(B) North, but not South, will be liable for the full amount of her damages.

(C) North and South will be jointly and severally liable for the full amount of her damages.

(D) North and South will each be partially liable to Prudence for the full amount of her damages apportioned between them according to their comparative fault.

Question 40

Assume the jurisdiction has not adopted the doctrine of Comparative Negligence. If North asserts a claim against South and Prudence, the most likely result is North will prevail against:

(A) South, but not Prudence.

(B) Prudence, but not South.

(C) Prudence and South.

(D) Neither Prudence nor South.

Questions 41–42 are based on the following facts:

Sailor and Builder entered into a written contract by which Builder agreed to construct a boat, in accordance with the detailed plans and specifications, and Sailor agreed to pay builder $25,000 for the boat upon completion. One provision in the contract read: "Sailor's liability is expressly conditioned on the main hatch being of genuine imported Malayan teak."

Thereafter, Sailor contracted in writing to sell the boat to Art. In this contract, there was the following: "This contract is contingent on Art obtaining financing at 7% interest." While the boat was under construction, the President of the United States, acting under proper legal authorization, banned the importation of specified wood products, including Malayan teak, and no Malayan teak was available in the United States. Builder, therefore, used first quality oak for the hatch. Art attempted to procure a loan from six separate institutions but found that he could not obtain financing at 7%, because his assets and annual income were not sufficient. A Carpenter had agreed in writing with Builder to construct a galley unit in the boat. The galley unit as constructed did not fit quite properly, although it was otherwise functional. Except for the hatch and the galley unit, the boat has been completed according to the plans and specifications.

Question 41

Assume that Sailor has refused to pay Builder because of his failure to meet the requirement that the hatch be Malayan teak. Builder sues on the contract. Which of the following arguments gives Builder the best chance to prevail?

(A) The requirement is a mere covenant which was satisfied by substantial performance.

(B) The requirement is an express condition which is excused by the supervening illegality resulting from the President's ban on importation.

(C) The requirement is an express condition which has been excused by impossibility of performance.

(D) The requirement, being nothing more than Sailor's personal whim, is a de minimis provision of the contract.

Question 42

Assume that Sailor has refused to pay Builder on the ground that the galley unit does not fit properly. Which of the following arguments is most likely to prevail?

(A) Sailor must pay Builder the full contract price because any damages resulting from the defective galley unit are recoverable only from Carpenter.

(B) Sailor must pay the contract price minus the diminished value of the boat because of the defective galley unit.

(C) Sailor must pay the full contract price without any offset for the defective galley unit because Builder substantially performed.

(D) Sailor is not required to pay for anything until the defect in the unit is completely remedied.

Question 43

Assume that Sailor has paid Builder the full price and now Sailor sues to enforce his contract with Art. Which of the following statements states the probable result of Sailor's lawsuit?

(A) Sailor will recover the full contract price, because Art's failure to obtain 7% financing is a breach of the agreement.

(B) Sailor will not recover because Art's duty to pay is conditional upon his obtaining 7% financing, which he attempted to do in good faith.

(C) Sailor will not recover, because the condition that art pay the price is excused by impossibility of performance.

(D) Sailor will recover a judgment requiring Art to obtain financing at a reasonable interest rate and thereafter to pay a purchase price adjusted to reflect the difference in the interest rate.

Question 44

Assume that Sailor has paid Builder the full contract price and that Sailor now sues the Carpenter for damages due to the defective galley unit, the probable results of the lawsuit will be that:

(A) Sailor will not recover because, by paying Builder and taking possession of the boat, he waived his right to claim damages.

(B) Sailor will not recover because he was not in privity with the Carpenter.

(C) Sailor will recover as a third-party beneficiary of the contract between Builder and Carpenter.

(D) Sailor will recover on the theory that, when he paid Builder, he acquired an implied assignment of any rights which Builder had against Carpenter.

Question 45

Owner loaned his new automobile to Friend to drive to Centerville. Owner specified that Friend should drive only on Interstate One. Friend took a different route to Centerville on an unpaved road. While Friend was driving, and without any fault on his part, a stone was thrown up by a passing car and chipped the paint on the side of Owner's car. The cracked paint can be fixed at a cost of $30.

If Owner asserts a claim against Friend, the likely result is that Friend is:

(A) Liable to Owner for the value of the car because friend took a different route.

(B) Liable to Owner for the value of the car because the car was damaged while in Friend's possession.

(C) Liable to Owner for the cost of fixing the chipped paint because Friend took a different route.

(D) Not liable to Owner because friend was not to blame for the stone hitting the car.

Question 46

Dick and John were neighbors and had been involved in a long-standing, bitter dispute over their boundary line, but neither person had ever used any force or threats of force. Shortly after a heated argument, Dick saw John come out of John's house carrying a shotgun over his shoulder. Dick, believing that John intended to shoot him, shot first and killed John. In fact, John was going to join some friends and go duck hunting.

If Dick is prosecuted for killing John, the likely result is:

(A) Excusable homicide, because Dick had mistaken John's intent.

(B) Justifiable homicide, because Dick had a privilege to kill if the circumstances were as he believed them to be.

(C) Manslaughter, because Dick killed John in the honest but unreasonable belief that it was necessary to do so to save his own life.

(D) Murder, because premeditation and deliberation will be implied from their long-standing, bitter dispute.

Question 47

Patient consented to an operation to be performed by Qualified, a surgeon whom Patient knew and in whom he had great confidence. Immediately before Patient's operation, Qualified became ill. There was no emergency, and Patient's operation could have been postponed. Without Patient's knowledge, the hospital substituted Skillful, another surgeon of equal competence. Skillful performed the operation satisfactorily.

If Patient asserts a claim based on battery against a Skillful, the likely result is that Patient will:

(A) Prevail only if the operation did not improve Patient's physical well-being.

(B) Prevail, regardless of whether the operation improved Patient's physical well-being.

(C) Not prevail because Skillful was as competent as Qualified.

(D) Not prevail, if Patient refused pay for the operation.

Question 48

The most accurate statement about a defendant in a criminal prosecution who claims that he used deadly force in self-defense is that he may properly rely on self-defense only if he:

(A) Retreated before using deadly force.

(B) Honestly believed deadly force was necessary to prevent bodily harm.

(C) Is charged with a criminal homicide.

(D) Was threatened with immediate and serious bodily harm and reasonably believed that deadly force was necessary.

Question 49

Tom, standing 10 feet behind Bill, pointed a pistol at Bill intending to shoot and kill him. Sam overpowered Tom before Tom could pull the trigger. Hearing the noise, Bill turned around and, for the first time, realized the danger to which he had been subjected.

If Bill asserts a claim for damages against Tom based on assault, the likely result is that Bill will:

(A) Recover because Tom attempted to kill Bill.

(B) Recover because when Bill turned around, he realized he would have been shot but for Sam's intervention.

(C) Not recover because Tom never carried out his intention to shoot Bill.

(D) Not recover because the danger had passed before Bill turned around.

Question 50

Andrew went to Sally's backyard sale. While Sally was answering the phone inside her home, Andrew saw a lamp he liked. The lamp was marked "Price—$25." Andrew waited 10 minutes for Sally. When Sally did not return to the backyard, Andrew took the lamp and left, intending to pay Sally if she found out he had taken the lamp.

Andrew is guilty of

(A) No crime.

(B) Larceny.

(C) Larceny by trick.

(D) Obtaining property by False Pretenses.

22

Multiple Choice Answers

Question 1 Answer

The correct answer is: (A) Succeed if Jeff's promise was also supported by consideration.

In order for a contract to be enforceable, it must be supported by consideration or a consideration substitute. Consideration is a bargained for exchange. Jeff made a gratuitous promise to pay for the damages without bargaining for anything in return. Therefore, his promise is unenforceable.

Answer choice (B) is incorrect because a unilateral mistake is not a defense to formation unless the other party knows or has reason to know about the mistake. (C) is incorrect because this contract is not required to be in writing. (Had the promise been to pay for the debt of another rather than a promise to pay for someone's losses, a writing would have been required.) Finally, answer choice (D) is incorrect because it is irrelevant that Don stole the car.

Professor's Guidance

This question tests you on the rules regarding consideration, mistake, and the Statute of Frauds. It also teaches us the importance of reading the call of the question and answer choices first. Had we not done that, we may have mistakenly set our focus on Criminal Law rather than Contracts had we jumped right into the facts. Notice also that the correct answer includes an otherwise missing element by using the qualifier "if."

Question 2 Answer

The correct answer is (B) Assault, Battery, or Recklessness.

Paul may be able to recover both compensatory and punitive damages depending on the theory he advances. Punitive damages are available to victims of intentional tort and may be available to victims of recklessness. However, punitive damages are not available in ordinary negligence cases. Therefore, if Paul alleges Assault, Battery, or Recklessness, he could recover punitive damages in addition to compensatory damages, increasing his amount of recovery.

Professor's Guidance

This question tests you on rules regarding torts damages. The takeaway here is that Plaintiff has to show malice, either through ill intent or reckless behavior, in order to recover punitive damages. If you know this rule, you could apply the True/False tip provided earlier and determine that the only answer choice that is true under the facts is answer choice (B).

Question 3 Answer

The correct answer is (C). Assault requires proof that Defendant intentionally placed another in reasonable fear of an imminent battery. Here, Marla's words constituted a threat of a future battery rather than the threat of an immediate battery. (A) and (B) are incorrect because even with an intent to frighten and a reasonable fear, it is not enough to prove assault without the element of immediate danger. (D) is incorrect because harmful or offensive contact is not an element required to prove assault.

Professor's Guidance

This question tests your knowledge of the elements required to prove assault. If you work your way through the fact pattern to determine what elements are present, you should quickly realize that the element of an imminent battery is missing, so you should look for the answer choice that either adds facts that allows for proof of that element or the answer choice that states that the element is missing. The True/False tip works here as well.

Question 4 Answer

The correct answer is (C) Yes, because Sarah intruded on the patients' seclusion.

Intrusion into Plaintiff's Seclusion is a form of Invasion of Privacy and requires proof that Defendant intentionally intruded upon the plaintiff's private affairs, the intrusion would be highly offensive to a reasonable person, Plaintiff had a reasonable expectation of privacy, and the intrusion caused Plaintiff mental anguish or suffering. Sarah's conduct was subjectively highly offensive, the patients had a reasonable expectation of privacy, and suffered mental anguish as a result. (A) is incorrect because malice is not a required element for Invasion of Privacy. (B) and (D) are incorrect because even if the patients cannot prove the Public Revelation of Private Facts or False Light forms of Invasion of Privacy, they can still prove Intrusion into Plaintiff's Seclusion.

Professor's Guidance

This question forces you to understand the differences between the various forms of Invasion of Privacy and what type of intent is required. The True/False tip works very well here in helping us eliminate answers (B) and (D), because it is not true that the patients will not prevail on an Invasion of Privacy Claim if they cannot prove publication or False Light under the facts provided. As you know, they can still prove Intrusion into Seclusion without those elements.

Question 5 Answer

The correct answer is (A) Murder. Murder requires a homicide plus malice. Here, Nurse caused the death of Brian by pulling the plug and acted with the intent for him to die, which is the same as the intent to kill form of malice. It does not matter that Brian asked her to do it or that she acted out of love. Absent a state statute to the contrary, the patient's consent does not serve as a justification or mitigation. Therefore, because both homicide and malice are present under the facts, murder is the correct charge.

Professor's Guidance

I like this question, because it forces you to remember the tip that you must never assume facts not in the question. A lot of students miss this one because they assume that there are laws that permit assisted suicide. Unless the facts tell you that such a statute is applicable, you cannot assume it exists. Therefore, you must treat it like any other question to see if the elements of each possible crime are met and keep your personal feelings out.

Question 6 Answer

The correct answer is (B) False Pretenses. False Pretenses requires that Defendant falsely represent a present or past material fact that causes the victim to pass title to his property to the Defendant, who knows his representation to be false and intends thereby to defraud the victim. Tim knowingly misrepresented the fact that a volcanic eruption was imminent causing Marion to pass the title to her property to him for less than market value. Marion did not want to sell her property and would not have sold it, especially for far less than market value, had Tim not lied about the volcano. Answer Choice (A) is incorrect, because although it is true that people are free to contract as they wish, they can still be guilty of a crime if their conduct is fraudulent. (C) and (D) are incorrect, because Larceny and Larceny by Trick requires Defendant to obtain custody of personal property rather than title to real or personal property.

Professor's Guidance

This was another good opportunity to practice testing yourself on the differences between the various theft crimes. It is also worth noting that every once in a while, even though you will see an otherwise true statement, such as "People are free to contract as they wish," don't get distracted, and keep your eye on the real issue. Always go back to the elements of each crime and see if they fit into the fact pattern. Similar to Question 5, if all of the elements are present, a crime has been committed.

Question 7 Answer

The correct answer is (D). Tracy will prevail because performance was not rendered impossible. Zach can still rent the space and open a shop, but cannot sell cigarettes, cigars, or other smoking paraphernalia. Answer choice (A) is incorrect because Tracy was unaware that Zach planned to open a smoke shop, so he cannot argue that the underlying purpose was frustrated as a defense. Answer choice (B) is incorrect because a shop could still be operated lawfully as long as it did not sell the prohibited items. Answer choice (C) is incorrect because the contract had been formed by the parties. It does not matter that Zach had not yet opened the store.

Professor's Guidance

This is a good review of the doctrines of impossibility and frustration of purpose. It also highlights the importance of reading the facts carefully. The answer would be different if Zach had made Tracy aware of the type of shop he wished to open.

Question 8 Answer

The correct answer is (A) No, because the landlord did not have notice of the dog's history. Although a landlord owes a duty to invitees to protect against dangerous conditions on his property such as rotting steps or slippery floors, a dog is not such a condition. Therefore, the landlord's duty was only to act reasonably under the circumstances. Because the landlord was not aware of the dog's vicious propensity, absent other facts indicating that the landlord was negligent in some way, the landlord is not liable. Answer (B) is an incorrect statement of the law. Answer (C) is incorrect because strict liability applies only to the owner or possessor of a dog he has reason to know is unreasonably dangerous. The dog does not belong to the landlord. Answer (D) is incorrect because the landlord only owes a duty of reasonable care in this situation.

Professor's Guidance

I included this question because it points out a fatal flaw made by many students applying landowner duty rules. Whenever you see the words landlord and tenant in a Torts question, you should always consider landowner duties. Hopefully, you have memorized the rules regarding the standard of care owed by landowners depending on the status of the Plaintiff. However, don't just assume that those status rules apply. Rather, look to see what the cause of Plaintiff's injury is. If the Plaintiff is not injured by a *dangerous condition* on the property, such as a broken step or slippery floor, you should apply the reasonable person standard of care. For example, let's say that a landowner is backing her car out of her garage and hits a child playing in her driveway. Her liability will depend on whether the landowner acted reasonably under the circumstances, not on the status of the child in the driveway.

It is also worth mentioning that the concept of strict liability is tested here as well. Don't just assume strict liability applies whenever you see a dangerous animal. Look to see if Defendant is in possession of the animal and whether he knows that the animal is dangerous.

Question 9 Answer

The correct answer is (D) Philip can pursue recovery from either paint company. The rule is that the obligee can recover from either the original obligor or the delegatee because the obligor is secondarily liable to the delagatee. So, if the delagatee (New Paint Company) fails to perform or if its performance is unsatisfactory, the obligee (Philip) can recover against either the original obligor (PaintPlus) or the delagatee (New Paint Company). Answer Choice (B) is incorrect for this reason as well. Answer choice (C) is incorrect because Philip had no choice but to allow the New Paint Company to Perform, as there was no prohibition of assignment. Answer Choice (A) is an incorrect statement of the law.

As long as the delegation is valid and there is no prohibition against assignment in the original contract, Philip can recover from either PaintPlus or the new paint company.

Professor's Guidance

This question is included because many students freak out and shut down when they have to use terms like Delagatee/Assignee, Obligor/Delegator/Assignor, and

Obligee. While these terms can cause some confusion, it helps to map out a quick chart of what happened in the fact pattern and then determine the labels used for each party. Once you do that, it will be easier to work through each answer choice to determine which is correct. It also helps to know the law so that you can quickly eliminate any answers that are not true statements of the law.

Question 10 Answer

The correct answer is (B) Not guilty, because Jack was not aware of Andy's conduct. Assault requires that Defendant intentionally place another in reasonable fear of an imminent battery. If Jack was not aware of Andy's conduct, there was no reasonable apprehension. Answer choice (A) is incorrect, because it doesn't matter if a reasonable person would have been frightened if the victim was not aware of the act. Answer Choice (C) is incorrect, because even though he was only joking, Andy's intent was to scare Jack. Answer choice (D) is incorrect, because it is not enough that the woman was present. We also need facts that show she was aware and suffered reasonable apprehension of a battery as a result.

Professor's Guidance

It is worth repeating here that you should *never assume facts not in the question* — especially if those facts would be conclusive proof of an element that is otherwise debatable. If that element is not included in the facts or is not otherwise offered as a permissive assumption in an answer choice, that element is lacking. In these facts, we have every element we need except for reasonable apprehension. We can safely connect the fact that Jack was asleep and was not aware of Andy's presence with the logical conclusion that there was no reasonable apprehension on his part. However, but we cannot safely connect the fact that a woman was in the store with the conclusion that she suffered reasonable apprehension without also having to assume that she saw or heard Andy and suffered reasonable apprehension as a result.

Question 11 Answer

The correct answer is (D) Paul's oral promise to guarantee the loan is enforceable because the "main purpose" rule applies. Although the promise to guarantee the debt of another is required to be in writing according to the Statute of Frauds, when the main purpose of the contract is for the economic benefit of the guarantor rather than for the interests of the debtor, an oral promise to guarantee the debt of another is enforceable as an exception to the Statute of Frauds. Answer choice (A) is not a true statement of the law under these facts. Answer Choice (B) is a true statement of the law under the facts provided, but is not the best answer, as it is not as complete as

Answer choice (D). Answer choice (C) is incorrect, because it does not matter whether Paul is a creditor.

Question 12 Answer

The correct answer is (D) Not recover because Dan used reasonable force to protect his property. A homeowner may use reasonable force to protect his property. The use of an electric fence is not meant to cause serious bodily injury or death. It was reasonable for Dan to use the fence to prevent trespassers from entering. As such, Joe will not be able to prove negligence. Answer choice (A) is incorrect, because the eggshell Plaintiff rule does not apply if Defendant was not negligent. Answer choice (B) is not the best answer, because Joe would be able to recover if the use of the fence was unreasonable. Answer choice (C) is incorrect, because it is an incorrect statement of the law.

Question 13 Answer

The correct answer is (C) Not convicted because the restaurant owner relied on the interpretation of the law provided by the fire chief. In general, mistake or ignorance of the law is not a defense to a crime. However, an exception exists when Defendant relies in good faith on an erroneous statement of the law contained in an administrative order or on an erroneous interpretation provided by a public official. Answer choice (A) is incorrect, because the strict liability rule is inapplicable here. The reasoning as presented applies to the law of Torts wherein Defendants are held strictly liable to injured Plaintiffs. Answer choice (B) is incorrect, because relying on advice provided by a private attorney is not a defense. Answer choice (D) is incorrect, because it states the wrong reasoning.

Question 14 Answer

The correct answer is (B) Not prevail because the Loan officer shared the information only with his friend. If Sally sues for Invasion of Privacy, it would likely be for the Public Disclosure of Private Facts. However, Sally cannot succeed on this claim, because the rule requires the disclosure to be made to the public at large. Because the loan officer only made the statement to his friend and Sally happened to overhear from a nearby table, this requirement is not met. Answer choice (A) is incorrect because the disclosure element is not met. Answer choice (C) is incorrect because the rule does not require publication, it requires disclosure to the public at large. Answer choice (D) is incorrect because it is irrelevant whether the statement is true. Truth is a defense to a Defamation claim but is not a defense to a claim for Public Disclosure of Private Facts.

Question 15 Answer

The correct answer is (C) The contract is not likely to be discharged because the couple bore the risk. While it is true that the purpose of the contract between the couple and the Botanical Gardens is frustrated if the couple is not able to get married at the venue due to Gary's illness, the couple bore the risk that the contingency could occur. It is foreseeable that the bride or groom could become ill before the wedding or that the wedding could be called off for any number of reasons. Absent a clause in the contract that would permit the couple to get out of the contract should the contingency occur, the contract will not be discharged. Answer choice (A) is incorrect because the couple bore the risk. Answer Choice (B) is incorrect because it states the incorrect reasoning. Also, Frustration of Purpose, rather than Impossibility is at issue. Answer choice (D) is incorrect because the frustration is substantial in that the wedding must be cancelled. Further, the couple bore the risk that Gary might become ill.

Question 16 Answer

The correct answer is (D). The employee is most likely to be convicted of common law Arson. At common law, Arson is defined as the malicious burning of the dwelling of another. The employee acted with malice by setting the front seat of the car on fire, knowing it was in the garage of the boss' home. Malice can be shown by proving that Defendant either intended to burn or acted recklessly. Answer choice (A) is incorrect, because "the dwelling of another" requirement is not met. Only the patio furniture was burned. Answer choice (B) is incorrect for the same reason. Burning the husband's personal belongings do not constitute arson under the common law. Answer choice (C) is incorrect, because the husband acted carelessly at most, rather than maliciously.

Question 17 Answer

The correct answer is (C) Yes, because a promise to pay the debt that is otherwise barred by the Statute of Limitations is enforceable without consideration. The rule is that a promise to pay a debt after the running of the Statute of Limitations has passed is enforceable without consideration. Answer Choice (A) is incorrect, because the defense is no longer applicable, since Stacey promised to pay her debt after the statute had run. Answer Choice (B) is incorrect, because such a promise is enforceable without consideration. Answer choice (D) is not the best answer, because the creditor could benefit from a gratuitous promise.

Question 18 Answer

The correct answer is (A) No crime. At common law, a Conspiracy is an agreement for an unlawful purpose. There must also be an intent to commit the crime committed. Because George only feigned agreement, he did not have the intent to commit the crime and therefore cannot be convicted of Burglary or Conspiracy. Answer choice (B) is incorrect, because George did not have the intent required to commit the crime. Answer choice (C) is incorrect, because Attempt is a specific intent crime, and George did not act with the intent to commit the crime. Answer Choice (D) is incorrect for the same reasons.

Question 19 Answer

The correct answer is (D) Pete will not recover because he was aware that some of the dogs in Max's yard could be dangerous. Those that engage in abnormally dangerous activities are strictly liable for any personal injuries resulting from that activity. However, Assumption of the Risk is a complete defense. Because Pete knew that dangerous dogs were in the yard and chose to enter the yard anyway, he assumed the risk that he could be injured and cannot recover in a strict liability action against Max. Answer choice (A) is incorrect, because even though Max was engaged in an abnormally dangerous activity, Pete assumed the risk. Answer choice (B) is incorrect, because Pete's status as a trespasser is irrelevant in a strict liability claim. Answer choice (C) is incorrect, because it is irrelevant to the action.

Question 20 Answer

The correct answer is (B) No, because there was no consideration to support the modification. The preexisting duty rule requires additional consideration to support the modification. Answer choice (A) is incorrect, because the modification would not be enforceable due to lack of consideration even if the modification was in writing. Choice (C) is incorrect, because mutual assent and good faith only apply to contracts that are governed by the UCC. This contract is governed by the common law. Answer choice (D) is incorrect, because the cost increase was not so significant or unforeseeable to either party to allow for the enforcement of the modification without consideration.

Question 21 Answer

The correct answer is (D) Stacy did not take any action to assist Ed. If a person aids, assists, or encourages another in the commission of a crime, they are an accomplice to the crime.

Accomplice liability requires an action. Stacy stood by and watched but did not encourage Ed to hurt Larry. Answer choice (A) is incorrect, because intent to commit the crime is not necessary for accomplice liability. Answer choice (B) is incorrect, as it is irrelevant. Answer choice (C) is incorrect because the "no duty to rescue" rule applies to tort, rather than criminal, liability.

Question 22 Answer

The correct answer is (A) First degree murder. It does not matter if Greg was not sure his actions would kill Larry; his intent was for Larry to die, and his action of hiding in the back seat and scaring Larry in the hope that Larry would have a heart attack were both premeditated and deliberate. Answer choices (B), (C), and (D) are all incorrect because Greg acted with premeditation and deliberation.

Question 23 Answer

The correct answer is (B) Nancy can sue Beverly as a donee beneficiary. Nancy is a third-party beneficiary to the contract created between Rob and Beverly. She is an intended donee beneficiary and has the right to sue Beverly if Beverly stops making payments. Answer choice (A) is incorrect because Nancy is not a creditor beneficiary. Answer choice (C) is incorrect because Nancy can sue as a donee beneficiary. Answer choice (D) is incorrect because Nancy can sue Beverly without suing Rob.

Question 24 Answer

The correct answer is (B) Succeed, if Billy can prove that the product was defective. Strict Products Liability requires proof of proper parties, defective product, causation, damages, and lack of defenses. Anyone in the commercial chain, including manufacturers and retailers, are proper parties. Home Spot is a retailer and is therefore a proper Defendant. Billy is a proper Plaintiff as a buyer and consumer of the product. Plaintiff must also prove that the product is defective by showing either a manufacturing defect, a design defect, or a failure to warn. If Billy can prove a defect, he can also show that the defect caused his injuries and recover against Home Spot.

Answer choice (A) is incorrect because it is irrelevant whether Ed assured Billy that there was nothing wrong with the ladder in a strict liability action against the retailer. Answer choice (C) is incorrect because, even though both manufacturers and retailers are proper Defendants in a strict products liability case, a plaintiff cannot succeed unless he can also prove defective product. Answer choice (D) is incorrect because both manufacturers and retailers are proper defendants in a strict liability case.

Question 25 Answer

The correct answer is (A) Succeed, if Becky can prove that the ladder was defective. Strict Products Liability requires proof of proper parties, defective product, causation, damages, and lack of defenses. Anyone foreseeably injured by the product, including users and bystanders, are proper parties. As a bystander, Becky is a proper Plaintiff. As long as she can prove that the ladder was defective, she will succeed, because all other elements can be established by the facts.

Answer choice (B) is incorrect because Becky is a proper Plaintiff. Answer Choice (C) is not the best answer because Becky's texting did not cause Billy to fall. Also, contributory/comparative negligence is not a traditional defense in a strict products liability case. Answer choice (D) is incorrect because even if Becky can prove proximate cause, she cannot recover unless she can also prove defective product.

Question 26 Answer

The correct answer is (A) Succeed, if Billy can establish Res Ipsa Loquitor. Negligence requires proving Duty, Breach, Causation, and Damages. In a case where Plaintiff is injured by a product, if Plaintiff can't prove breach by showing that Defendant acted unreasonably, he must use the doctrine of Res Ipsa Loquitor to establish breach. If Billy can prove Res Ipsa Loquitor, he will be able to succeed in a negligence action, because all of the other elements are established by the facts.

Answer choice (B) is incorrect because defective product is an element of a strict liability claim. Answer choice (C) is incorrect because Billy can recover even if Ed was off duty based on a Res Ipsa Loquitor theory. Answer choice (D) is incorrect because it is irrelevant whether Billy was warned about the danger of climbing a ladder. Further, the facts showed that warnings were included in the directions.

Question 27 Answer

The correct answer is (C) Buyer can avoid performance if the June 1 date was an express condition precedent. The failure of a condition precedent can prevent a duty from arising, while the failure of a condition subsequent has the effect of terminating an existing duty. If the June 1 date was an express condition precedent to the obligation to pay for the units, then Buyer's duty to pay does not arise. If the June 1 date was a promise rather than a condition, then Buyer's duty to pay still arises, but she can get damages for any harm suffered by the breach.

Answer Choice (A) is incorrect because there is a question with regard to whether the June 1 date was a promise or condition. Answer Choice (B) is incorrect because if the June 1 date was a promise, Buyer would have a duty to perform. Answer Choice (D) is incorrect because a condition subsequent exists when the failure of the condition terminates an existing duty. The June 1 date is either a condition precedent or a promise.

Question 28 Answer

The correct answer is (D) Collect both actual and consequential damages as a result of Molly's breach. This contract contained a liquidated damages clause. Liquidated damages clauses will be enforced as long as they are valid. In order to be valid, the damages must be difficult to ascertain in advance and the amount selected must be a reasonable estimate of possible loss rather than a penalty. Here, the damages may be difficult to ascertain in advance, but the $500,000 amount stipulated is exceedingly high, considering it would apply for both major and minor breaches. It is therefore a penalty and will not be enforced. Instead, the non-breaching party can recover any actual and consequential damages suffered.

Answer Choice (A) is incorrect because the liquidated damages clause is not enforceable. Answer Choice (B) is not correct because you cannot require specific performance from a service providing party. Choice (C) is incorrect because Tom is also entitled to recover any lost profits he may suffer due to having to hire a less popular comedian to replace Molly.

Question 29 Answer

The correct answer is (A) Convicted. This is a strict liability crime. Andrew's intent or mistake with regard to whether his previous crime was a felony is irrelevant. Answer choices (B), (C), and (D) are incorrect for the same reason.

Question 30 Answer

The Correct answer is (D) The University is liable if Andrew was negligent in approaching the students with a gun. Under the doctrine of respondeat superior, employers are liable for the negligent acts of their employees. Therefore, if Andrew was negligent, the university can be held liable. Answer Choice (A) is incorrect, because while it is true that a criminal act can break the chain of causation, Andrew's criminal act of violating the state statute was not the cause of Larry's injuries. Answer Choice (B) is incorrect because the gun fired accidentally when Andrew tripped. Andrew did not shoot Larry in self-defense. Answer Choice (C) is incorrect because it is irrelevant whether the University acted reasonably. Because the doctrine of respondeat superior is applicable, Andrew's behavior is at issue.

Question 31 Answer

The correct answer is (D) Not recover because she learned of Joe's deception before the date for the proposed examination.

Assault requires intentionally placing another in reasonable apprehension of an imminent battery. Because Mary learned of Joe's deception before the date for the proposed examination, there was no imminent battery, and therefore no assault.

Answer choice (A) is incorrect because even though Joe intended to touch her, that touch was not imminent. Answer choice (B) is incorrect because fraud is not a required element of assault. Answer choice (D) is a better answer than answer choice

(C) because establishing a defense is not necessary unless a prima facie case for assault is first established. Had a prima facie case for assault been established, Mary could recover even though she had consented under these facts.

Question 32 Answer

The correct answer is (A) Recover damages for battery.

Battery requires an intentional touching that causes harm or offense. Had the examination taken place, Mary could prove an offensive touching and could therefore be able to recover damages for battery. Answer choice (A) is better than answer choice (B), because the examination involved a physical touching contact, which is a required element of battery. Further, battery is an injury to the person, whereas fraud and misrepresentation generally result in injury to property. Answer choice (C) is incorrect because Mary's consent was fraudulently obtained. Answer choice (D) is incorrect because physical harm is not required. Either harm or offense will suffice.

Question 33 Answer

The correct answer is (A) Seller, because of their past course of dealing.

When a contract does not provide for time of payment, past course of dealing can establish the parties' intention with regard to that term. Because Buyer always paid on the first of each month, that became the agreed time of payment. Buyer cannot now refuse to pay in advance and hold Seller responsible for damages. Answer choice (B) is incorrect because no provision was made for time of payment, and the UCC allows for either a reasonable time or for past course of dealing to establish such a term. Answer choices (C) and (D) are incorrect because the parties' past course of dealing is relevant.

Question 34 Answer

The correct answer is (D) No, because Buyer's order was disproportionate to his normal requirements.

In a requirements contract, a buyer can order all that in good faith he requires but cannot enforce an order that is disproportionate to his normal requirements. Because Buyer had never ordered fuel for August delivery over the past five years, an order of 5,000 gallons of fuel for August delivery is disproportionate to his normal requirements. Answer choice (B) is incorrect because it does not matter whether Seller had a sufficient supply, because Buyer's order was disproportionate. Answer choice (C) is incorrect because even though there was no expressed limit stated in the agreement, the proportionality rules still applies.

Question 35 Answer

The correct answer is (C) Buyer was not obligated to purchase from Seller any amount in excess of his monthly requirement, and his normal September requirement was zero.

In a requirements contract, a buyer can order all that in good faith he requires, even if those requirements are zero, but cannot enforce an order that is disproportionate to his normal requirements. Here, Buyer's normal requirements for September are zero, which is disproportionate to his 3,500-gallon September order. Because he could not enforce the order against Seller, his best argument is that he is not obligated to purchase the fuel from Seller because his usual September requirement is zero. Answer choice (A) is incorrect because courts will enforce requirements contracts even though they may be illusory. Answer choice (B) is incorrect because a decline in market price is something that can be anticipated by both parties. Answer choice (D) is incorrect, because courts favor the enforcement of requirements contracts.

Question 36 Answer

The correct answer is (D) That Seller's duty to deliver more than 2,500 gallons was excused.

A party's duty to perform can be excused if the performance due becomes illegal. Because the regulation subsequently prohibited Seller from delivering the amount required, Seller's duty to perform is excused. Answer choice (A) is incorrect because performance is still physically possible, as Seller could find another way to fill the order. Answer choice (B) is incorrect because the contract itself is not illegal. Answer choice (C) is irrelevant.

Question 37 Answer

The correct answer is (C) No, because duress does not excuse killing of an innocent person.

The rule is that duress will never excuse the killing of an innocent person. Therefore, answer choices (A) and (B) are incorrect. Answer choice (D) is an incorrect statement of the law. Duress can excuse the commission of other felonies.

Question 38 Answer

The correct answer is (D) S prevails, because the note sent with C's check constitutes a writing sufficient to satisfy the Statute of Frauds.

The Statute of Frauds requires that contracts for the sale of goods of more than $500 be in writing. The writing must contain price, and quantity, and be signed by the party to be charged. This contract is subject to the Statute of Frauds, as it is for the sale of 1200 lamps at $1 each. The note constitutes a writing sufficient to satisfy the statute. Answer choice (A) is incorrect for this reason. Answer choice (B) is incorrect because the note is specific enough to satisfy the Statute of Frauds. It is by C and indicates that the price was one dollar per lamp. Answer choice (C) is irrelevant.

Question 39 Answer

The correct answer is (C) North and South will be jointly and severally liable for the full amount of her damages.

Both North and South were negligent and caused the accident. Therefore, they are jointly and severally liable for Prudence's damages. Answer choices (A) and (B) are incorrect because both North and South contributed to the accident. Answer choice (D) is incorrect because the doctrines of contributory negligence and comparative fault are only applicable as defenses for a situation wherein the Plaintiff was also negligent. There are no facts indicating that Prudence was negligent.

Question 40 Answer

The correct answer is (D) Neither Prudence nor South.

A Plaintiff that caused his own injury cannot prevail in a claim for negligence. Here, although South was negligent in failing to pay attention, North would not have hit Prudence's car had he not been following so closely. Therefore, North cannot recover against either South or Prudence.

Question 41 Answer

The correct answer is (C) The requirement is an express condition which has been excused by impossibility of performance.

A duty of performance can be discharged by impossibility, impracticability, or frustration of purpose. Because of the ban on the material, Builder can successfully argue that the express condition to use Malayan teak was excused due to impossibility of performance. Answer choice (A) is incorrect because the words "expressly conditioned upon" create a condition rather than a covenant. Answer choice (D) is incorrect for the same reason. Answer choice (B) is incorrect because the ban on importation did not make the condition illegal. Rather, it made it impossible to perform.

Question 42 Answer

The correct answer is (C) Sailor must pay the full contract price without any offset for the defective galley unit because Builder substantially performed.

The galley unit is defective because it does not fit properly but is otherwise functional. Therefore, this is a minor breach. In the case of a minor breach, the non-breaching party must continue to perform, but can sue for damages caused by the breach. Answer choices (B) and (D) are incorrect for this reason. Answer choice (A) is incorrect because Sailor contracted with Builder for the boat. If there is any breach, whether caused by Builder or Carpenter, Sailor can recover from Builder.

Question 43 Answer

The correct answer is (B) Sailor will not recover, because Art's duty to pay is conditional upon his obtaining 7% financing, which he attempted to do in good faith.

Art's duty to perform is conditioned upon his ability to obtain a loan at 7% financing. Art has a duty of good faith to attempt to secure the financing. If in good faith he fails to do so, the condition is not satisfied, and his duty of performance terminates. Art attempted to obtain the loan at six institutions and was denied because his income and assets were insufficient. This constitutes a good faith effort. Answer choice (A) is incorrect because Art's performance is excused. Answer choice (C) is incorrect because it is the failure of a condition, rather than the doctrine of impossibility, that discharges Art's duty to perform. Answer choice (D) is incorrect because courts will not change the terms of a contract.

Question 44 Answer

The correct answer is (C) Sailor will recover as a third-party beneficiary of the contract between Builder and Carpenter.

Builder contracted with Carpenter for the benefit of Sailor. Therefore, Sailor can recover from either Builder as a party to the original contract or from Carpenter as a third-party beneficiary of the contract between Builder and Carpenter. Answer choice (A) is incorrect, because Sailor had a duty to perform under the contract because Builder substantially performed. Paying and taking possession did not result in a waiver of his right to recover for damages caused by Carpenter. Answer choice (B) is incorrect because privity is not required for a third-party beneficiary to enforce his rights. Answer choice (D) is incorrect because there was no assignment of rights. Rather, Sailor is a third-party beneficiary.

Question 45 Answer

The correct answer is (C) Liable to Owner for the cost of fixing the chipped paint because Friend took a different route.

Trespass to chattel refers to the intentional and wrongful interference of another individual's personal property without their permission. Defendant will be liable for any damaged caused by the interference. Answer choices (A) and (B) are incorrect because Friend is only liable for the damaged caused rather than for the value of the car. Had Friend totaled the car, Owner could sue for conversion and recover for the value of the car. Answer choice (D) is incorrect because Friend took the car on a dirt road without Owner's permission.

Question 46 Answer

The correct answer is (C) Manslaughter, because Dick killed John in the honest but unreasonable belief that it was necessary to do so to save his own life.

Murder can be reduced to Manslaughter if the doctrine of imperfect self-defense applies. Imperfect self-defense applies if Defendant kills in the honest but unreasonable belief that deadly force is necessary to protect himself. Answer choice (A) is incorrect because Dick's mistake was unreasonable given that force or threat of force had never been used. Answer choice (B) is incorrect because Dick was not privileged to use self-defense under these facts. Answer choice (D) is incorrect because the facts indicate that Dick was reacting to John coming outside with a shotgun, and no force or threat of force had ever been used.

Question 47 Answer

The correct answer is (B) Prevail, regardless of whether the operation improved Patient's physical well-being.

Battery is an intentional touching without Plaintiff's consent that causes harm or offense. While Patient consented to Qualified performing the surgery, he did not consent to Skillful performing the surgery. Allowing Skillful to operate without Patient having an opportunity to consent is offensive. Answer choice (A) is incorrect because it does not matter whether Patient's physical well-being is improved. What matters is that Skillful touched Plaintiff without her consent. Answer choice (C) is incorrect because it does not matter whether Skillful was as competent nor does it matter whether Patient refused to pay for the surgery. As such, answer choice (D) is incorrect as well.

Question 48 Answer

The correct answer is (D) Was threatened with immediate and serious bodily harm and reasonably believed that deadly force was necessary.

The rule regarding self-defense is that Defendant is entitled to use deadly force to protect himself if he is threatened with immediate and serious bodily harm and reasonably believes that deadly force is necessary. Answer (A) is incorrect because retreat is not always necessary. Answer choice (B) is incorrect because the belief must be reasonable. Answer choice (C) is incorrect because not everyone who is charged with a criminal homicide may be able to claim self-defense.

Question 49 Answer

The correct answer is (D) Not recover because the danger had passed before Bill turned around.

An assault occurs when Defendant intentionally places Plaintiff in reasonable apprehension of an imminent battery. Plaintiff must be aware of the threat. Therefore, Bill cannot recover, because the threat of an immediate battery had already passed before he turned around. Answer choice (A) is incorrect because it is not enough that Tom acted with intent. Answer choice (B) is incorrect because the threat of the battery must be imminent. Answer choice (C) is incorrect because it does not matter whether the battery was completed.

Question 50 Answer

The correct answer is (B) Larceny.

A larceny occurs when Defendant intentionally takes and caries away the personal property of another with the intent to permanently deprive. Because Andrew took the lamp with the intent not to pay for it unless Sally found out about it, all elements are met. Answer choice (A) is incorrect for this reason. Answer choice (C) is incorrect because Andrew did not trick Sally into giving him possession of the lamp. Answer choice (D) is incorrect because Andrew did not obtain title to the lamp by misrepresenting facts to Sally.

Hopefully with this practice and guidance, you now have some strategies to help you conquer more practice multiple-choice questions. As you practice, do the best you can and make sure you completely understand why each correct answer choice is correct and why each incorrect answer choice is incorrect. Doing so will help fill in any gaps in your knowledge of the substantive law. If you are preparing for the FYLSE or the bar exam, practice as many questions as you can. Finally, make sure to practice under timed pressure.

For Additional Practice:

For more practice, most schools have accounts that allow you to access Cali.org, the Center for Computer Assisted Legal Instruction. There are many lessons that include multiple choice questions. Some are quite simple in an effort to help you understand the topic, while others are much more involved. This site is especially helpful for students studying for final exams and learning how to use IRAC.

Your school may also give you access to Westlaw's school site, lawschool.westlaw.com. Westlaw has a resource section where you can access study and exam materials for tips on legal writing and exam preparation. You can ask your law librarian if you have access to these resources or if there is another available resource in your library that is recommended.

You can also review these materials and practice on actual past bar questions via PassTheFYLSE.com.

Rule Statements

23

Student Workbook:
Contracts Rule Statements

You cannot pass a Contracts exam without collecting and memorizing all of the applicable rules. Use the following pages to collect rule statements for each of the topics that may be tested. You can find many of the rules in this book or in your course materials. You can also check your work at PassTheFYLSE.com

Contract Formation:

Mutual Assent:

Offer:

Acceptance:

Consideration:

Objective Theory of Contract:

Revocation:

Rejection:

Mailbox Rule:

UCC 2-205:

Mirror Image Rule:

UCC 2-206:

UCC 2-207:

Common Law Contract Modification:

UCC Contract Modification:

Statute of Frauds:

Parol Evidence Rule:

Defense of Fraud/Mistake:

Capacity to Contract:

Express Condition:

Implied Conditions:

Condition Subsequent:

Condition Precedent:

Waiver of Condition:
Forfeiture:

Impossibility:

Impracticability:

Frustration of Purpose:

Anticipatory Breach:

Adequate Assurance:

Retraction:

Present Breach:

Major Breach:

Minor Breach:

Time to Cure:

Substantial Performance:

Divisible Contract:

Liquidated Damages:

Expectation Damages:

Reliance Damages:

Natural/Standard Damages:

Consequential Damages:

Restitution:

Rescission:

Injunction:

Specific Performance:

Third Party Beneficiary:

Intended Third Party Beneficiary:

Incidental Third Party Beneficiary:

Creditor Beneficiary:

Donee Beneficiary:

Assignment:

Delegation:

24

Student Workbook: Torts Rule Statements

You cannot pass a Torts exam without collecting and memorizing all of the applicable rules. Use the following pages to collect rule statements for each of the topics that may be tested. You can find most of the rule statements in this book or in your course materials. You can also check your work at PassTheFYLSE.com

Intentional Torts:

Intent:

Battery:

Assault:

False Imprisonment:

Intentional Infliction of Emotional Distress:

Malicious Prosecution:

Wrongful Institution of Civil Proceedings:

Abuse of Process:

Invasion of Privacy:

Intrusion into the Plaintiff's Seclusion:

Public Revelation of Private Facts:

Commercial Appropriation:

False Light:

Trespass to Land:

Trespass to Chattels:

Conversion:

Public Nuisance:

Private Nuisance:

Deceit:

Inducing Breach of Contract:

Interfering with Prospective Business Advantage:

Consent:

Authority:

Private Necessity:

Public Necessity:

Self Defense:

Defense of Others:

Defense of Property:

Negligence:

Duty:

Cordozo's View:

Andrew's View:

Standard of Care:

Variations from the General Standard of Care:

Breach:

Negligence Per Se:

Learned Hand Test:

Res Ipsa Loquitor:

Actual Cause:

But/For Test:

Substantial Factor:

Summers v. Tice:

Market Share:

Proximate Cause:

Types of Proximate Cause Issues:

Eggshell Plaintiff Rule:

Contributory Negligence:

Comparative Negligence:

Assumption of the Risk:

Negligent Infliction of Emotional Distress:

Strict Liability:

Wild Animals:

Abnormally Dangerous Activities:

Theories of Liability when Defendant Creates a Defective Product:

Implied Warranty of Merchantability:

Implied Warranty of Fitness for a Particular Purpose:

Strict Products Liability:

Ways to Prove Defective Product:

Manufacturing Flaw:

Design Defect:

Lack of Warning:

Ways to prove Design Defect:

Consumer Contemplation Test:

Feasible Alternative Test:

Product Misuse:

Assumption of The Risk:

Applicability of comparative fault to Strict Liability:

Defamation:

Libel:

Slander:

Libel Per Se:

Libel Per Quad:

Public Figure:

Private Plaintiff:

Matter of Public Concern:

Matter of Private Concern:

Proof of Actual Malice Required:

Proof of Negligence Required:

Defamation Defenses:

Defamation Privileges:

Tort Remedies:

25

Student Workbook: Criminal Law Rule Statements

You cannot pass a Criminal Law exam without collecting and memorizing all of the applicable rules. Use the following pages to collect rule statements for each of the topics that may be tested. You can find many of the rules in this book or in your course materials. You can also check your work at PassTheFYLSE.com

Assault:

Battery:

Rape:

Mayhem:

False Imprisonment/Kidnapping:

Murder:

Homicide:

Malice:

Intent to Kill:

Deadly Weapon Doctrine:

Depraved Heart:

Intent to Cause Serious Bodily Injury:

Felony Murder:

Vicarious Liability Limitations:

First Degree Murder:

Premeditation:

Deliberation:

Second Degree Murder:

Justification Defenses:

Prevention of a Crime:

Apprehension of a Fleeing Felon:

Self Defense:

Defense of Others:

Reasonable Mistake:

Excuse Defenses:

Youth:

Mental Illness (Insanity Tests):

Voluntary Intoxication:

Involuntary Intoxication:

M'Naghten Test:

Irresistible Impulse Test:

Substantial Capacity (MPC) Test:

Durham Test:

Mitigating Factors:

Good Faith Mistake:

Adequate Provocation/Anger:

Coercion/Necessity:

Involuntary Manslaughter:

Larceny:

Robbery:

Embezzlement:

Larceny by Trick:

False Pretenses:

Burglary:

Arson:

Solicitation:

Conspiracy:

Attempt:

Overt Act:

Merger:

Withdrawal:

Legal Impossibility:

Factual Impossibility:

26

Words of Encouragement

I sincerely hope that you found the advice and practice contained in this book helpful. I know that studying for your exams and/or the FYLSE is a daunting task, but I promise you that it is worth it. It truly takes a village to get through law school and I am honored to be a part of your success. Please feel free to reach out to me anytime through PassTheFYLSE.com for support and encouragement! Again, you can do this!

Last, but certainly not least, a former student of mine, Jessyca Henderson, was kind enough to agree to share her FYLSE experience and advice as well. I found it appropriate to include here and am sure you will find it both encouraging and useful as exam day approaches.

Words of Encouragement from a Former Student

If you're preparing to take the FYLSE, chances are you're already facing some of the unique challenges and opportunities that come along with attending an online or unaccredited law school program. You're here because you're taking the road less traveled — and while that can sometimes feel lonely, you should also know that you're in good company. People from all walks of life, from many different law schools, and under a variety of personal circumstances sit for the FYLSE, successfully. Beginning with a sense of community will benefit you in many ways as you begin this journey.

If there is one advantage to taking the FYLSE, it is that you get a crack at experiencing testing conditions that are similar to the actual bar exam. This may seem like a minor detail, but experiencing the big convention hall room full of test takers, the downpour-like sound of hundreds of people typing, and the pressure of timed conditions will all help you to prepare for your ultimate goal: passing the California Bar Exam. Another bit of good news is that the Bar is now only two days, so by taking the FYLSE, you're "halfway there" in terms of the stamina it takes to get through the full two days of testing. Take stock in that silver lining as you prepare for one tough, but manageable testing day.

Read the examination rules carefully and consider your comfort first and foremost. How well do you do with noise? It may seem like the room will be quiet, but there are squeaking chairs, a cacophony of typing, coughs, people getting up and down — if you don't do well with ambient noise, bring earplugs — several pairs. Look carefully at what's permitted and bring whatever you need within the bounds of the rules that will help you have the best testing experience possible. Get plenty of rest, eat well and exercise in the weeks or months leading up to the exam so you are in peak physical performance for exam day.

You cannot expect to be successful on the FYLSE, nor later the Bar Exam, if you do not adequately prepare. Having a preparation plan will be vital to your success, and that starts with good materials, a good frame of mind, and time enough to do the necessary work. Memorization must be done iteratively, not all at once, so making sure that you can work with your materials many, many times with understanding as a chief goal is very important. If you do not understand a concept, you will not be able to memorize it in a meaningful way. First, understand, then memorize, then practice — over and over again.

Remember, you've made it through your first grueling year of law school, likely with many other challenges that you've overcome along the way. Did you go through a few days or a few weeks caring for a sick child or relative while also juggling your school work? Did you give up free time, fun, and hobbies while working a job and attending law school at night or online? Think about all that you did to successfully get through your first year — and then remind yourself: this is just one more day. This is just one more test. You've done so much to get to where you are: you can do this too. This too shall pass.

On the last day of the California Bar Exam in July 2016, as the proctor said "time, stop typing, stop writing," there was a collective sigh that fell across the room filled with over four thousand exam takers. We all waited patiently for the words "you are dismissed." Growing from a few cautious claps into the crescendo of thousands of hands applauding, the room roared with joyful congratulations. We did it: no matter the score, no matter the outcome — we'd made it through the California Bar. And you can too — but your first step to accomplishing that big goal is the FYLSE. Have faith in yourself, do the work, and one fine day, you'll be celebrating your own success.